Learn CentOS Linux
Network Services

Antonio Vazquez

Apress®

Learn CentOS Linux Network Services

Antonio Vazquez
Madrid, Madrid, Spain

ISBN-13 (pbk): 978-1-4842-2378-9   ISBN-13 (electronic): 978-1-4842-2379-6

DOI 10.1007/978-1-4842-2379-6

Library of Congress Control Number: 2016960292

Distributed to the book trade worldwide by Springer Science+Business Media New York, 233 Spring Street, 6th Floor, New York, NY 10013. Phone 1-800-SPRINGER, fax (201) 348-4505, e-mail orders-ny@springer-sbm.com, or visit www.springer.com. Apress Media, LLC is a California LLC and the sole member (owner) is Springer Science + Business Media Finance Inc (SSBM Finance Inc). SSBM Finance Inc is a **Delaware** corporation.

For information on translations, please e-mail rights@apress.com, or visit www.apress.com.

Apress and friends of ED books may be purchased in bulk for academic, corporate, or promotional use. eBook versions and licenses are also available for most titles. For more information, reference our Special Bulk Sales-eBook Licensing web page at www.apress.com/bulk-sales.

Any source code or other supplementary materials referenced by the author in this text are available to readers at www.apress.com. For detailed information about how to locate your book's source code, go to www.apress.com/source-code/.

Printed on acid-free paper

This book is dedicated to my family, especially to my parents, who recently had to endure some difficult times. I love you both.

Contents at a Glance

Contents

About the Author

Antonio Vazquez is an IT professional who has been working with Linux for more than a decade. He studied computer engineering at university in Spain, and he currently holds many IT certifications from the main vendors in the industry. At present, he works for a public institution and is in charge of almost a thousand Linux servers spread across the country, providing web services, FTP services, file services, virtualization, and more.

About the Technical Reviewer

Massimo Nardone has more than 22 years of experience in security, web/mobile development, and cloud and IT architecture. His true IT passions are security and Android.

He has been programming and teaching how to program with Android, Perl, PHP, Java, VB, Python, C/C++, and MySQL for more than 20 years. He holds a master of science degree in computer science from the University of Salerno, Italy.

He has worked as a project manager, software engineer, research engineer, chief security architect, information security manager, PCI/SCADA auditor, and senior lead IT security/cloud/SCADA architect for many years. His technical skills cover security, Android, cloud, Java, MySQL, Drupal, Cobol, Perl, web and mobile development, MongoDB, D3, Joomla, Couchbase, C/C++, WebGL, Python, Pro Rails, Django CMS, Jekyll, and Scratch, among others. He currently works as Chief Information Security Officer (CISO) for Cargotec Oyj.

He was a visiting lecturer and supervisor for exercises at the Networking Laboratory of the Helsinki University of Technology (Aalto University). He holds four international patents (related to PKI, SIP, SAML, and Proxy).

Massimo has reviewed more than 40 IT books for various publishing companies, and he is the coauthor of *Pro Android Games* (Apress, 2015).

Acknowledgments

I'd like to extend my gratitude to everybody at Apress, especially to those with whom I've had the pleasure of working directly: Louise Corrigan and Nancy Chen. I would also like to thank the technical reviewer, Massimo Nardone. They all helped me a lot.

Of course, I can't forget my wife, who is also my biggest fan and always offers me her support and patience.

Introduction

Many things have changed since that day in which a young Finnish student named Linus Torvalds decided to post a message in a forum, searching for help with the development of a new operating system. He hardly could have imagined that there would be so many people eager to collaborate. And what had started as a hobby became an efficient operating system (OS) used today by thousands of companies and users around the world.

Linus decided to make this OS free for everybody to use, share, study, and modify the code. So he licensed the code under the GNU license. This way, it was possible for everybody to have access to the source code and modify it according to their likes and/ or needs. This resulted in many companies, universities, etc., having their own Linux distributions.

Even though many of these distributions have remained confined to small areas of influence, such as universities or official departments, a few have achieved general recognition over the years. A few well-known examples include Red Hat, SUSE, Debian, and Ubuntu.

The Red Hat Linux distribution system, developed by the Red Hat company is, undoubtedly, one of the most important and influential. Red Hat has made many relevant contributions to the Linux community, for example, the Red Hat Package Manager (RPM), used by several other distributions, and Suse.

Red Hat used to publish desktop, as well as server, editions of its OS, and these were made freely available for anyone to use. But in the year 2004, the company decided that its OS would be provided only to clients. Obviously, this concerns only the binary distributions, as the source code has to be made publicly available to comply with the GNU license.

From that moment on, two new projects emerged with the aim of trying to maintain a Red Hat clone that would be freely available to everyone. The first project was called Fedora. It was sponsored by Red Hat itself and was conceived as some sort of beta Red Hat platform.

Many users thought that Fedora was OK as a desktop platform, but it was by no means a reliable enterprise solution. In order to fulfill this gap, many Linux professionals and enthusiasts gathered around a new project called CentOS (Community Enterprise Operating System), whose main goal was to become a freely available robust enterprise operating system.

Today, CentOS is a reliable, efficient server operating system used by hundreds of companies to provide critical services.

Audience

Some experience with computers is expected of readers of this book. Some previous Linux experience is useful, if not absolutely necessary. The only requirement, however, is the will to learn!

Conventions

The Code style attribute has been applied to file names, paths, commands, and URLs.

Feedback

I would really appreciate your opinions, suggestions, questions, or criticisms regarding this book. Please feel free to e-mail me at antoniojvv@yahoo.es. Note, however, that I cannot promise to respond to everyone.

CHAPTER 1

Installation

1.1. CentOS 6

As it usually happens, there is more than one way to install CentOS on a computer. So, depending on the way we initially boot the server and the source of the installation packages, we have many options.

- We can boot and install the system from a DVD. This is probably the most straightforward option, and the right choice if you only have to install a couple of servers. We boot the server from the DVD, and we install all the software from the DVD too.

- We can also use a CentOS Network netinstall DVD to boot the server and then install the packages from a server in our local network or from the Internet. This is a good choice if we have to install a lot of servers.

- We could also use a USB device to boot the server. In this case, we first prepare the USB device by using software packages such as UNetbootin,[1] and we also have to download the CentOS installation files. Once the USB device is ready, we can use it to boot the server and then choose whether to install from a local or a network repository.

In addition, independent of the type of installation we choose, we can also automate the installation by using kickstart. The use of kickstart is beyond the scope of this book, but it basically consists of passing a special parameter to the installer with the location of a script file that contains instructions for the installation.

---

[1]SourceForge, "UNetbootin: Bootable live USB creator for Ubuntu, Fedora, and Linux distributions," https://sourceforge.net/projects/unetbootin/, 2016.

© Antonio Vazquez 2016
A. Vazquez, *Learn CentOS Linux Network Services*, DOI 10.1007/978-1-4842-2379-6_1

Nevertheless, in order to keep things simple, in this book, we will avail ourselves only of the typical DVD installation. The first thing one must do is to get the installation DVDs. These can be downloaded from the CentOS official site.[2] At the time of writing this book, the ISO files could be downloaded from the links available from http://wiki.centos. org/Download.[3] We can choose the exact version we want to install, the architecture (32 or 64 bits), and the type of installation (minimal, network, etc.). We will download and burn the ISO files CentOS-6.2-i386-bin-DVD1.iso and CentOS-6.2-i386-bin-DVD2.iso. Once we have the DVDs, installation is fairly simple. We make sure that the computer is configured to boot from a DVD, and we restart it with the first installation DVD inside. After a few seconds, we'll see the screen in shown in Figure 1-1.

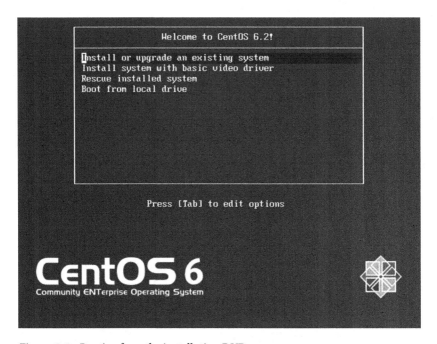

Figure 1-1. *Booting from the installation DVD*

We'll select the first option, "Install or upgrade an existing system." This will launch the actual installation program. Now we are offered the possibility of checking the installation media (Figure 1-2). Once we are sure that there is no problem with the DVDs, we click Skip.

---

[2]CentOS, "The CentOS Project," http://centos.org/, 2016.
[3]CentOS, http://wiki.centos.org/Download, 2016.

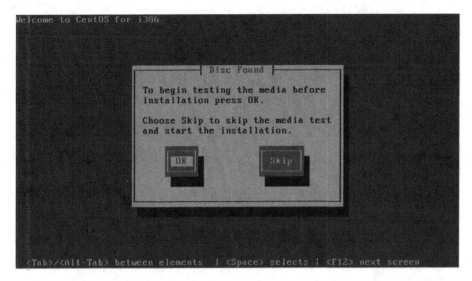

Figure 1-2. *Checking the installation media*

Now the system will init the graphical installer (Figure 1-3).

Figure 1-3. *The graphical installer*

From the next screens, we'll have to choose the language and the keyboard layout (Figures 1-4 and 1-5).

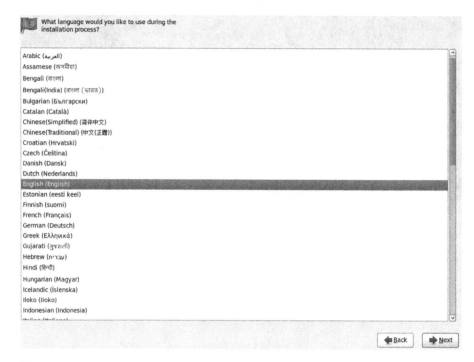

Figure 1-4. Language

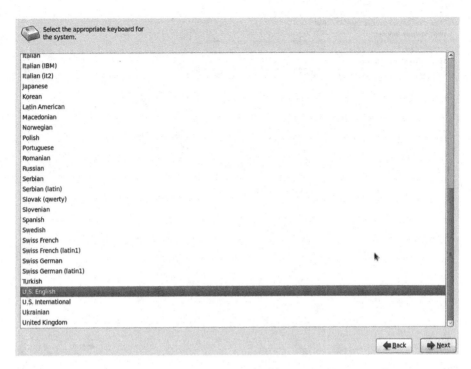

Figure 1-5. *Keyboard*

Now we have to choose whether to install CentOS in a standard disk or in a special device, such as a SAN, LUN, iSCSI drive, etc. As we'll be installing standard disks most of the time, we will choose the first option (Figure 1-6).

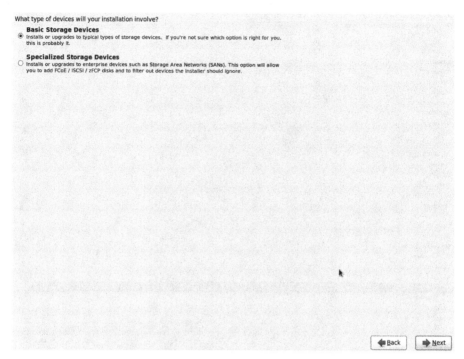

Figure 1-6. *Choosing where to install the OS*

After clicking the Next button, a warning appears (Figure 1-7), telling us that all data in the disk will be lost. As this is either a blank disk or a disk whose data are no longer needed, we click Yes.

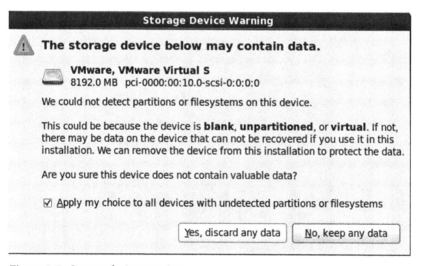

Figure 1-7. *Storage device warning*

The program now requests us to enter the name and the domain of the computer we are about to install (Figure 1-8). We can write this information now or do it once the installation is complete. We click Next.

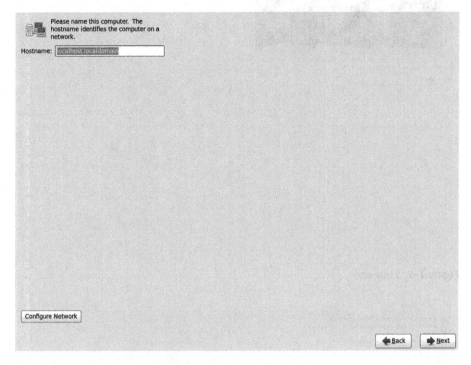

Figure 1-8. *Computer name and domain*

From the upcoming screens, we'll have to choose the time zone as well as the root password (Figures 1-9 and 1-10).

Figure 1-9. *Time zone*

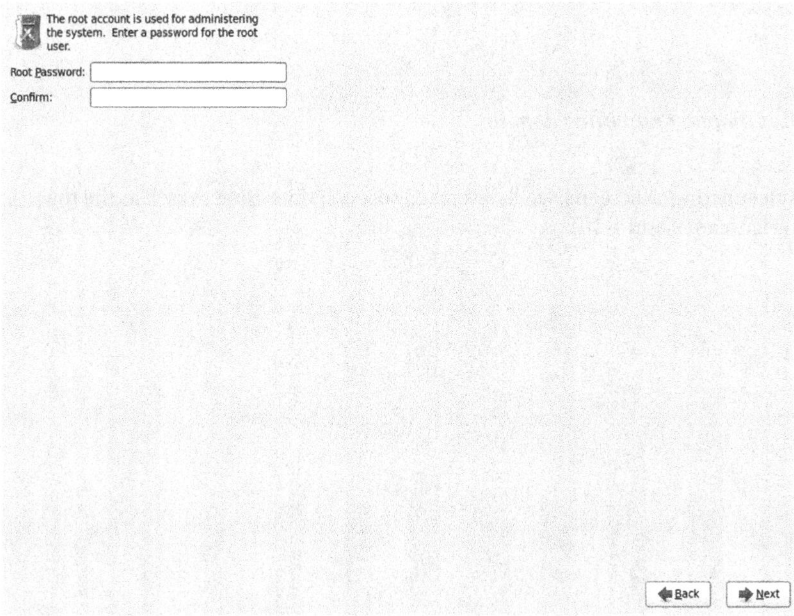

Figure 1-10. *Root password*

Now we are offered several options before starting the actual installation (Figure 1-11). We can choose to use the whole disk, no matter what Linux or non-Linux partitions might exist on the disk, use only free disk space, customize the disk partitioning, etc. As the default partitioning scheme is acceptable to start, we choose the first option. Although, if we already had clearly in mind the role the server was to play in the network, we would probably have to customize the partitioning layout to create separate partitions or volumes for the different directories: /home, /var, etc.

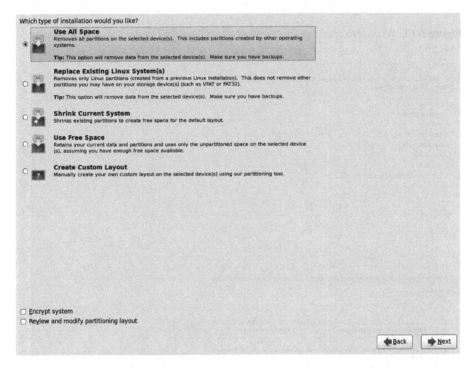

Figure 1-11. Partitioning layout

We receive another warning (Figure 1-12), reminding us that the changes are going to be written on disk, and we are requested to specify what software package we want to install. There are several predefined sets of software, database server, web server, etc. We'll choose the Minimal option (Figure 1-13) and install later the different software packages, as we need them.

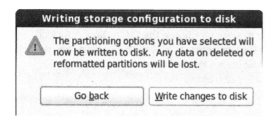

Figure 1-12. *Writing to disk*

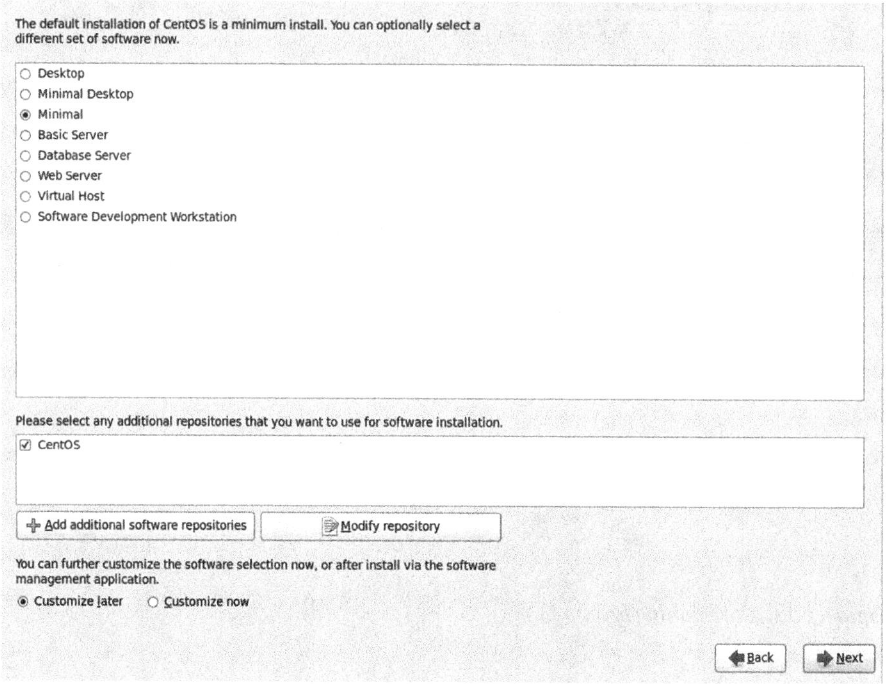

The default installation of CentOS is a minimum install. You can optionally select a different set of software now.

○ Desktop
○ Minimal Desktop
◉ Minimal
○ Basic Server
○ Database Server
○ Web Server
○ Virtual Host
○ Software Development Workstation

Please select any additional repositories that you want to use for software installation.

☑ CentOS

⊹ Add additional software repositories   🗟 Modify repository

You can further customize the software selection now, or after install via the software management application.

◉ Customize later   ○ Customize now

⬅ Back   ➡ Next

Figure 1-13. *Software selection*

And, finally, the actual installation process begins (Figure 1-14).

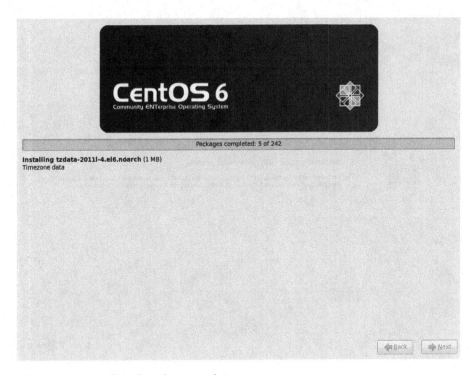

Figure 1-14. Installing the software packages

After a few minutes, the installation will be over (Figure 1-15), and we'll have to reboot the system.

Figure 1-15. *Congratulations!*

Once the boot process is complete, we have a working CentOS server (Figure 1-16).

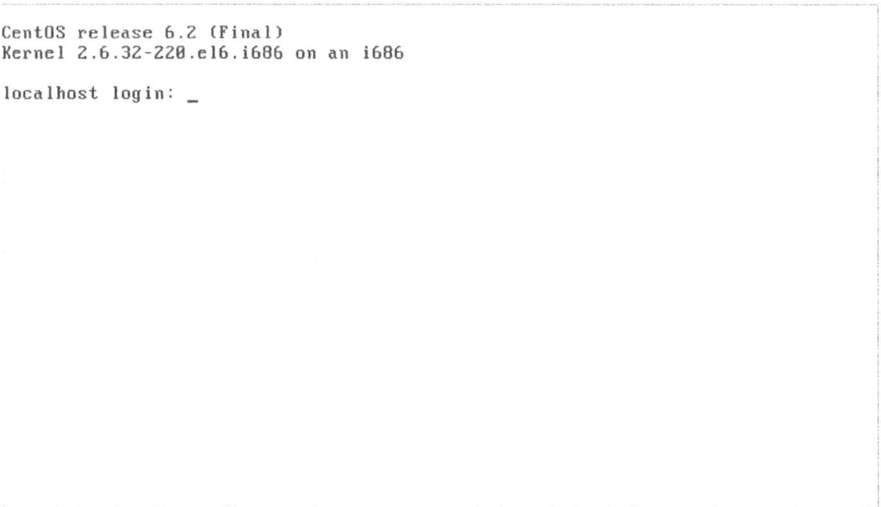

```
CentOS release 6.2 (Final)
Kernel 2.6.32-220.el6.i686 on an i686

localhost login: _
```

Figure 1-16. *Our brand new server*

1.2. CentOS 7

As you saw in section "CentOS 6," there are many types of installations to choose from. As we did previously when installing CentOS 6, we'll also install CentOS 7 from the installation DVD. At the time of writing of this book, this could be downloaded from the official site.[4] After downloading the ISO file, we can burn it onto a DVD. After that, we are ready to boot a server with the installation DVD inserted, as long as the computer is configured to boot from a DVD. After a few seconds, we'll see the screen shown in Figure 1-17.

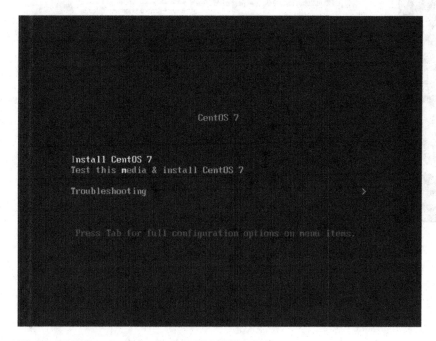

Figure 1-17. *Booting from the CentOS 7 DVD*

---

[4]CentOs, http://www.centos.org/download/, 2016.

We select the first option: Install CentOS 7. The computer now will start the graphical installer, and we'll be asked about the language we want to use during the install (Figure 1-18).

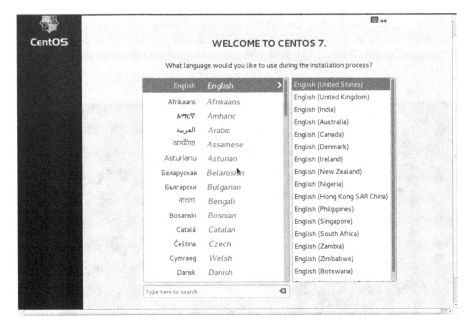

Figure 1-18. *Installing CentOS 7*

After we click the Continue button, we can see a brief summary of the installation (Figure 1-19).

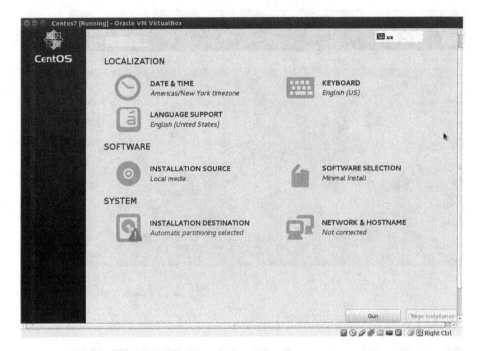

Figure 1-19. Installing CentOS 7

From this screen, we can set the time zone (Figure 1-20) or change the keyboard layout (Figure 1-21).

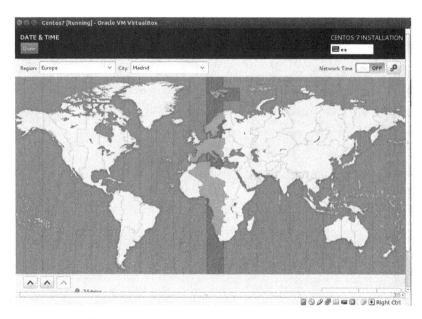

Figure 1-20. Choosing the time zone

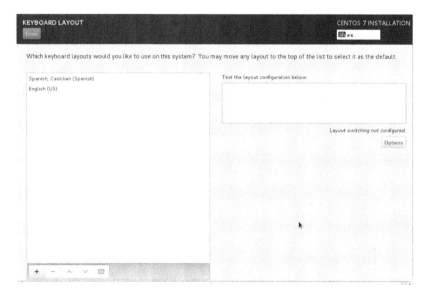

Figure 1-21. Selecting the keyboard layout

We can also select the software packages we want to install (Figure 1-22). By default, a minimum install is selected, but there are many other collections of packages available, such as Basic Web Server or Virtualization Host. We will keep the default selection: Minimal Install.

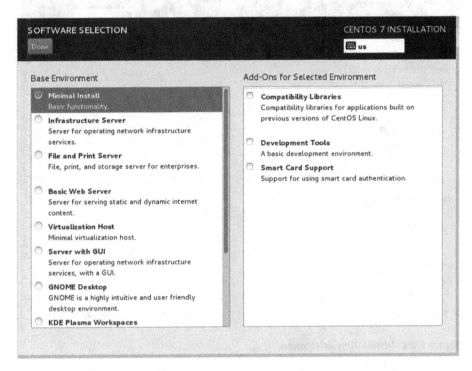

Figure 1-22. Software selection

Before beginning the actual installation, we must choose the installation destination (Figure 1-23).

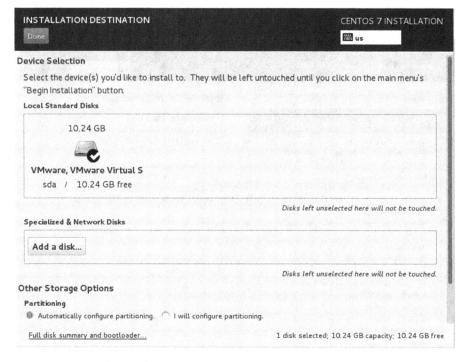

Figure 1-23. *Installation destination*

In most cases, we select the local hard disk, but we could also select other devices, such as SAN disks.

At this point, we could also set up the network, but, as we prefer to do it after the installation, we can omit this step and click the Begin Installation button.

While the system is copying files (Figure 1-24), we can set the root password and create additional users (Figures 1-25 and 1-26).

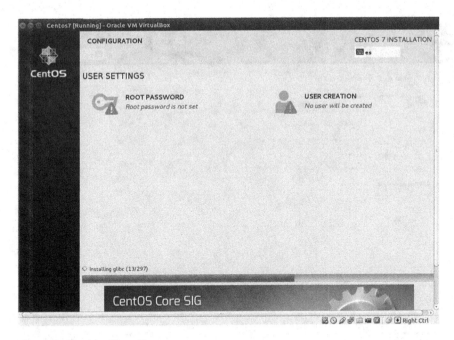

Figure 1-24. Installing the system

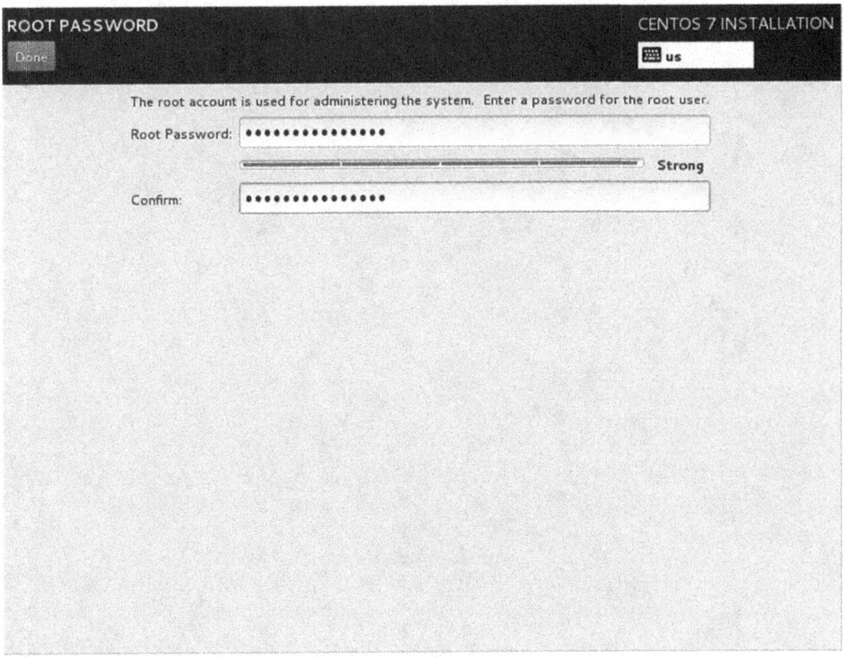

ROOT PASSWORD   CENTOS 7 INSTALLATION

Done   ⌨ us

The root account is used for administering the system. Enter a password for the root user.

Root Password: ●●●●●●●●●●●●●●●●●

                                                                                    Strong

Confirm: ●●●●●●●●●●●●●●●●●

Figure 1-25. Setting the root password

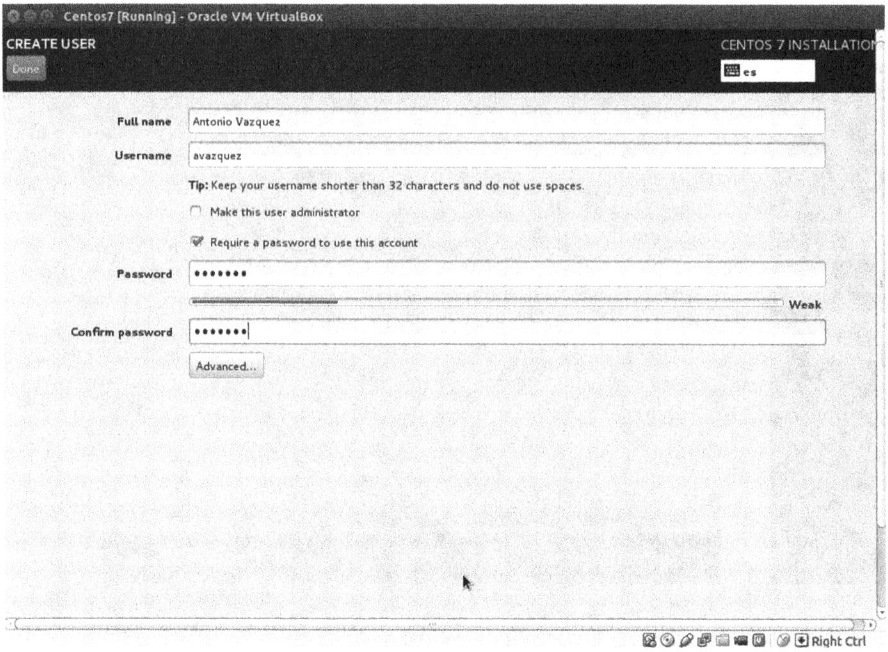

Figure 1-26. *Creating an additional user*

When the installation completes (Figure 1-27), we can reboot the computer and start using CentOS 7.

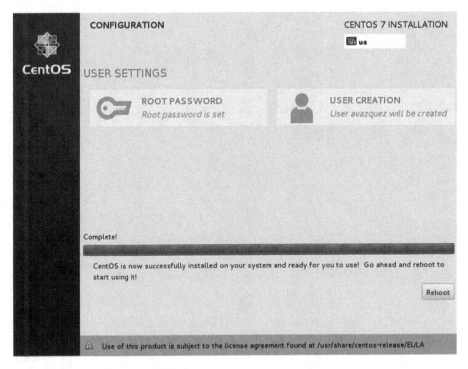

Figure 1-27. *Installation complete!*

CHAPTER 2

∎ ∎ ∎

Basic Administration

Once the system is installed and ready, it's time to start doing something useful with it. This is not a book about Linux basic administration, but I will try to explain briefly the most important commands a Linux systems administrator has to know.

2.1. Basic Commands

Most of this chapter applies to both versions of CentOS covered in this book (6 and 7). There are, however, some sections that differ, depending on the version you're working with. In such cases, to avoid confusing the reader, I will identify explicitly the version to which the section applies.

2.1.1. Directories and Their Contents (ls and cd)

Once we log on to the system as the root user, with the password we specified when installing the server, we are shown a prompt. Initially, we will be located in the root home directory (/root). We can confirm it with the command pwd. If we want to list the files and subdirectories inside /root, we can do so by typing "ls."

As in real life, we can have different folders to organize our documents. We can do the same thing in the server. Thus, we can create directories with the command mkdir directory_name. Now, to access this directory, we type cd directory_name. Later, we can go back to the parent directory by adding two dots as a parameter to the cd command (Figure 2-1).

© Antonio Vazquez 2016

A. Vazquez, *Learn CentOS Linux Network Services*, DOI 10.1007/978-1-4842-2379-6_2

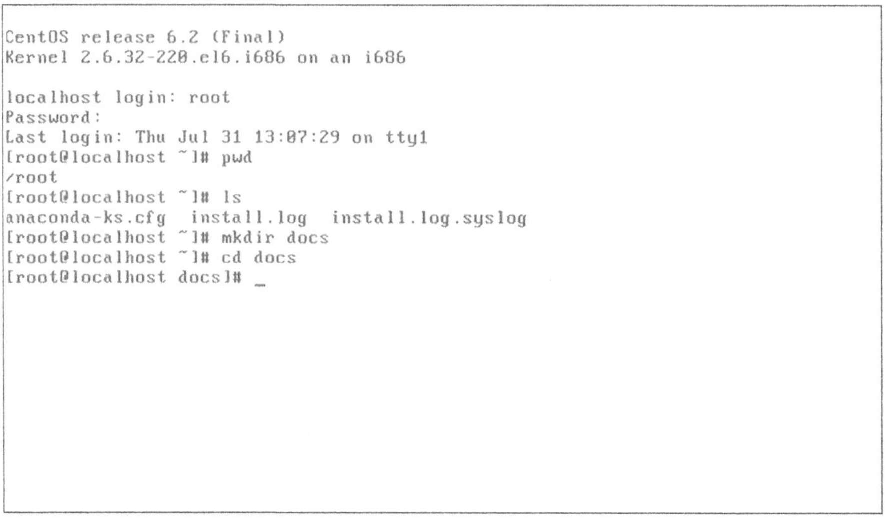

CHAPTER 2 ■ BASIC ADMINISTRATION

```
CentOS release 6.2 (Final)
Kernel 2.6.32-220.el6.i686 on an i686

localhost login: root
Password:
Last login: Thu Jul 31 13:07:29 on tty1
[root@localhost ~]# pwd
/root
[root@localhost ~]# ls
anaconda-ks.cfg  install.log  install.log.syslog
[root@localhost ~]# mkdir docs
[root@localhost ~]# cd docs
[root@localhost docs]# _
```

Figure 2-1. *Some basic commands*

2.1.2. Creating Users

Previously, we logged in as root. This is acceptable for a test system, but it's not advisable to do this on a production system. Instead, you should log in as a normal user and switch to the root account when performing administrative tasks. Let's see how to do it.

First, we should create the normal user with useradd. useradd can accept many parameters, but in this case, we will only use -m, in order to create the home directory of the user. If we are not sure about the list of parameters of any command, we can (almost) always type command -h, and a brief help text will appear.

So, we type useradd -m antonio and create the user. Now we have to assign this user a new password. We do this with the passwd username.

```
1  [root@delphos ~]# useradd -m antonio
2  [root@delphos ~]# passwd antonio
3  Changing password for user antonio.
4  New password:
5  BAD PASSWORD: it is based on a dictionary word
6  BAD PASSWORD: is too simple
7  Retype new password:
8  passwd: all authentication tokens updated successfully.
```

Now that we have created the normal user, we log out with exit and log back in with the user we just created. From now on, if we have to perform an administrative task, we can switch to root with the su command. Once we're done, we type "exit" to switch back to the normal account. If we are not sure about the user we are currently logged in as, we can use the whoami command at any time.

```
1    [antonio@delphos ~]$ pwd
2    /home/antonio
3    [antonio@delphos ~]$ su root
4    Password:
5    [root@delphos antonio]# whoami
6    root
7    [root@delphos antonio]# exit
8    exit
9    [antonio@delphos ~]$ whoami
10   antonio
```

2.2. Creating and Editing Files

When administering a server, one of the most repeated actions is editing configuration files. This is done by using text editors. Linux includes many of them, either in text or in graphic mode.

2.2.1. vi

Perhaps the most widely used text editor in the Linux and Unix world is vi. For that reason, it is advisable for any Linux administrator to know at least the basics of the vi editor. To create a new text file or edit an existing one, we pass the file name as a parameter. For instance, we could type vi new_file. A new blank screen will appear (Figure 2-2). But before we type any text, we have to press the *i* key. When doing this, we switch from "command mode" into "insert mode."

Figure 2-2. Creating a new file with vi

Once we enter into insert mode, we can type the text (Figure 2-3).

```
Once upon a time there was a king...█
~
~
~
~
~
~
~
~
~
~
~
~
~
~
~
~
~
~
~
-- INSERT --
```

Figure 2-3. *Inserting text in* vi

If we make a mistake, or we want to delete or change something, we must switch back to command mode, by pressing the Esc key. Now we can move the cursor with the arrow keys and supress a character, by hitting the *x* key. For example, if we want to substitute the word *king* for *queen*, we place the cursor over the letter *k* and press the *x* key four times. Once we delete the word *king*, we have to type the new text. In order to do this, we must switch to insert mode again, by pressing the *i* key.

We'll have to repeat the process whenever we want to change or delete something, navigating through the text with the cursor keys. And when we are done, we save the file and leave vi. To save the file at any time, we switch to command mode and type ":w" (without the quotes; Figure 2-4). To exit the program, we do the same thing, but instead of ":w" we type ":q". It is also possible to save and exit at once, with ":wq". Finally, if we want to exit and discard the changes, we type ":q!".

```
Once upon a time there was a queen...
~
~
~
~
~
~
~
~
~
~
~
~
~
~
~
~
~
~
~
~
~
~
~
:w
```

Figure 2-4. *Saving the text file*

2.2.2. nano

Another well-known text editor in the Linux world is nano. It is not as widespread as vi, but, on the other hand, many people find it far more friendly. nano is usually not installed by default, so we'll have to install it with yum (see section "Redirecting Output").

```
1   [root@delphos ~]# nano
2   -bash: nano: command not found
3   [root@delphos ~]# yum provides nano
4   Loaded plugins: fastestmirror
5   Loading mirror speeds from cached hostfile
6    * c6-media:
7   nano-2.0.9-7.el6.i686 : A small text editor
8   Repo     : c6-media
9   Matched from:
10
11  [root@delphos ~]# yum install nano
```

To open or create a file, we only have to type "nano filename," for example, nano another_text_- file.txt. Once we launch nano (Figure 2-5), we can type the text directly, using the keys as we would in any WYSIWYG (what you see is what you get) word processor. Once we have finished, we press Ctrl+X to save the file.

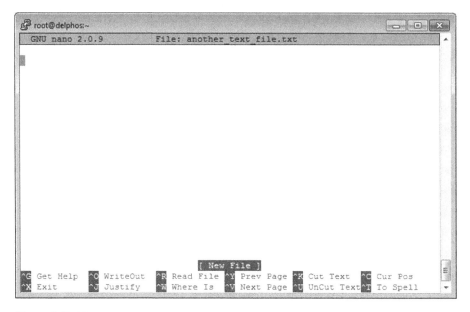

Figure 2-5. *Nano*

2.2.3. gedit

For those who prefer a graphical text editor, CentOS, as well as most Linux distributions, includes gedit. gedit is very easy to use and quite similar to Windows's Notepad. Most systems administrators find it much more user friendly than vi or nano.

Usually, it is not installed by default, so we'll probably have to install it. In the upcoming section "Installing Software," you'll see in detail how to install additional software in CentOS. Once installed, it can be launched by typing "gedit". However, we must take into account that this is a graphical application.

To work, the application has to use a series of graphical libraries. If you have followed the instructions in the book so far, the graphical libraries won't be installed yet in the server, so you won't be able to execute gedit from the server itself. One solution would be to install the graphical environment, as described in the section "Graphical Environment." After that, you could execute gedit.

Another solution would be to connect to the server from a computer that already has a working graphical environment installed. This scenario will be covered in more detail in Chapter 6.

In any case, after successfully executing gedit, you'll see the following screen (Figure 2-6):

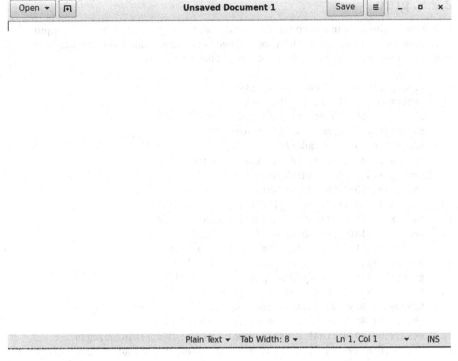

Figure 2-6. *gedit*

From this screen, you can open a file, create a new document, save it, etc.

2.2.4. cat

Another command we could use is cat. It will simply show on the screen the contents of the file passed as a parameter. For example, if we wanted to see the contents of the /etc/group file, we would type this:

```
1   [root@localhost named]# cat /etc/group
2   root:x:0:root
3   bin:x:1:root,bin,daemon
4   daemon:x:2:root,bin,daemon
5   sys:x:3:root,bin,adm
6   adm:x:4:root,adm,daemon
7   tty:x:5:
8   .
9   .
10  .
```

2.2.5. grep

This is one of the most useful commands for the admin. It receives a file or the output of a command as an input and shows only those lines that contain a certain pattern. For example, to see the contents of the /etc/passwd file, we can use cat.

```
1   [root@delphos ~]# cat /etc/passwd
2   root:x:0:0:root:/root:/bin/bash
3   bin:x:1:1:bin:/bin:/sbin/nologin
4   daemon:x:2:2:daemon:/sbin:/sbin/nologin
5   adm:x:3:4:adm:/var/adm:/sbin/nologin
6   lp:x:4:7:lp:/var/spool/lpd:/sbin/nologin
7   sync:x:5:0:sync:/sbin:/bin/sync
8   shutdown:x:6:0:shutdown:/sbin:/sbin/shutdown
9   halt:x:7:0:halt:/sbin:/sbin/halt
10  mail:x:8:12:mail:/var/spool/mail:/sbin/nologin
11  uucp:x:10:14:uucp:/var/spool/uucp:/sbin/nologin
12  operator:x:11:0:operator:/root:/sbin/nologin
13  games:x:12:100:games:/usr/games:/sbin/nologin
14  gopher:x:13:30:gopher:/var/gopher:/sbin/nologin
15  ftp:x:14:50:FTP User:/var/ftp:/sbin/nologin
16  nobody:x:99:99:Nobody:/:/sbin/nologin
17  dbus:x:81:81:System message bus:/:/sbin/nologin
18  vcsa:x:69:69:virtual console memory owner:/dev:/sbin/nologin
19  saslauth:x:499:76:"Saslauthd user":/var/empty/saslauth:/sbin/nologin
20  postfix:x:89:89::/var/spool/postfix:/sbin/nologin
21  qpidd:x:498:499:Owner of Qpidd Daemons:/var/lib/qpidd:/sbin/nologin
22  sshd:x:74:74:Privilege-separated SSH:/var/empty/sshd:/sbin/nologin
23  named:x:25:25:Named:/var/named:/sbin/nologin
24  ntp:x:38:38::/etc/ntp:/sbin/nologin
25  dhcpd:x:177:177:DHCP server:/:/sbin/nologin
26  tcpdump:x:72:72::/:/sbin/nologin
27  apache:x:48:48:Apache:/var/www:/sbin/nologin
28  antonio:x:500:500::/home/antonio:/bin/bash
```

But if we wanted to see only the line of the root user, we could pass this output to the grep command. To do this, we have to connect the two commands with the symbol "|", called, a "pipe." We would type this:

```
1   [root@delphos ~]# cat /etc/passwd | grep root
2   root:x:0:0:root:/root:/bin/bash
```

The command now only shows the line that contains the word *root*.

Another useful option of grep is "-v". This option shows all the lines that DO NOT contain a certain word or pattern. For example, many configuration files have a lot of lines that start with a comment sign (#). In such cases, it is much clearer to watch only the lines that are uncommented.

```
 1    [root@delphos ~]# cat /etc/ssh/sshd_config | grep -v "#"
 2
 3    .
 4    .
 5    .
 6    Protocol 2
 7    SyslogFacility AUTHPRIV
 8    .
 9    .
10    PasswordAuthentication yes
11    ChallengeResponseAuthentication no
12    .
13    .
```

2.2.6. more

If the file we try to see with the cat command is too long, we won't be able to see all the content in a single screen, as the text will immediately scroll down. If we want to see the full content, we can use the more command. This way, we'll be able to see the whole text one screen at a time, manually passing to the next one (Figure 2-7).

```
 1    [root@localhost ~]# more /var/log/messages
```

```
Jul 31 09:05:01 localhost kernel: imklog 4.6.2, log source = /proc/kmsg started.
Jul 31 09:05:01 localhost rsyslogd: [origin software="rsyslogd" swVersion="4.6.2
" x-pid="977" x-info="http://www.rsyslog.com"] (re)start
Jul 31 09:05:01 localhost kernel: Initializing cgroup subsys cpuset
Jul 31 09:05:01 localhost kernel: Initializing cgroup subsys cpu
Jul 31 09:05:01 localhost kernel: Linux version 2.6.32-220.el6.i686 (mockbuild@c
6b18n3.bsys.dev.centos.org) (gcc version 4.4.6 20110731 (Red Hat 4.4.6-3) (GCC)
) #1 SMP Tue Dec 6 16:15:40 GMT 2011
Jul 31 09:05:01 localhost kernel: KERNEL supported cpus:
Jul 31 09:05:01 localhost kernel:   Intel GenuineIntel
Jul 31 09:05:01 localhost kernel:   AMD AuthenticAMD
Jul 31 09:05:01 localhost kernel:   NSC Geode by NSC
Jul 31 09:05:01 localhost kernel:   Cyrix CyrixInstead
Jul 31 09:05:01 localhost kernel:   Centaur CentaurHauls
Jul 31 09:05:01 localhost kernel:   Transmeta GenuineTMx86
Jul 31 09:05:01 localhost kernel:   Transmeta TransmetaCPU
Jul 31 09:05:01 localhost kernel:   UMC UMC UMC UMC
Jul 31 09:05:01 localhost kernel: Disabled fast string operations
Jul 31 09:05:01 localhost kernel: BIOS-provided physical RAM map:
Jul 31 09:05:01 localhost kernel: BIOS-e820: 0000000000000000 - 000000000009f800
 (usable)
Jul 31 09:05:01 localhost kernel: BIOS-e820: 000000000009f800 - 00000000000a0000
 (reserved)
--More--(0%)
```

Figure 2-7. *Seeing the content of a file with more*

2.2.7. less

less is pretty similar to more. We can see a long file one screen at the time, the only difference being that less allows us to go back to a previous page. With more, once we advance to the next page, we can't go back (unless we exit more and execute it again).

2.2.8. head

We've seen that we can use cat to see the content of a file. Nevertheless, if the file is too long, the content will fill many screens. We could use more or less to see one page at a time, but maybe we just want to see the first lines. In this case, we can simply type "head filename", and we'll see the first 10 lines (by default) of the file.

```
1    [root@localhost named]# head /etc/group
2    root:x:0:root
3    bin:x:1:root,bin,daemon
4    daemon:x:2:root,bin,daemon
5    sys:x:3:root,bin,adm
6    adm:x:4:root,adm,daemon
7    tty:x:5:
8    disk:x:6:root
9    lp:x:7:daemon,lp
10   mem:x:8:
11   kmem:x:9:
12   [root@localhost named]#
```

If we wanted to see just the first three lines, we'd use -n 3. For example:

```
1    [root@localhost named]# head -n 3 /etc/group
2    root:x:0:root
3    bin:x:1:root,bin,daemon
4    daemon:x:2:root,bin,daemon
5    [root@localhost named]#
```

2.2.9. tail

tail is a command similar to head, but it will show the last lines of the file instead of the first ones. So, to see the last four lines of the file /etc/group, we can do this:

```
1    [root@localhost named]# tail -n 4 /etc/group
2    qpidd:x:499:
3    sshd:x:74:
4    antonio:x:500:
5    named:x:25:
6    [root@localhost named]#
```

A really useful option of the `tail` command is `-f`. The last lines of the file will appear on the screen, which will also show the new lines added in real time. For instance, if we want to see what system events are taking place right now, we can open the `/var/log/messages` file with the `-f` option. Once we're done, we exit by pressing Ctrl+C.

2.3. Redirecting Output

When discussing the `grep` command, you saw that we could associate the output of a program to the input of another program. When we typed "cat /etc/passwd | grep root," what we were actually doing was passing the output data of the `cat` command as an input parameter for the `grep` program.

We could also redirect the output to a file. For example, if we wanted to have a list with the content of the `/etc` folder, we could redirect the output to the file `cat.txt`. Then, we would only have to open the file with whatever tool we wanted.

```
1   [root@delphos ~]# ls /etc/ > etc.txt
2   [root@delphos ~]# cat etc.txt
3   adjtime
4   aliases
5   aliases.db
6   alternatives
7   anacrontab
8   .
9   .
10  .
```

2.4. Installing Software

One of the main tasks an administrator has to deal with is installing new software. This is done mainly in CentOS with the `rpm` and `yum` utilities. This is valid for CentOS 6 as well as for CentOS 7. However, when working with `yum`, we'll see that there are some minor differences between the two CentOS versions, so we'll study them in two different subsections.

The application `rpm` was developed by Red Hat as a software package manager. It allows the user to install new packages very easily, and it keeps a database with all the software installed in the system. The `rpm` file contains the binary code that will be installed, as well as the scripts that have to be executed before or after the installation, to copy the files to the final destination, create directories, etc. For example, if we have mounted the DVD in `/media/cdrom`, we could install an `rpm` like this:

```
1   [root@delphos ~]# rpm -ivh /media/cdrom/Packages/gedit-2.28.4-3.el6.
    i686.rpm
2   Preparing...
    ######################################## [100%]
3           package gedit-1:2.28.4-3.el6.i686 is already installed
```

We tell rpm to install (-i) the package gedit, to show us the progress of the installation (-h) and to show as much information as possible (-v). At that moment, we can check with rpm the software currently installed in the system.

```
1   [root@delphos ~]# rpm -qa
2   libnl-1.1-14.el6.i686
3   ca-certificates-2010.63-3.el6_1.5.noarch
4   python-iwlib-0.1-1.2.el6.i686
5   centos-release-6-2.el6.centos.7.i686
6   pciutils-3.1.4-11.el6.i686
7   iwl5000-firmware-8.83.5.1_1-1.el6_1.1.noarch
8   lsof-4.82-2.el6.i686
9   xorg-x11-drv-ati-firmware-6.14.2-7.el6.noarch
10  libedit-2.11-4.20080712cvs.1.el6.i686
11  iwl4965-firmware-228.61.2.24-2.1.el6.noarch
12  libpcap-1.0.0-6.20091201git117cb5.el6.i686
13  .
14  .
15  .
```

If we want to check that the package named gedit is installed, we can do so by combining the former command and grep.

```
1   [root@delphos ~]# rpm -qa | grep -i gedit
2   gedit-2.28.4-3.el6.i686
```

And, finally, if we want to erase the new installed package, it is also very easy to do.

```
1   [root@delphos ~]# rpm -e gedit
2   [root@delphos ~]# rpm -qa | grep -i gedit
3   [root@delphos ~]#
```

Every rpm file also states the rpms it depends on, that is, the rpms that have to be installed before, so that the one we are installing at the moment will work. So it could happen, and it usually does, that, to work, a software depends on a certain library, which, in turn, depends on another component, and so on. For example, if we try to install logwatch, we'll get the following message:

```
1   [root@delphos ~]# rpm -ivh /media/cdrom/Packages/logwatch-7.3.6-49.el6.
    noarch.rp\
2   m
3   error: Failed dependencies:
4           mailx is needed by logwatch-7.3.6-49.el6.noarch
5           perl(Date::Manip) is needed by logwatch-7.3.6-49.el6.noarch
```

This has been called "dependency hell," and it's been a nightmare for every Linux administrator over the years. To solve this problem, yum was created. yum tries to check and solve automatically the dependencies every package has, so that software installation runs smoothly.

2.4.1. Configuring yum in CentOS 6

yum can be configured to search for software packages in different repositories. By default, it is configured to get the package from http://mirror.centos.org. If you are not connected to the Internet, you'll have to tell yum to use the local DVD as a repository. This repository is already configured, but it is disabled by default. In the /etc/yum.repos.d directory, we can see the files associated with the yum repositories.

```
1   [root@delphos ~]# ls /etc/yum.repos.d/
2   CentOS-Base.repo    CentOS-Debuginfo.repo    CentOS-Media.repo
```

We can edit the CentOS-Media.repo file to enable the repository, but we can also use yum for this. If we type the yum command, it will show us the different options associated on the screen. To see the current repositories, we execute yum repolist.

```
1   [root@delphos ~]# yum repolist
2   Loaded plugins: fastestmirror
3   Loading mirror speeds from cached hostfile
4   Could not retrieve mirrorlist http://mirrorlist.centos.
    org/?release=6&arch=i386&\
5   repo=os error was
6   14: PYCURL ERROR 6 - "Couldn't resolve host 'mirrorlist.centos.org'"
7   repo id                 repo name                          status
8   base                    CentOS-6 - Base                    0
9   extras                  CentOS-6 - Extras                  0
10  updates                 CentOS-6 - Updates                 0
11  repolist: 0
```

To make sure that yum uses only the local DVD repository, we'll have to disable all the repositories and then enable the repository c6-media. We can do that with the –disablerepo and –enablerepo options. So, the full command to list the software packages available in the local DVD would be this: yum –disablerepo=* –enablerepo=c6-media list.

Now, if we execute the yum list command, we will see all the packages available in this repository, as long as the DVD is mounted. If it is not, we can mount it at any time, with the mount command. For example, to mount the CD-ROM in the directory /media/cdrom, we create the directory (if it doesn't exist) and execute the mount /dev/cdrom /media/cdrom command.

```
1   [root@delphos ~]# mkdir /media/cdrom
2   [root@delphos ~]# mount /dev/cdrom /media/cdrom/
3   mount: block device /dev/sr0 is write-protected, mounting read-only
```

We can see part of the listing of available packages.

```
1   [root@delphos ~]# yum --disablerepo=* --enablerepo=c6-media list
2   Loaded plugins: fastestmirror
3   Loading mirror speeds from cached hostfile
4    * c6-media:
5   Installed Packages
```

35

6	ConsoleKit.i686	0.4.1-3.el6	@anaconda\
7	-CentOS-201112130233.i386/6.2		
8	ConsoleKit-libs.i686	0.4.1-3.el6	@anaconda\
9	-CentOS-201112130233.i386/6.2		
10	GConf2.i686	2.28.0-6.el6	@c6-media
11	MAKEDEV.i686	3.24-6.el6	@anaconda\
12	-CentOS-201112130233.i386/6.2		
13	ORBit2.i686	2.14.17-3.1.el6	@c6-media
14	acl.i686	2.2.49-6.el6	@anaconda\
15	-CentOS-201112130233.i386/6.2		
16	aic94xx-firmware.noarch	30-2.el6	@anaconda\
17	-CentOS-201112130233.i386/6.2		
18	alsa-lib.i686	1.0.22-3.el6	@c6-media
19	apr.i686	1.3.9-3.el6_1.2	@c6-media
20	apr-util.i686	1.3.9-3.el6_0.1	@c6-media
21	apr-util-ldap.i686	1.3.9-3.el6_0.1	@c6-media
22	atk.i686	1.28.0-2.el6	@c6-media
23	atmel-firmware.noarch	1.3-7.el6	@anaconda\
24	-CentOS-201112130233.i386/6.2		
25	attr.i686	2.4.44-7.el6	@anaconda\
26	-CentOS-201112130233.i386/6.2		
27	audit.i686	2.1.3-3.el6	@anaconda\
28	-CentOS-201112130233.i386/6.2		
29	audit-libs.i686	2.1.3-3.el6	@anaconda\
30	-CentOS-201112130233.i386/6.2		
31	authconfig.i686	6.1.12-5.el6	@anaconda\
32	-CentOS-201112130233.i386/6.2		
33	avahi-libs.i686	0.6.25-11.el6	@c6-media
34	b43-openfwwf.noarch	5.2-4.el6	@anaconda\
35	-CentOS-201112130233.i386/6.2		
36	basesystem.noarch	10.0-4.el6	@anaconda\
37	-CentOS-201112130233.i386/6.2		
38	bash.i686	4.1.2-8.el6.centos	@anaconda\
39	-CentOS-201112130233.i386/6.2		
40	.		
41	.		
42	.		

2.4.2. Configuring yum in CentOS 7

By default, in CentOS 7, there isn't any predefined repository to use the DVD. So, we'll have to create it by hand. In the /etc/yum.repo.d/ folder, we'll see the following:

```
1  [root@Centos7 ~]# ls /etc/yum.repos.d/
2  CentOS-Base.repo CentOS-Debuginfo.repo CentOS-Sources.repo CentOS-
   Vault.repo
3  [root@Centos7 ~]#
```

For this new repository, we have to create a new file named CentOS-Media.repo. We can create it from scratch, or we can use the following nice example, with comments from the Internet:[1]

```
1  [root@Centos7 yum.repos.d]# cat CentOS-Media.repo
2  [c7-media]
3  name=CentOS-$releasever - Media
4  baseurl=file:///media/cdrom/
5  gpgcheck=0
6  enabled=0
```

We'll have to create the /media/cdrom directory and mount the CD-ROM too.

```
1  [root@Centos7 ~]# mkdir /media/cdrom
1  [root@CentOS7 ~]# mount /dev/cdrom /media/cdrom/
1  mount: block device /dev/sr0 is write-protected, mounting read-only
```

Now we can check whether this new repository works, by listing the available packages.

```
1   [root@Centos7 yum.repos.d]# yum --disablerepo=* --enablerepo=c7-media list
2
3   Installed Packages
4   ModemManager-glib.x86_64      1.1.0-6.git20130913.el7          @anaconda
5   NetworkManager.x86_64         1:0.9.9.1-13.git20140326.4dba720.el7 @ana\
6   conda
7   NetworkManager-glib.x86_64    1:0.9.9.1-13.git20140326.4dba720.el7 @ana\
8   conda
9   NetworkManager-tui.x86_64     1:0.9.9.1-13.git20140326.4dba720.el7 @ana\
10  conda
11  acl.x86_64                    2.2.51-12.el7                    @anaconda
12  aic94xx-firmware.noarch       30-6.el7                         @anaconda
13  alsa-firmware.noarch          1.0.27-2.el7                     @anaconda
14  alsa-lib.x86_64               1.0.27.2-3.el7                   @anaconda
15  alsa-tools-firmware.x86_64    1.0.27-4.el7                     @anaconda
16  audit.x86_64                  2.3.3-4.el7                      @anaconda
17  audit-libs.x86_64             2.3.3-4.el7                      @anaconda
18  authconfig.x86_64             6.2.8-8.el7                      @anaconda
19  avahi.x86_64                  0.6.31-13.el7                    @anaconda
20  avahi-autoipd.x86_64          0.6.31-13.el7                    @anaconda
21  avahi-libs.x86_64             0.6.31-13.el7                    @anaconda
22  basesystem.noarch             10.0-7.el7.centos                @anaconda
23 .
24 .
```

---

[1]https://github.com/cloudrouter/centos-repo/blob/master/CentOS-Media.repo

2.4.3. yum Options

yum is quite a versatile tool. We have seen how to list the packages, but we can also list collections of packages called groups. To list these groups, we could type yum -disablerepo=* -enablerepo=c6- media grouplist. After that, we would see on the screen a list with the groups already installed and those which are available to install. In this example, there might be some differences between CentOS 6 and CentOS 7, as the yum versions are different. For instance, some groups might not appear by default in CentOS 7. In this case, we should use the option group list hidden.

In CentOS 6:

```
1   [root@delphos ~]# yum --disablerepo=* --enablerepo=c6-media grouplist
2   Loaded plugins: fastestmirror
3   Loading mirror speeds from cached hostfile
4    * c6-media:
5   Setting up Group Process
6   Checking for new repos for mirrors
7   Installed Groups:
8      Client management tools
9      E-mail server
10     Graphical Administration Tools
11     Messaging Client Support
12     Systems Management Messaging Server support
13  Installed Language Groups:
14     Arabic Support [ar]
15     Armenian Support [hy]
16     Georgian Support [ka]
17  .
18  .
19  .
```

In CentOS 7:

```
1   [root@CentOS7 ~]# yum --disablerepo=* --enablerepo=c7-media group list
2   Loaded plugins: fastestmirror
3   Loading mirror speeds from cached hostfile
4   Available environment groups:
5      Minimal Install
6      Infrastructure Server
7      File and Print Server
8      Basic Web Server
9      Virtualization Host
10     Server with GUI
11     GNOME Desktop
12     KDE Plasma Workspaces
13     Development and Creative Workstation
14  Installed groups:
15     System Administration Tools
```

```
16    Available Groups:
17       Compatibility Libraries
18       Console Internet Tools
19       Development Tools
20       Graphical Administration Tools
21       Legacy UNIX Compatibility
22       Scientific Support
23       Security Tools
24       Smart Card Support
25       System Management
26    Done
27
28    [root@CentOS7 ~]# yum --disablerepo=* --enablerepo=c7-media group list
      hidden
29    Loaded plugins: fastestmirror
30    Loading mirror speeds from cached hostfile
31    Available environment groups:
32       Minimal Install
33       Infrastructure Server
34       File and Print Server
35       Basic Web Server
36       Virtualization Host
37       Server with GUI
38       GNOME Desktop
39       KDE Plasma Workspaces
40       Development and Creative Workstation
41    Installed groups:
42       Core
43       E-mail Server
44       Network Infrastructure Server
45       System Administration Tools
46    Available Groups:
47       Additional Development
48       Anaconda Tools
49       Backup Client
50       Backup Server
51       Base
52       Compatibility Libraries
53       Conflicts (Client)
54       Conflicts (Server)
55       Conflicts (Workstation)
56       Console Internet Tools
57       DNS Name Server
58       Debugging Tools
59       Desktop Debugging and Performance Tools
60       Development Tools
61       Dial-up Networking Support
62       Directory Client
```

39

63	Directory Server
64	Emacs
65	FTP Server
66	File and Storage Server
67	Fonts
68	GNOME
69	GNOME Applications
70	Graphical Administration Tools
71	Graphics Creation Tools
72	Guest Agents
73	Guest Desktop Agents
74	Hardware Monitoring Utilities
75	High Availability
76	Identity Management Server
77	Infiniband Support
78	Input Methods
79	Internet Applications
80	Internet Browser
81	Java Platform
82	KDE
83	KDE Applications
84	KDE Multimedia Support
85	Large Systems Performance
86	Legacy UNIX Compatibility
87	Legacy X Window System Compatibility
88	Load Balancer
89	Mainframe Access
90	MariaDB Database Client
91	MariaDB Database Server
92	Multimedia
93	Network File System Client
94	Networking Tools
95	Office Suite and Productivity
96	PHP Support
97	Performance Tools
98	Perl Support
99	Perl for Web
100	Platform Development
101	PostgreSQL Database Client
102	PostgreSQL Database Server
103	Print Server
104	Printing Client
105	Python
106	Remote Desktop Clients
107	Remote Management for Linux
108	Resilient Storage
109	Ruby Support
110	Scientific Support

```
111     Security Tools
112     Smart Card Support
113     System Management
114     Technical Writing
115     Virtualization Client
116     Virtualization Hypervisor
117     Virtualization Platform
118     Virtualization Tools
119     Web Server
120     Web Servlet Engine
121     X Window System
120  Done
```

If we wanted to install one of these groups, such as "Hardware monitoring utilities," we could get some more information about it with the groupinfo parameter.

```
1   [root@delphos www]# yum --disablerepo=* --enablerepo=c6-media groupinfo
    "Hardwar\
2   e monitoring utilities"
3   Loaded plugins: fastestmirror
4   Loading mirror speeds from cached hostfile
5    * c6-media:
6   Setting up Group Process
7   Checking for new repos for mirrors
8
9
10  Group: Hardware monitoring utilities
11   Description: A set of tools to monitor server hardware
12   Default Packages:
13      smartmontools
14   Optional Packages:
15      edac-utils
16      lm_sensors
```

As you can see, the group consists of one default package and two optional packages. The default package will be installed whenever we install the group, whereas the optional packages will be installed only if we specify them. So, to install the group with its additional packages, we would use the following command: 'yum –disablerepo=* -enablerepo=c6-media -setopt=group_package_types=optional groupinstall "Hardware monitoring utilities"'. An information screen will appear later asking for confirmation. We respond yes (y).

```
1   [root@delphos ~]# yum --disablerepo=* --enablerepo=c6-media
    --setopt=group_packa\
2   ge_types=optional groupinstall "Hardware monitoring utilities"
3   Loaded plugins: fastestmirror
4   Loading mirror speeds from cached hostfile
5    * c6-media:
```

```
 6    Setting up Group Process
 7    Checking for new repos for mirrors
 8    Resolving Dependencies
 9    --> Running transaction check
10    ---> Package edac-utils.i686 0:0.9-14.el6 will be installed
11    ---> Package lm_sensors.i686 0:3.1.1-10.el6 will be installed
12    --> Finished Dependency Resolution
13
14    Dependencies Resolved
15
16    ========================================================================
17     Package        Arch      Version        Repository      Size
18    ========================================================================
19    Installing:
20     edac-utils     i686      0.9-14.el6     c6-media        40 k
21     lm_sensors     i686      3.1.1-10.el6   c6-media       122 k
22
23 Transaction Summary
24    ========================================================================
25    Install    2 Package(s)
26
27    Total download size: 162 k
28    Installed size: 415 k
29    Is this ok [y/N]: y
30    Downloading Packages:
31    ------------------------------------------------------------------------
32    Total                              2.0 MB/s | 162 kB     00:00
33    Running rpm_check_debug
34    Running Transaction Test
35    Transaction Test Succeeded
36    Running Transaction
37      Installing : lm_sensors-3.1.1-10.el6.i686                    1/2
38      Installing : edac-utils-0.9-14.el6.i686                      2/2
39
40    Installed:
41      edac-utils.i686 0:0.9-14.el6        lm_sensors.i686 0:3.1.1-10.el6
42
43    Complete!
```

Another useful characteristic of yum is its ability to identify in which package a command is located. Among the most helpful tools for a Linux administrator are the man pages. These provide the user with a lot of information about the different commands and configuration files of the system.

As we have performed a minimum install of CentOS, man will not be installed by default. Nevertheless, we can identify the package to install, thanks to the yum command.

```
1   [root@delphos ~]# man
2   -bash: man: command not found
3   [root@delphos ~]# yum --disablerepo=* --enablerepo=c6-media provides man
4   Loaded plugins: fastestmirror
5   Loading mirror speeds from cached hostfile
6    * c6-media:
7   man-1.6f-29.el6.i686 : A set of documentation tools: man, apropos and
     whatis
8   Repo        : c6-media
9   Matched from:
```

As we can see, the package to install is called—not surprisingly—man. In this case, the name of the package is very intuitive, but it is not always like this, and, in these cases, yum is very helpful. Now we just type "yum –disablerepo=* –enablerepo=c6-media install man", and we can use man to obtain information about any command.

```
1   [root@delphos ~]# yum --disablerepo=* --enablerepo=c6-media install man
2   [root@delphos ~]# man ls
3
4   LS(1)                          User Commands                          LS(1)
5
6   NAME
7          ls - list directory contents
8
9   SYNOPSIS
10         ls [OPTION]... [FILE]...
11
12  DESCRIPTION
13         List information about the FILEs (the current directory by
            default).
14         Sort entries alphabetically if none of -cftuvSUX nor --sort is
            speci
15         fied.
16
17         Mandatory arguments to long options are mandatory for short
            options
18         too.
19
20         -a, --all
21                do not ignore entries starting with .
22
23         -A, --almost-all
24                do not list implied . And ..
25  .
26  .
27  .
```

2.5. Graphical Environment

2.5.1. CentOS 6

After performing a minimal installation, there will be no graphical environment. If we want to start the server in graphic mode, we'll have to install a series of packages. We can combine the required groups in the same yum command, as follows:

```
1   [root@localhost ~]# yum -y --disablerepo=* --enablerepo=c6-media
    groupinstall "D\
2   esktop" "Desktop Platform" "X Window System" "Fonts"
```

In this case, we specified the "-y" option, in order not to be asked for confirmation before installing the software. As we haven't configured networking yet, we'll have to install from the CD repository by specifying the –disablerepo and –enablerepo options.

Once the required packages have been installed, we can switch to graphical mode with the init 5 command.

```
1   [root@localhost ~]# init 5
```

The first time, we'll see a welcome screen (Figure 2-8) and the usual license information (Figure 2-9). Next, the system will ask us to create a normal (non-root) user (Figure 2-10).

Figure 2-8. Installing the graphical environment

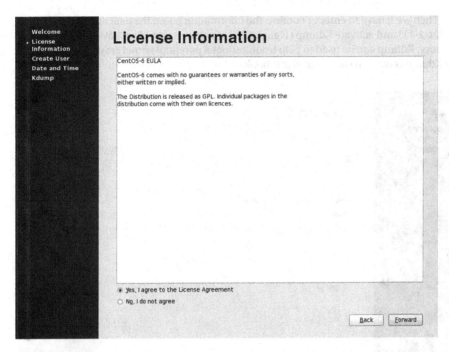

Figure 2-9. *License information*

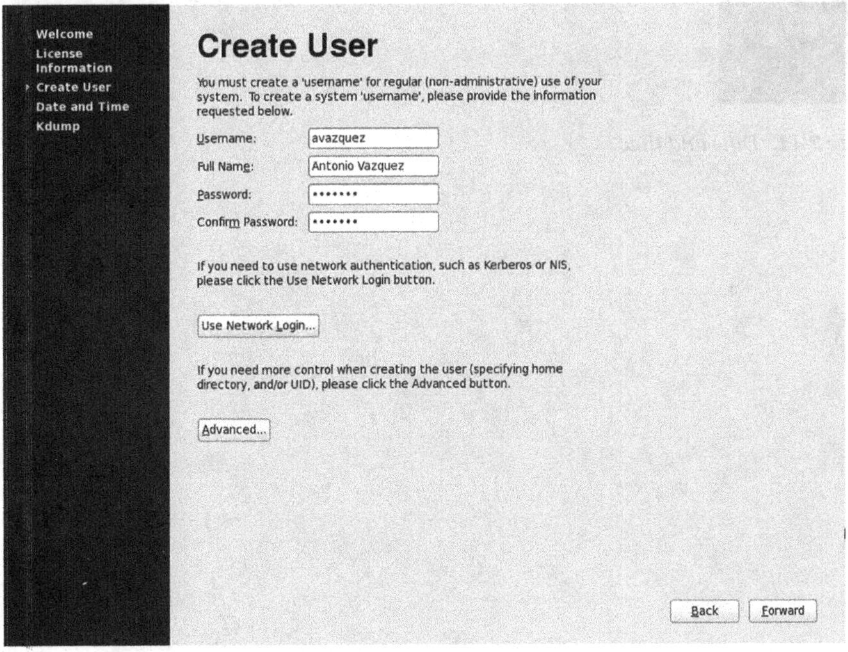

Figure 2-10. *Creating a user*

Then we'll have to enter or confirm the information about the date and time (Figure 2-11) and activate Kdump (Figure 2-12), if we want to and we have enough memory. Kdump can be used to help troubleshoot a potential kernel crash. The way to use Kdump is beyond the scope of this book.

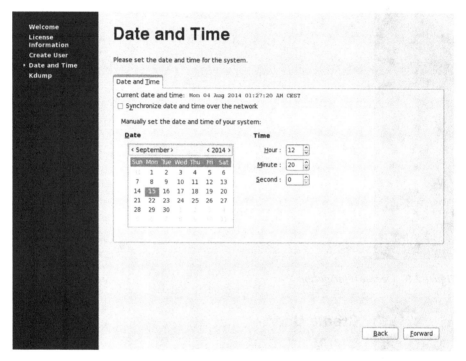

Figure 2-11. *Date and time*

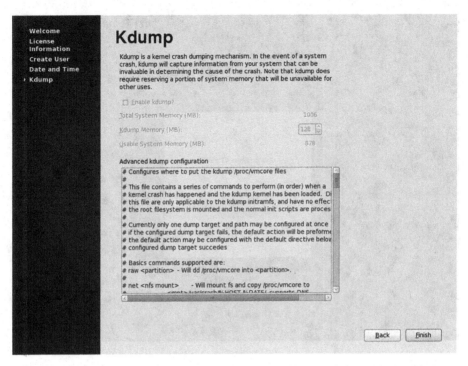

Figure 2-12. *Kdump*

Finally, we see the graphical login screen (Figure 2-13).

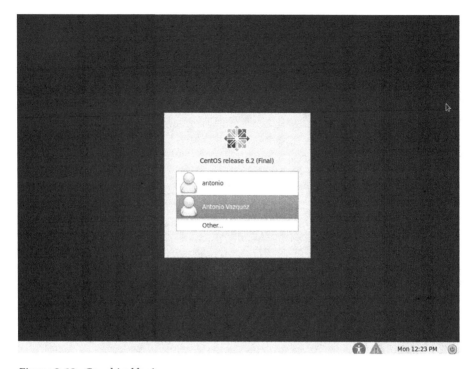

Figure 2-13. *Graphical login*

2.5.2. CentOS 7

If we're using CentOS 7, the packages we need to install are the following:

```
1   [root@CentOS7 ~]# yum --disablerepo=* --enablerepo=c7-media group
    install "X Win\
2   dow System"
3   [root@CentOS7 ~]# yum --disablerepo=* --enablerepo=c7-media group
    install "Gnome\
4   Desktop"
```

We can only use the local repository we created in the section "Configuring yum in CentOS 7," which searches for the software packages in the local CD/DVD. Later, when we configure networking, we can use the default network repositories instead.

When the installation completes, we can launch the graphical desktop with startx.

```
1   [root@CentOS7 ~]# startx
```

After a moment, we'll see the following (Figure 2-14).

Figure 2-14. *Initial setup*

As we can see, the license information is missing, so we click "LICENSE INFORMATION" and accept the license (Figure 2-15).

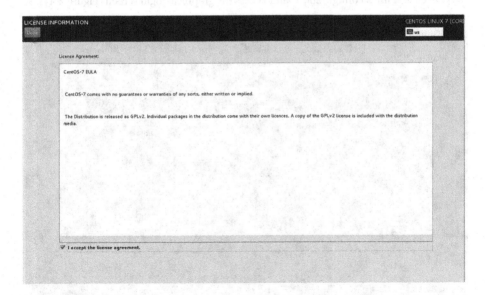

Figure 2-15. *License information*

After accepting the license and clicking the Done button, we can see now that the license has been accepted (Figure 2-16).

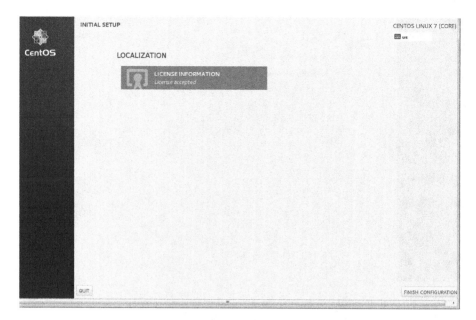

Figure 2-16. *Finishing the configuration*

We click "Finish configuration" and access the graphical login screen (Figure 2-17).

Figure 2-17. *Graphical login*

2.6. Other Useful Commands

2.6.1. chmod

Every file in a Linux system has an associated set of permissions, that is, not every user can read or modify the file. Some users might open the file and execute it (if it is a binary or a script file); some others might modify its content, etc. Traditionally, every file in Linux has three sets of permissions associated: for the owner, the group, and the rest of the users. We can see these permissions with the ls -l command. For example:

```
1    [root@localhost named]# ls -l /etc/init.d/named
2    -rwxr-xr-x. 1 root root 6806 Dec  7  2011 /etc/init.d/named
```

In this case, the owner (root) can read (r), write (w), and execute (x) the /etc/init.d/named script file.

The group(root) can only read it and execute it. And the rest of the users can read and execute the file too.

If for some reason we have to change the permissions, we can do so with chmod. We have to say what set of permissions we want to modify: u (owner), g (group), o (other) or a (all three). We also specify whether we want to add (+) or remove (-) the permission. Let's see a couple of examples.

```
1    [root@localhost named]# chmod o+w /etc/init.d/named
2    [root@localhost named]# ls -l /etc/init.d/named
3    -rwxr-xrwx. 1 root root 6806 Dec 7   2011 /etc/init.d/named
```

We have added (+) the write (w) permission to the rest of users (o).

```
1    [root@localhost named]# chmod o-w /etc/init.d/named
2    [root@localhost named]# ls -l /etc/init.d/named
3    -rwxr-xr-x. 1 root root 6806 Dec  7   2011 /etc/init.d/named
```

And now we revert the situation by removing (-) the write (w) permission.

2.6.2. tee

We've already seen that we can redirect the output of a command to a file.

```
1    [root@delphos ~]# ls /var/ > var_folder.txt
2    [root@delphos ~]# cat var_folder.txt
3    cache
4    db
5    empty
6    games
7    lib
8    local
9    lock
10   log
```

```
11    mail
12    named
13    nis
14    opt
15    preserve
16    run
17    spool
18    tmp
19    www
20    yp
```

But sometimes we might be interested in watching the output of a command while redirecting it to another file. We can do this with tee.

```
1     [root@delphos ~]# ls /var/ | tee var_folder.txt
2     cache
3     db
4     empty
5     games
6     lib
7     local
8     lock
9     log
10    mail
11    named
12    nis
13    opt
14    preserve
15    run
16    spool
17    tmp
18    www
19    yp
20    [root@delphos ~]# cat var_folder.txt
21    cache
22    db
23    empty
24    games
25    lib
26    local
27    lock
28    log
29    mail
30    named
31    nis
32    opt
33    preserve
34    run
```

2.6.3. rm

Sometimes, we have to remove files or directories. To do this, we can use rm. For example, to remove a file called file_to_delete.txt, we'd simply type

```
1    [root@delphos ~]# rm file_to_delete.txt
2    rm: remove regular empty file `file_to_delete.txt'? y
```

By default, rm asks for confirmation before deleting a file, but this can be overridden by using the -f parameter. If we want to delete a folder, we have to use the -r (recursive) parameter.

```
1    [root@delphos ~]# rm -f file_to_delete.txt
2    rm: descend into directory `folder_to_delete'? y
3    rm: remove regular file `folder_to_delete/one.txt'? y
4    rm: remove regular file `folder_to_delete/two.txt'? y
5    rm: remove regular file `folder_to_delete/three.txt'? y
```

2.6.4. ps

Another command used every day by systems administrators is ps, which is used to show current processes. When executed without any options, it shows the processes associated with the terminal from which the command is executed. We can use the -e option to see all the processes, not only those associated with the current terminal. Another interesting option we can use with the command is -f, which shows a bit more of information about the processes, such as the effective user they're executing as or the process ID of their parent process.

```
1    [root@delphos ~]# ps -ef
2    UID          PID  PPID  C STIME TTY        TIME CMD
3    .
4    .
5    .
6    named      17881     1  0 17:35 ?      00:00:00 /usr/sbin/named -u named
7    .
8    .
9    .
```

In this case, we can see that the named service is executing as the named user (UID=named), and its parent process ID(PPID) is 1. That is the init process (in CentOS 6) or the systemd process (in CentOS 7).

2.7. SELinux

SELinux (Security Enhanced Linux) is a mandatory access control (MAC) security mechanism implemented in the kernel that was developed by the United States National Security Agency (NSA). It creates another layer of protection against unauthorized access and limits the damage a hacker can do to the system.

In every Linux system, SELinux could be in one of these three states:

- *Disabled.* SELinux is not executing, and it won't perform any action.

- *Permissive.* SELinux is monitoring the system behavior, and it logs the activity, but it won't restrict any action the system performs.

- *Enforcing.* SELinux is executing and, depending on the configuration, it might block certain actions performed by processes.

We can see if SELinux is executing with the following command:

```
1   [root@localhost named]# sestatus
2   SELinux status:              enabled
3   SELinuxfs mount:             /selinux
4   Current mode:                enforcing
5   Mode from config file:       enforcing
6   Policy version:              24
7   Policy from config file:     targeted
```

In this case, we can see that SELinux is enabled and in enforcing mode. When in enforcing mode, SELinux will block any action that is not allowed by the SELinux settings. We could switch the current mode to permissive, which would permit any action SELinux would normally block but also write a log with details about every action executed that violated SELinux settings. This permissive mode is very useful when tuning SELinux. We can switch to this mode with setenforce.

```
1   [root@centosv6 ~]# setenforce permissive
```

We can check that the change was successful either with the getenforce or the sestatus command.

```
1   [root@centosv6 ~]# getenforce
2   Permissive
3   [root@centosv6 ~]# sestatus
4   SELinux status:              enabled
5   SELinuxfs mount:             /selinux
6   Current mode:                permissive
7   Mode from config file:       enforcing
8   Policy version:              24
9   Policy from config file:     targeted
```

It is possible to disable SELinux completely too. This can be achieved by editing the /etc/syscon- fig/selinux file. There should be a line beginning with SELINUX=, which could take three values: enforcing, permissive, or disabled. When assigning it the value disabled, SELinux will be disabled the next time the computer is rebooted.

SELinux assigns "labels" to processes, files, and folders. According to these labels, usually called contexts, the processes will be allowed or not allowed to perform certain actions.

We can check the security context of any folder with the command ls -Z.

```
1   [root@centosv6 ~]# ls -Z /home/
2   drwx------. antonio antonio unconfined_u:object_r:user_home_dir_t:s0
    antonio
3   drwx------. Jose    jose    unconfined_u:object_r:user_home_dir_t:s0 jose
```

Different folders have different contexts associated with them.

```
1   [root@centosv6 ~]# ls -Z /var/www/
2   drwxr-xr-x. root root system_u:object_r:httpd_sys_script_exec_t:s0 cgi-bin
3   drwxr-xr-x. root root system_u:object_r:httpd_sys_content_t:s0 error
4   drwxr-xr-x. root root system_u:object_r:httpd_sys_content_t:s0 html
5   drwxr-xr-x. root root system_u:object_r:httpd_sys_content_t:s0 icons
```

For example, in order for Apache to access the html files of a web site, the folder should have the httpd_sys_content_t context assigned. We must take this into account when configuring any service on CentOS, and, of course, we should also assign read, write, and/or execute permissions, when necessary.

If we have to change the context of a file or folder, we can use chcon.

```
1   [root@centosv6 ~]# mkdir test
2   [root@centosv6 ~]# ls -Zd test
3   drwxr-xr-x. root root unconfined_u:object_r:admin_home_t:s0 test
4   [root@centosv6 ~]# chcon -t httpd_sys_content_t test/
5   [root@centosv6 ~]# ls -dZ test
6   drwxr-xr-x. root root unconfined_u:object_r:httpd_sys_content_t:s0 test
```

We can also see the context associated to a running process with ps -Z.

```
1   [root@CentOS7 ~]# ps -Z
2   LABEL                          PID TTY          TIME CMD
3   unconfined_u:unconfined_r:unconfined_t:s0-s0:c0.c1023 40884 pts/0
    00:00:00 bash
4   unconfined_u:unconfined_r:unconfined_t:s0-s0:c0.c1023 45546 pts/0
    00:00:01 ps
```

By default, SELinux also keeps a series of Boolean values that influence the behavior of the system. We can get a list of these values with the getsebool command.

```
1   [root@centosv6 ~]# getsebool -a
2   abrt_anon_write --> off
3   abrt_handle_event --> off
4   allow_console_login --> on
5   allow_cvs_read_shadow --> off
6   allow_daemons_dump_core --> on
7   allow_daemons_use_tcp_wrapper --> off
```

```
 8   allow_daemons_use_tty --> on
 9   allow_domain_fd_use --> on
10   allow_execheap --> off
11   allow_execmem --> on
12   .
13   .
14   .
```

We can change any of these Boolean values with setsebool.

```
1   [root@centosv6 ~]# setsebool abrt_anon_write on
2   [root@centosv6 ~]# getsebool abrt_anon_write
3   abrt_anon_write --> on
```

The change will take effect immediately, but when the server is rebooted again, the parameter will be assigned its former value. In order to make the change permanent, we have to add -P to the preceding command.

```
1   [root@centosv6 ~]# setsebool -P abrt_anon_write on
```

Another useful tool when managing SELinux is semanage. Usually it is not installed by default, so if we want to use it, we'll have to install the policycoreutils-python package.

With semanage, we can receive a list of the different contexts.

```
 1   [root@centosv6 ~]# semanage fcontext -l
 2   SELinux fcontext               type           Context
 3
 4   /                              directory      system_u:o\
 5   bject_r:root_t:s0
 6   /.*                            all files      system_u:o\
 7   bject_r:default_t:s0
 8   /[^/]+                         regular file   system_u:o\
 9   bject_r:etc_runtime_t:s0
10   /\. Autofsck                   regular file   system_u:o\
11   bject_r:etc_runtime_t:s0
12   /\.autorelabel                 regular file   system_u:o\
13   bject_r:etc_runtime_t:s0
14   /\.journal                     all files      <<None>>
15   /\.suspended                   regular file   system_u:o\
16   bject_r:etc_runtime_t:s0
17   /a?quota\.(user|group)         regular file   system_u:o\
18   bject_r:quota_db_t:s0
19   /afs                           directory      system_u:o\
20   bject_r:mnt_t:s0
21   /bin                           directory      system_u:o\
22   bject_r:bin_t:s0
23   /bin/.*                        all files      system_u:o\
```

```
24  bject_r:bin_t:s0
25  /bin/alsaunmute                             regular file    system_u:o\
26  bject_r:alsa_exec_t:s0
27  /bin/bash                                   regular file    system_u:o\
28  bject_r:shell_exec_t:s0
29  /bin/bash2                                  regular file    system_u:o\
30  bject_r:shell_exec_t:s0
31  /bin/d?ash                                  regular file    system_u:o\
32  bject_r:shell_exec_t:s0
33  .
34  .
35  .
```

We can also get a list of SELinux Booleans with a short description.

```
1   [root@centosv6 ~]# semanage boolean -l
2   SELinux boolean                   State    Default Description
3
4   ftp_home_dir                      (off, off)  Allow ftp to read and write
    files \
5   in the user home directories
6   smartmon_3ware                    (off, off)  Enable additional
    permissions need\
7   ed to support devices on 3ware controllers.
8   xdm_sysadm_login                  (off, off)  Allow xdm logins as sysadm
9   xen_use_nfs                       (off, off)  Allow xen to manage nfs
    files
10  mozilla_read_content              (off, off)  Control mozilla content
    access
11  ssh_chroot_rw_homedirs            (off, off)  Allow ssh with chroot env to
    read \
12  and write files in the user home directories
13  tftp_anon_write                   (off, off)  Allow tftp to modify public
    files \
14  used for public file transfer services.
15  allow_console_login               (on,  on)  Allow direct login to the
    console \
16  device. Required for System 390
17  spamassassin_can_network          (off, off)  Allow user spamassassin
    clients to\
18  use the network.
19  .
20  .
21  .
```

Throughout the book, we'll use these tools to configure SELinux to allow the execution of different network services.

CHAPTER 3

Networking

In this day and age, a computer that is completely isolated from the outer world is pretty much useless. Many everyday tasks, such as sending or receiving e-mail, sharing files, or querying a database, require an external connection.

In order to communicate, computers use a software component called a network protocol. I won't go into detail about the different network protocols, as there are already many books on the subject. There are actually many network protocols, but the de facto standard is the TCP/IP protocol.

3.1. IPv4

This protocol was developed in the '70s by the Defense Advanced Research Projects Agency (DARPA). It is a hierarchical model that assigns every computer an IP address in the form of four octets: x.x.x.x. Every address has an associated mask that also consists of four octets. You'll see this subsequently in a little more detail.

As I mentioned earlier, an IP address is represented by four numbers whose values range from 0 to 255. For example, 192.168.10.19, 198.165.30.40, 88.43.53.12, etc. And this number has another associated parameter, the subnet mask. The subnet mask could be 255.255.255.0, 255.255.0.0, 255.240,0.0, etc. Let's imagine we have a computer with the following parameters:

IP Address: 192.168.10.19

Network Mask: 255.255.255.0

Now we must introduce a new concept, the network address. This value will tell us whether two computers are in the same or in different networks. To obtain the network address, we check the values of the IP address and the network mask in binary.

IP Address: 11000000.10100100.00001010.00010011

Network Mask: 11111111.11111111.11111111.00000000

The network address will be the part of the IP address that corresponds to the part of the network mask that has the 1's digits. In our example, it will be

Network Address: 11000000.10100100.00001010 192.168.10

As the network address has to have a length of four octets too, the rest of the address will be completed with 0's.

Network Address: 11000000.10100100.00001010.00000000 192.168.10.0

© Antonio Vazquez 2016
A. Vazquez, *Learn CentOS Linux Network Services*, DOI 10.1007/978-1-4842-2379-6_3

For two computers to communicate directly, they must have the same network address. In our example, if we already have a server with the 192.168.10.19 IP address, and the network mask is 255.255.255.0, we should use the same network address (and, of course, a different IP) for a new computer. One of the many valid IP address could be this one:

IP Address: 192.168.10.20

Network Mask: 255.255.255.0

Network Address: 192.168.10.0

So, an IP address must always have an associated mask; otherwise, one wouldn't be able to determine the network it belongs to. In the preceding examples, the IP address and the network mask were specified as two independent values, but they can be represented in an abbreviated form. Let's take the last example.

IP Address: 192.168.10.20

Network Mask: 255.255.255.0

If we translate the values into binary, we have this:

IP Address: 11000000.10101000.00001010.00010010

Network Mask: 11111111.11111111.11111111.00000000

The network mask has 24 1's, so we could represent the IP address and mask like this: 192.168.10.20/24.

IP addresses can also be classified in many categories:

Class A:

The address begins with a 0. That is to say, every address from 1.x.x.x up to 127.x.x.x is considered to be a Class A IP address.

Class B:

The address begins with 10. These IP addresses range from 128 to 191.x.x.x.

Class C:

In this case, the address begins with 110. The valid range of addresses is 192.x.x.x to 224.x.x.x.

There are also a Class D and Class E, used for specific purposes, but I won't get into the details of these.

3.1.1. Special Addresses

There are also a few addresses that are defined for specific purposes.

One example is the IP address 127.0.0.1, called loopback. Every single device that uses the TCP protocol is automatically assigned this address, even if it doesn't have a network device and it hasn't been assigned any other IP. By using this loopback address, we can test the TCP protocol locally.

Some other network addresses are meant to be used in private LANs but not on the Internet, as they might not be unique. These addresses are

10.0.0.0/8 172.16.0.0/12 192.168.0.0/16

So, every IP address belonging to any of these networks is considered a private address.

3.1.2. Unicast, Multicast, and Broadcast

An IPv4 device can communicate directly with another IPv4 device, establishing a one-to-one relation. This is called unicast.

But maybe this device wants to communicate with all the devices with the same network address. This is called a broadcast, and it consists of the network address plus all the host bit filled with 1's. For example, if a computer has the 192.168.1.20/24 address and wants to send a broadcast, it will send it to the 192.168.1.255 address.

There is also a third scenario, in which a computer wants to communicate with a few other computers in the same network, but not all of them. For this to work, these computers should share a multicast address. And this type of communication is called multicast.

3.1.3. IPv4 Configuration in CentOS
3.1.3.1. CentOS 6

To assign temporarily an IP address to our CentOS server, we can use the `ifconfig` command. Executed with the -a parameter, it will show all the network interfaces present, ignoring whether they are configured or not.

```
1   [root@delphos ~]# ifconfig -a
2   eth0      Link encap:Ethernet HWaddr 00:0C:29:78:4C:B1
3             UP BROADCAST RUNNING MULTICAST MTU:1500 Metric:1
4             RX packets:0 errors:0 dropped:0 overruns:0 frame:0
5             TX packets:0 errors:0 dropped:0 overruns:0 carrier:0
6             collisions:0 txqueuelen:1000
7             RX bytes:0 (0.0 b) TX bytes:55678099 (0.0 b)
8             Interrupt:19 Base address:0x2000
9
10  lo        Link encap:Local Loopback
11            inet addr:127.0.0.1 Mask:255.0.0.0
12            inet6 addr: ::1/128 Scope:Host
13            UP LOOPBACK RUNNING MTU:16436 Metric:1
14            RX packets:19843 errors:0 dropped:0 overruns:0 frame:0
15            TX packets:19843 errors:0 dropped:0 overruns:0 carrier:0
16            collisions:0 txqueuelen:0
17            RX bytes:19601819 (18.6 MiB) TX bytes:19601819 (18.6 MiB)
```

We can see there are two network interfaces in our server, lo (loopback), a virtual network interface used internally, and eth0, which corresponds to an ethernet card. This last is the interface we'll have to use to configure the IP address of our server.

```
1   [root@delphos ~]# ifconfig eth0 192.168.1.20 netmask 255.255.255.0 up
```

With `ifconfig`, we can add a temporary IP, but in order to make this change persistent, we'll have to modify the network configuration of the system. We can do this by manually editing the /etc/sysconfig/network-scripts/ifcfg-eth0 file and adding the following lines:

```
1   IPADDR=192.168.10.19
2   BOOTPROTO=none
3   NETMASK=255.255.255.0
4   TYPE=Ethernet
```

61

We'll also have to change the line ONBOOT=no to ONBOOT=yes, so that the network interface gets activated after every reboot. This procedure works perfectly, but it is probably more convenient to use an automatic configuration tool, such as system-config-network. This program is probably not installed by default, so we'll have to install it now. As you saw in the previous chapter, we can use yum to identify the package associated to a command.

```
1    [root@delphos ~]# yum --disablerepo=* --enablerepo=c6-media provides
     system-conf\
2    ig-network
3    Loaded plugins: fastestmirror
4    Loading mirror speeds from cached hostfile
5    * c6-media:
6    file:///media/CentOS/repodata/repomd.xml: [Errno 14] Could not open/
     read file://\
7    /media/CentOS/repodata/repomd.xml
8    Trying other mirror.
9    file:///media/cdrecorder/repodata/repomd.xml: [Errno 14] Could not
     open/read fil\
10   e:///media/cdrecorder/repodata/repomd.xml
11   Trying other mirror.
12   c6-media | 4.0 kB 00:00 ...
13   Warning: 3.0.x versions of yum would erroneously match against
     filenames.
14   You can use "*/system-config-network" and/or "*bin/system-config-
     network" to ge\
15   t that behaviour
16   No Matches found
17   [root@delphos ~]# yum --disablerepo=* --enablerepo=c6-media provides */
     system-co\
18   nfig-network
19   Loaded plugins: fastestmirror
20   Loading mirror speeds from cached hostfile
21   * c6-media:
22   system-config-network-tui-1.6.0.el6.2-1.el6.noarch : The Network
     Adminstration
23                                                       : Tool
24   Repo        : c6-media
25   Matched from:
26   Filename    : /usr/share/system-config-network
27   Filename    : /usr/bin/system-config-network
28   Filename    : /etc/pam.d/system-config-network
29   Filename    : /etc/security/console.apps/system-config-network
30   Filename    : /usr/sbin/system-config-network
```

So, we install the package system-config-network-tui with this command: yum -disablerepo=* - enablerepo=c6-media install system-config-network-tui. Once the package is installed, we can launch the program with system-config-network (Figure 3-1).

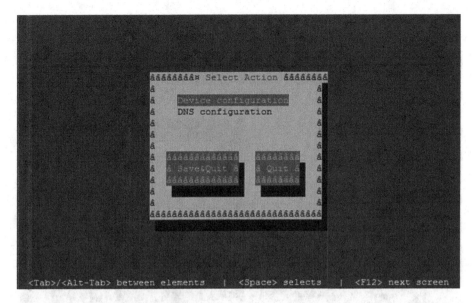

Figure 3-1. *system-config-network*

We select the Device configuration option and press Enter. A list with the network interfaces (Figure 3-2) now appears on the screen. In this case, there is only one. We choose it and press Enter again.

Figure 3-2. *Selecting an interface*

63

We fulfill the form and click Ok ➤ Save ➤ Save & Hit (Figure 3-3).

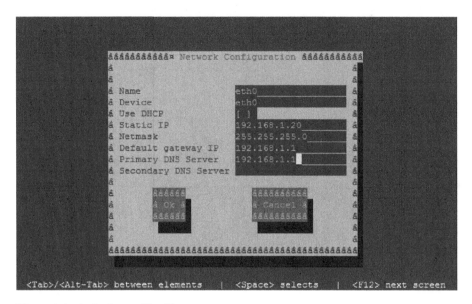

Figure 3-3. *Assigning an IP address*

If we check the /etc/sysconfig/network-scripts/ifcfg-eth0 file again, we'll see that it has updated the file contents. Nevertheless, we'll still have to manually change the parameter ONBOOT=no to ONBOOT=yes.

Finally, we restart the service.

```
1   [root@delphos ~]# service network restart
```

3.1.3.2. CentOS 7

In CentOS 7, the ifconfig command is not installed by default, as it is considered deprecated. The use of the utility ip is encouraged instead. We can add an IP address this way:

```
1   [root@Centos7 ~]# ip address add 192.168.1.202/24 dev enp0s3
```

We can also list the interfaces and their associated IP addresses.

```
1   [root@Centos7 ~]# ip address show
2   1: lo: <LOOPBACK,UP,LOWER_UP> mtu 65536 qdisc noqueue state UNKNOWN
3       link/loopback 00:00:00:00:00:00 brd 00:00:00:00:00:00
4       inet 127.0.0.1/8 scope host lo
5          valid_lft forever preferred_lft forever
```

```
6        inet6 ::1/128 scope host
7            valid_lft forever preferred_lft forever
8    2: enp0s3: <BROADCAST,MULTICAST,UP,LOWER_UP> mtu 1500 qdisc pfifo_fast
     state UP \
9    qlen 1000
10       link/ether 08:00:27:a0:46:d2 brd ff:ff:ff:ff:ff:ff
11       inet 192.168.1.202/24 scope global enp0s3
12           valid_lft forever preferred_lft forever
```

As happened in CentOS 6, the IP address we have just assigned will be temporary. If we want to make it persistent, we'll have to edit the /etc/sysconfig/network-scripts/ ifcfg-enp0s3 file and add the following lines:

```
1    IPADDR=192.168.10.19
2    BOOTPROTO=static
3    NETMASK=255.255.255.0
4    TYPE=Ethernet
```

We'll have to set the parameter ONBOOT=yes, so that the network interface gets activated every time the system boots. This way, we have assigned a static IP address to the server, but it is more convenient to use a network utility. In CentOS 6 we used system-config-network, but this command is not available in CentOS 7. Instead, we must use nmtui (Figures 3-4 and 3-5).

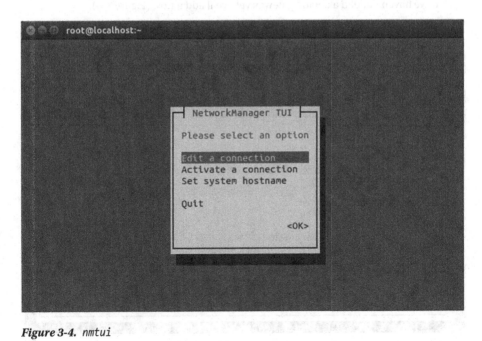

Figure 3-4. nmtui

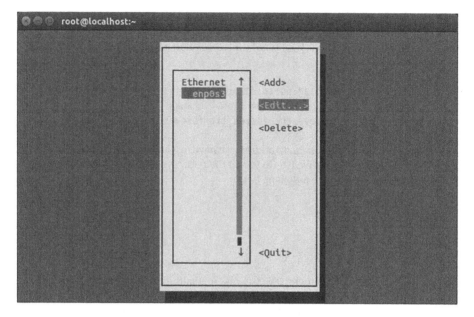

Figure 3-5. *Editing a connection with* nmtui

As we haven't added a default gateway yet, we'll add it now (Figure 3-6).

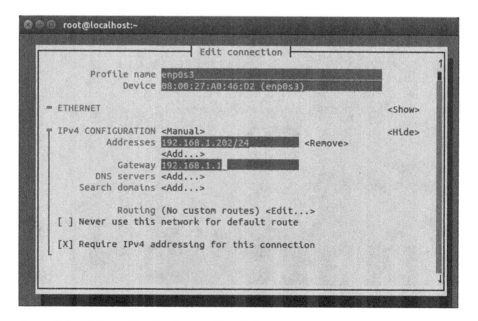

Figure 3-6. *Adding a default gateway with* nmtui

We accept the changes (Figure 3-7).

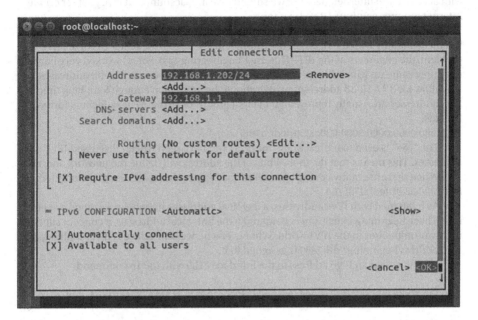

Figure 3-7. Adding a default gateway with nmtui

And we restart the network service.

```
1  [root@localhost ~]# service network restart
2  Restarting network (via systemctl):                    [ OK ]
```

Now we can check the default gateway currently configured with the ip command.

```
1  [root@localhost ~]# ip route show
2  default via 192.168.1.1 dev enp0s3 proto static metric 1024
3  192.168.1.0/24 dev enp0s3 proto kernel scope link src 192.168.1.202
```

3.2. IPv6

When the Internet grew in popularity, at one point it became clear that there would come a day when there would be no more IPv4 addresses available. IPv4 addresses are 4 bytes long, which allows for a maximum of approximately 4.2 billion addresses, whereas the human population is about 7 billion. Obviously, not every human being has a computer with an Internet connection—this is especially true in developing countries—but every day, more and more people get access to the Internet, and it is not at all unusual to have a computer at the office, another computer at home, and a smartphone—all of them with access to the Internet. Besides, we should take into account that every server on the Internet requires a unique IP address too.

Considering the facts, it seems pretty reasonable to think that IPv4 will no longer be able to comply with the needs of the Internet in the upcoming years. To solve this problem, the engineers of the IETF (Internet Engineering Task Force) worked very hard, until they came up with a new protocol that they call IPv6. IPv6 uses 128-bit addresses that allow for 3.4 * 10^38 addresses, which should be more than enough for a long time. IPv6 addresses are usually represented in eight groups of 16 bits in hexadecimal format, like this:

fe80:0000:0000:0000:020c:29ff:fedf:d786/64

The "/64" is used to represent the mask, as you have seen when I discussed IPv4 addresses. This means that the first 64 bits of the address will define the network address.

When there are many consecutive zeros, the bigger group of zeros can be omitted: fe80::020c:29ff:fedf:d786/64.

As happened with IPv4 addresses, a few IPv6 addresses have been assigned a special role. Those beginning in fe80 are considered to be link-local addresses, a concept similar to private addresses in the IPv4 world. Whenever a network interface is Ipv6-enabled, an IPv6 address beginning with fe80 is assigned to it.

We can assign an IPv6 address to the interface eth0 with the ip command.

```
1    [root@delphos ~]# ip address add 2000::20c:29ff:fe78:4cb1/64 dev eth0
```

Now we can see the new IP assigned.

```
1    [root@delphos ~]# ifconfig eth0
2    eth0      Link encap:Ethernet  HWaddr 00:0C:29:78:4C:B1
3              inet addr:192.168.1.20 Bcast:192.168.1.255 Mask:255.255.255.0
4              inet6 addr: 2000::20c:29ff:fe78:4cb1/64 Scope:Global
5              inet6 addr: fe80::20c:29ff:fe78:4cb1/64 Scope:Link
6              UP BROADCAST RUNNING MULTICAST MTU:1500 Metric:1
7              RX packets:3911047 errors:25 dropped:14 overruns:0 frame:0
8              TX packets:264248 errors:0 dropped:0 overruns:0 carrier:0
9              collisions:0 txqueuelen:1000
10             RX bytes:387910100 (369.9 MiB) TX bytes:57615841 (54.9 MiB)
11             Interrupt:19 Base address:0x2000
12
13   [root@delphos ~]# ip address show dev eth0
14   2: eth0: <BROADCAST,MULTICAST,UP,LOWER_UP> mtu 1500 qdisc pfifo_fast
     state UNKNO\
15   WN qlen 1000
16       link/ether 00:0c:29:78:4c:b1 brd ff:ff:ff:ff:ff:ff
17   inet 192.168.1.20/24 brd 192.168.1.255 scope global eth0
18   inet6 2000::20c:29ff:fe78:4cb1/64 scope global
19       valid_lft forever preferred_lft forever
20   inet6 fe80::20c:29ff:fe78:4cb1/64 scope link
21       valid_lft forever preferred_lft forever
```

3.3. Networking Tools
3.3.1. netstat

Every time a program has to communicate with the network, it uses what the TCP protocol calls "ports." A port is a means to identify a network service in the network. For example, to communicate with a web server, a server would use port 80. To connect to an FTP server, one would have to access port 21, etc. That is, for every network service running in the server, there must be (at least) one open TCP port.

If we want to know how many open ports we currently have, we can use netstat. By default, it will show only the ports with an established connection.

```
1   [root@localhost ~]# netstat
2   Active Internet connections (w/o servers)
3   Proto Recv-Q Send-Q Local Address          Foreign Address        Stat\
4   e
5   tcp        0      0 192.168.1.20:ssh        192.168.1.1:49775      ESTA\
6   BLISHED
7   Active UNIX domain sockets (w/o servers)
8   Proto RefCnt Flags      Type      State      I-Node Path
9   unix 2       [ ]        DGRAM                8587   @/org/kernel/
    udev/udevd
10  unix 10      [ ]        DGRAM                10473  /dev/log
11  .
12  .
13  .
```

In this case, we can see that we have a single connected TCP port, the ssh port. The command shows many open unix sockets, but we'll ignore them for now. We can pass many options to netstat. Some of the more useful are: -a, to show ALL the open ports and not only those already connected; -p, to identify the program that opened the port; -t, for TCP; -u, for UDP; or -n, to show the port number instead of the port name. Let's see an example.

```
1   [root@localhost ~]# netstat -aptn
2   Active Internet connections (servers and established)
3   Proto Recv-Q Send-Q Local Address          Foreign Address        Stat\
4   e        PID/Program name
5   tcp        0      0 0.0.0.0:22              0.0.0.0:*              LIST\
6   EN       1107/sshd
7   tcp        0      0 127.0.0.1:25            0.0.0.0:*              LIST\
8   EN       1183/master
9   tcp        0      0 0.0.0.0:5672            0.0.0.0:*              LIST\
10  EN       1196/qpidd
11  tcp        0      0 192.168.1.20:22         192.168.1.1:50316      ESTA\
12  BLISHED 6738/sshd
```

```
13  tcp      0     0 :::22                    :::*              LIST\
14  EN    1107/sshd
15  tcp      0     0 ::1:25                   :::*              LIST\
16  EN    1183/master
```

We get a list of all the open TCP ports, showing the port numbers and their associated programs.

3.3.2. lsof

Another really useful tool is lsof. It will probably not be installed by default, but we can install it with yum, as we have seen before.

```
1  [root@localhost ~]# yum --disablerepo=* --enablerepo=c6-media provides
   lsof
2  Loaded plugins: fastestmirror
3  Loading mirror speeds from cached hostfile
4   * c6-media:
5  lsof-4.82-2.el6.i686 : A utility which lists open files on a Linux/UNIX
   system
6  Repo        : c6-media
7  Matched from:
8
9  [root@localhost ~]# yum --disablerepo=* --enablerepo=c6-media install lsof
```

This tool lists the open files in the system, but we can use it to see what process is listening in a given port.

```
1  [root@localhost ~]# lsof -i :53
2  COMMAND  PID  USER   FD  TYPE DEVICE SIZE/OFF NODE NAME
3  named   8616 named  20u IPv6  27844      0t0 TCP *:domain (LISTEN)
4  named   8616 named  21u IPv4  27849      0t0 TCP localhost:domain
   (LISTEN)
5  named   8616 named  22u IPv4  27851      0t0 TCP 192.168.1.20:domain
   (LISTEN)
6  named   8616 named 512u IPv6  27843      0t0 UDP *:domain
7  named   8616 named 513u IPv4  27848      0t0 UDP localhost:domain
8  named   8616 named 514u IPv4  27850      0t0 UDP 192.168.1.20:domain
```

3.3.3. nmap

Sometimes we have to know the open ports that can be accessed through the network. It could happen that a service is listening in a port in the local machine, but a firewall or a filter of some kind exists between the server and the client. In this case, obviously, there would be no communication between the two computers. To prove whether a port is accessible or not, we can use nmap.

The basic syntax is nmap name_or_ip.

```
1   [root@localhost named]# nmap 192.168.1.20
2
3   Starting Nmap 5.21 ( http://nmap.org ) at 2014-08-03 02:31 CEST
4   mass_dns: warning: Unable to determine any DNS servers. Reverse DNS is
    disabled.\
5    Try using --system-dns or specify valid servers with --dns-servers
6   Nmap scan report for 192.168.1.20
7   Host is up (0.00071s latency).
8   Not shown: 998 filtered ports
9   PORT   STATE SERVICE
10  22/tcp open ssh
11  53/tcp open domain
12  MAC Address: 00:0C:29:78:4C:B1 (VMware)
13
14  Nmap done: 1 IP address (1 host up) scanned in 5.29 seconds
15  [root@localhost named]#
```

We can also specify the ports we want to check.

```
1   [root@localhost named]# nmap -p 80,22 192.168.1.20
2
3   Starting Nmap 5.21 ( http://nmap.org ) at 2014-08-03 03:05 CEST
4   mass_dns: warning: Unable to determine any DNS servers. Reverse DNS is
    disabled.\
5    Try using --system-dns or specify valid servers with --dns-servers
6   Nmap scan report for 192.168.1.20
7   Host is up (0.00024s latency).
8   PORT   STATE    SERVICE
9   22/tcp open     ssh
10  80/tcp filtered http
11  MAC Address: 00:0C:29:78:4C:B1 (VMware)
12
13  Nmap done: 1 IP address (1 host up) scanned in 0.08 seconds
14  [root@localhost named]#
```

We can also get some more information about the services listening in every port.

```
1   [root@localhost named]# nmap -sV 192.168.1.20
2
3   Starting Nmap 5.21 ( http://nmap.org ) at 2014-08-03 03:07 CEST
4   Nmap scan report for delphos.olimpus.local (192.168.1.20)
5   Host is up (0.00034s latency).
6   Not shown: 998 filtered ports
7   PORT   STATE SERVICE VERSION
```

```
 8   22/tcp open   ssh      OpenSSH 5.3 (protocol 2.0)
 9   53/tcp open   domain
10   MAC Address: 00:0C:29:78:4C:B1 (VMware)
11
12   Service detection performed. Please report any incorrect results at
     http://nmap.\
13   org/submit/ .
14   Nmap done: 1 IP address (1 host up) scanned in 16.86 seconds
15   [root@localhost named]#
```

3.3.4. ping

One of the simplest and most useful utilities to diagnose networking problems is ping. With ping, we simply send a small data packet to a destination. If the packet arrives, the destination usually will answer back.

```
1   [root@delphos ~]# ping 192.168.10.23
2   PING 192.168.10.23 (192.168.10.23) 56(84) bytes of data.
3   64 bytes from 192.168.10.23: icmp_seq=1 ttl=63 time=2.76 ms
4   64 bytes from 192.168.10.23: icmp_seq=2 ttl=62 time=1.59 ms
```

3.3.5. ping6

Ping6 is the IPv6 version of the ping command. It works the same way, but by using IPv6 addresses.

```
1   [root@CentOS7 ~]# ping6 2001::20c:29ff:fe78:4cb2
2   PING 2001::20c:29ff:fe78:4cb2(2001::20c:29ff:fe78:4cb2) 56 data bytes
3   64 bytes from 2001::20c:29ff:fe78:4cb2: icmp_seq=1 ttl=64 time=0.083 ms
4   64 bytes from 2001::20c:29ff:fe78:4cb2: icmp_seq=2 ttl=64 time=0.080 ms
```

If we try to ping a link-local address (those starting with fe80), we have to specify the interface. Otherwise, we receive an error.

```
 1   [root@delphos ~]# ping6 fe80::20c:29ff:fe78:4cb1
 2   connect: Invalid argument
 3   [root@delphos ~]# ping6 -I eth0 fe80::20c:29ff:fe78:4cb1
 4   PING fe80::20c:29ff:fe78:4cb1(fe80::20c:29ff:fe78:4cb1) from
     fe80::20c:29ff:fe78\
 5   :4cb1 eth0: 56 data bytes
 6   64 bytes from fe80::20c:29ff:fe78:4cb1: icmp_seq=1 ttl=64 time=3.70 ms
 7   64 bytes from fe80::20c:29ff:fe78:4cb1: icmp_seq=2 ttl=64 time=0.111 ms
 8   64 bytes from fe80::20c:29ff:fe78:4cb1: icmp_seq=3 ttl=64 time=0.044 ms
 9   ^C
10   --- fe80::20c:29ff:fe78:4cb1 ping statistics ---
11   3 packets transmitted, 3 received, 0% packet loss, time 2300ms
12   rtt min/avg/max/mdev = 0.044/1.285/3.701/1.708 ms
```

CHAPTER 4

DNS

The number of interconnected computers is growing day by day. It is possible to design a hierarchical network addressing schema that assigns network addresses according to a computer's physical location, but even in this case, it will always be easier to refer to computers by using names instead of IP addresses. A local DNS (Domain Name System) server will allow us to establish a direct relationship between a computer name and an IP address, which, in turn, will make it much easier to identify a local machine.

Today, DNS service is a critical part of IT infrastructure, as many other services depend on it to work properly. Unfortunately, this characteristic makes it an interesting target for hackers too. In order to minimize the risks of an attack, a lot of attention must be paid when configuring the service.

4.1. DNS Service

In order to communicate with one another, every computer in the network must be assigned a unique IP address. It could be said that there is a certain analogy with a phone network, in which a phone number identifies a single device and makes it possible for it to communicate with the other phones.

Working with IP addresses is fine for computers, but it is cumbersome for people. It would be necessary to remember the IP address of every single device a user wanted to connect to. It is definitely much more convenient to employ names such as www.google.es or www.apress.com, which are much easier to remember.

Internally, computers communicate with each other by using their IP addresses, not their associated domain names. So, it is necessary to have a system that is able to determine the IP address(es) associated with a domain name.

For example, when we type "www.google.es" in our favorite web browser, our PC has to be able to know the actual IP address associated with the name www.google.es. Once it finds out that the IP address is 173.194.41.215, it establishes a connection and reveals the web page to the user.

If we had written "http://173.194.41.215" in the address bar, it wouldn't have been necessary to ask about the IP address of www.google.es.

© Antonio Vazquez 2016

A. Vazquez, *Learn CentOS Linux Network Services*, DOI 10.1007/978-1-4842-2379-6_4

A DNS server is a machine that keeps a list of associated names–IP addresses. In the early days of the Internet, this was achieved with a single text file that all computers had to know in order to communicate with one another. This file is /etc/hosts, and it is still present in every computer. It can be used to provide some sort of basic name resolution. For example, we could open the file /etc/hosts and add the following line:

```
1    192.168.10.19              www.dummy-domain.com
```

From now on, every time our computer has to know the address of www.dummy-domain.com, it will assume the IP address for this is 192.168.10.19.

```
1    [root@delphos ~]# cat /etc/hosts
2    127.0.0.1  localhost localhost.localdomain localhost4 localhost4.
     localdomain4
3    ::1        localhost localhost.localdomain localhost6 localhost6.
     localdomain6
4    192.168.10.19     dummy-server.example.com
5    192.168.10.19     www.dummy-domain.com
6    [root@localhost ~]# ping www.dummy-domain.com
7    PING www.dummy-domain.com (192.168.10.19) 56(84) bytes of data.
8    64 bytes from dummy-server.example.com (192.168.10.19): icmp_seq=1
     ttl=64 time=0\
9    056 ms
10   64 bytes from dummy-server.example.com (192.168.10.19): icmp_seq=2
     ttl=64 time=0\
11   .058 ms
12   64 bytes from dummy-server.example.com (192.168.10.19): icmp_seq=3
     ttl=64 time=0\
13   .052 ms
14   ^C
15   --- www.dummy-domain.com ping statistics ---
16   3 packets transmitted, 3 received, 0% packet loss, time 2459ms
17   rtt min/avg/max/mdev = 0.052/0.055/0.058/0.006 ms
```

Using a host file for name resolution remains appropriate for small networks, but as the Internet began to grow, it became pretty clear that a new name-resolution system was required, and so, the DNS service was developed.

A DNS server maintains a database with all the IP addresses and names included in its domain. Of course, a single DNS server can't store all the IP addresses that exist in the world. On the contrary, they usually hold only the information about their domain.

DNS servers are organized in a hierarchical way, as can be seen in Figure 4-1. So, when the assigned DNS can't resolve a name, it will pass the request to another DNS server from an upper layer. It's easy to understand with an example.

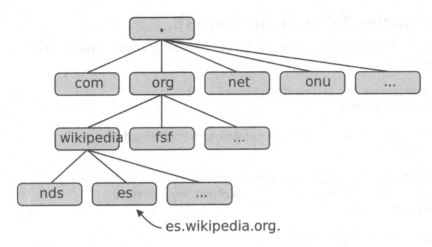

Figure 4-1. DNS hierarchy

Let's say we are sitting in front of a computer in the acme.net domain, and we want to access the web es.wikipedia.org. The computer will query its local DNS server about the name es.wikipedia.org, but this server only knows about www.acme.net, mail.acme.net, etc., so it decides to query the .net server. The .net server doesn't know about es.wikipedia.org, so it has to query the root (.) server. The root server doesn't know the exact address of es.wikipedia.org, but it knows the address of the .org server, so it passes the query to this server. The .org server will then query the wikipedia.org server, and this server will finally contact the IP address associated with the name es.wikipedia.org. The answer will be passed back to the DNS server in acme.net, which, in turn, will provide that information to the computer that requested it.

4.2. Installing a DNS Server

To illustrate the preceding, we are going to install a working DNS server. The package we'll have to install is bind. If we already have an Internet connection, we can use yum without the –disablerepo and –enablerepo options, as it will download the software from the preconfigured Internet repositories. We can also pass the -y parameter to automatically answer yes to any confirmation message. Otherwise, if we still haven't got an Internet connection, we'll have to use the options we saw earlier and make sure that the DVD is mounted.

```
1    [root@delphos ~]# yum -y install bind
```

4.2.1. Starting the Service in CentOS 6

Once installed, we should have a new script in the /etc/init.d directory. This script will be called named.

```
1  [root@delphos ~]# ls /etc/init.d/named
2  /etc/init.d/named
```

We can check the status of this new installed service by calling the script with the status parameter.

```
1  [root@delphos ~]# /etc/init.d/named status
2  rndc: neither /etc/rndc.conf nor /etc/rndc.key was found
3  named is stopped
```

Or we can use the service command.

```
1  [root@localhost ~]# service named status
2  rndc: neither /etc/rndc.conf nor /etc/rndc.key was found
3  named is stopped
```

In both cases, we're told that named is stopped. And a couple of files seem to be missing too. I'll provide more details in a moment. Anyway, we can start the service with the following command:

```
1  [root@delphos ~]# service named start
2  Starting named:                                    [ OK ]
3  [root@delphos ~]# service named status
4  rndc: neither /etc/rndc.conf nor /etc/rndc.key was found
5  named (pid  1570) is running...
```

Now we should make sure that the service starts every time the system boots. We can check this with chkconfig.

```
1  [root@delphos ~]# chkconfig --list named
2  named          0:off   1:off   2:off   3:off   4:off   5:off   6:off
```

We can see that, right now, named is not configured to be active on any of the six runlevels. We will change this.

```
1  [root@delphos ~]# chkconfig named on
2  [root@delphos ~]# chkconfig --list named
3  named          0:off   1:off   2:on    3:on    4:on    5:on    6:off
```

Now, named will be started in every runlevel except 0 (shutdown), 1 (single user), or 6 (reboot) We haven't talked about runlevels so far, but I can say that a runlevel is the means by which the OS identifies whether the machine is shut down (runlevel 0), in single-user mode (runlevel 1), in multiuser text mode with limited networking, in multiuser text mode with full networking (runlevel 3), in graphic multiuser mode (runlevel 5), or rebooting (runlevel 6).

With the ps command, we can check the user a service is running.

```
1    [root@delphos ~]# ps -ef | grep named
2    named      1848     1  0 20:44 ?        00:00:00 /usr/sbin/named -u named
```

In this case, the named service is running as the named user. In the past, some people used to execute this with the root user, which can be very dangerous if the service becomes compromised. In recent versions of the software, however, the default configuration starts the service with the named user. We can see this by examining the associated script file (/etc/init.d/named). This file is very long, but at the start() section, we'll see the line that actually launches the service.

```
1    daemon --pidfile "$ROOTDIR$PIDFILE" /usr/sbin/"$named" -u named
     ${OPTIONS};
```

By passing the -u named parameter, the service will execute with the effective rights of the named user. So, if the service becomes compromised, the consequences will be far less serious than they could be if the service was being executed as root.

If we wanted, we could even customize this script a bit further. We could create a new user, grant it the appropriate rights, and then use it to execute the named service by employing the -u flag.

4.2.2. Starting the Service in CentOS 7

With CentOS 7, service management has undergone many changes, and the system no longer uses scripts in /etc/init.d, except for a few services. All other services are managed by systemd.

To check the status of a service, we have to use the systemctl command.

```
1    [root@Centos7 ~]# systemctl status named
2    named.service - Berkeley Internet Name Domain (DNS)
3       Loaded: loaded (/usr/lib/systemd/system/named.service; disabled)
4       Active: inactive (dead)
```

We can see that the service has stopped, so we start it.

```
1    [root@Centos7 ~]# systemctl start named
2    [root@Centos7 ~]# systemctl status named
3    named.service - Berkeley Internet Name Domain (DNS)
4       Loaded: loaded (/usr/lib/systemd/system/named.service; disabled)
5       Active: active (running) since dom 2014-11-23 01:05:36 CET; 4s ago
6       Process: 2855 ExecStart=/usr/sbin/named -u named $OPTIONS
         (code=exited, status\
7    =0/SUCCESS)
8       Process: 2853 ExecStartPre=/usr/sbin/named-checkconf -z /etc/named.conf
         (code=\
9    exited, status=0/SUCCESS)
```

```
10   Main PID: 2857 (named)
11   CGroup: /system.slice/named.service
12              └─2857 /usr/sbin/named -u named
13
14   nov 23 01:05:37 Centos7 named[2857]: validating @0x7fa9c062ff10: . NS:
     veri...un
15   nov 23 01:05:37 Centos7 named[2857]: validating @0x7fa9c062ff10: . NS:
     no v...nd
16   nov 23 01:05:37 Centos7 named[2857]: error (no valid RRSIG) resolving
     './NS...53
17   nov 23 01:05:37 Centos7 named[2857]: error (network unreachable)
     resolving ...53
18   nov 23 01:05:37 Centos7 named[2857]: validating @0x7fa9c062ff10: . NS:
     veri...un
19   nov 23 01:05:37 Centos7 named[2857]: validating @0x7fa9c062ff10: . NS:
     no v...nd
20   nov 23 01:05:37 Centos7 named[2857]: error (no valid RRSIG) resolving
     './NS...53
21   nov 23 01:05:37 Centos7 named[2857]: validating @0x7fa9c062ff10: . NS:
     veri...un
22   nov 23 01:05:37 Centos7 named[2857]: validating @0x7fa9c062ff10: . NS:
     no v...nd
23   nov 23 01:05:37 Centos7 named[2857]: error (no valid RRSIG) resolving
     './NS...53
24   Hint: Some lines were ellipsized, use -l to show in full.
```

The service is running now, but we have to make sure that it starts every time the system boots.

```
1   [root@Centos7 ~]# systemctl enable named
2   ln -s '/usr/lib/systemd/system/named.service' '/etc/systemd/system/
    multi-user.ta\
3   rget.wants/named.service'
```

We can check that the service is actually enabled, with the following command:

```
1   [root@Centos7 ~]# systemctl list-unit-files --type=service
```

It will list all the services installed in the computer.

```
1   UNIT FILE                               STATE
2   auditd.service                          enabled
3   .
4   .
5   .
6   named.service                           enabled
7   .
8   .
9   .
```

As I mentioned when talking about CentOS 6, with the ps command, we can check that the effective user named is running.

```
1   [root@Centos7 ~]# ps -ef | grep named
2   named    17881    1  0 17:35 ?         00:00:00 /usr/sbin/named -u named
```

We see that the service is running as the named user. This is correct, as it limits the damage an attacker can do if the service is compromised. A bad practice from the past was to execute the service as the root user. If we take a look at the associated unit file (lib/systemd/system/named.service), we'll see the following line:

```
1   ExecStart=/usr/sbin/named -u named $OPTIONS
```

in which we tell the named service to execute with the rights associated to the named user.

As I said before in the previous section, we can customize this a bit further and execute the named service with another user. We only have to launch the named service with the -u new_user option.

4.3. Installing a Master Server

Before we move on to the next step, I'll talk a bit more about the types of DNS servers.

As we already know, a DNS server translates names into IP addresses. But it can do this through different approaches.

- *Cache only server.* In this case, the server doesn't hold any information about the associated name–IP addresses, so it has to query another server. But once it gets an answer, it keeps it in the cache, so that when another client performs the same query, it can respond quickly, without forwarding the request to another server.

- *Master server.* This is a server that holds a copy of the names and IP addresses of the computers belonging to the domain in what is called a zone. A master server has the authority to change an IP associated with a certain name, as well as to add or delete new registers.

- *Slave server.* This type of server holds a copy of the zone too, but it is a read-only one. A slave server has all the information it needs to answer queries about the domain, but it cannot change, add, or delete any register.

Deciding how to combine these types of name servers depends on the size of the network. Obviously, one always needs a master server to add, delete, or modify DNS entries, but one also needs at least a slave server, so that a workload can be distributed. Besides, if the master server crashes or gets hacked, one can replace it with a slave server.

So far, we have already installed the necessary software, but, obviously, we still haven't configured it. Let's assume we manage a domain called olimpus.local, and a few machines called prometheus, zeus, aphrodite, etc., and we want to make sure that when a client computer searches for the computer aphrodite.olimpus.com, it gets its associated IP address. In order to achieve this, we'll have to create the zone. Let's take the procedure step-by-step.

The main configuration file of the DNS server is /etc/named.conf. Right after a fresh installation, it will look like this:

```
1   //
2   // named.conf
3   //
4   // Provided by Red Hat bind package to configure the ISC BIND named(8)
    DNS
5   // server as a caching only nameserver (as a localhost DNS resolver
    only).
6   //
7   // See /usr/share/doc/bind*/sample/ for example named configuration
    files.
8   //
9
10  options {
11          listen-on port 53 { 127.0.0.1; };
12          listen-on-v6 port 53 { ::1; };
13          directory       "/var/named";
14          dump-file       "/var/named/data/cache_dump.db";
15          statistics-file "/var/named/data/named_stats.txt";
16          memstatistics-file "/var/named/data/named_mem_stats.txt";
17          allow-query     { localhost; };
18          recursion yes;
19
20          dnssec-enable yes;
21          dnssec-validation yes;
22          dnssec-lookaside auto;
23
24          /* Path to ISC DLV key */
25          bindkeys-file "/etc/named.iscdlv.key";
26  };
27
28  logging {
29          channel default_debug {
30                  file "data/named.run";
31                  severity dynamic;
32          };
33  };
34
35  zone "." IN {
```

```
36          type hint;
37          file "named.ca";
38  };
39
40  include "/etc/named.rfc1912.zones";
```

This is the configuration file of a CentOS 6 server. In a CentOS 7 server, the file is slightly different, but the way to configure it is exactly the same in both cases.

These are some of the most important options:

```
1  listen-on port 53 { 127.0.0.1; };
2  listen-on-v6 port 53 { ::1; };
```

The server will listen only in the local host address, that is, it won't be accessible from other computers on the network. As we want to be able to query the DNS server from other computers, we will change these two lines.

```
1  listen-on port 53 { 192.168.1.21; };
2  listen-on-v6 port 53 { fe80::a00:27ff:feac:da50; };
```

This way, we tell the server to listen on the interface with the IPv4 address 192.168.1.21 (and the IPv6 address fe80::a00:27ff:feac:da50), that is, the IP connected to the same local area network (LAN) as the DNS clients. We could have used the keyword *any*, and the name server would listen in all of its interfaces, but it is safer to listen only in the interface the clients will connect to.

```
1  directory          "/var/named";
```

This only means that the default directory for the zone files will be in /var/named. We don't need to change this.

```
1  allow-query          { localhost; };
```

We want the server to answer queries from any computer in our network, so we change this value accordingly.

```
1  allow-query          { 192.168.1.0/24; fe80::/64; };
```

We could have used the word *any* to allow queries from any device independently of its IP address, but there are a couple of drawbacks to this approach. First, our servers could be overloaded by requests from devices outside of our network. Second, we could be allowing a malicious user to get information from the DNS.

```
1  zone "." IN {
2          type hint;
3          file "named.ca";
4  };
```

This is the only zone defined so far in the configuration file—the topmost zone in the hierarchy. If we open the /var/named/named.ca file, we will see that it contains the address of the root servers on the Internet. Here, we will have to tell the server about our domain olimpus.local. Below the . zone definition, we will type the following:

```
1   zone "olimpus.local" IN {
2       type master;
3       file "olimpus.local.zone";
4   };
```

We can now save the changes. To make sure the syntax of the file named.conf is correct, we can use named-checkconf.

```
1   [root@delphos ~]# named-checkconf
2   [root@delphos ~]#
```

As we can see, the program didn't show any output, so we can assume that the syntax is correct. If there were a syntax error, the program would tell us about it. For example, if we had forgotten a curly bracket, we might receive a message such as this:

```
1   [root@delphos ~]# named-checkconf
2   /etc/named.conf:26: '}' expected near  ';'
```

But now we have to create the /var/named/olimpus.local.zone file. As expected, the file must have a proper syntax. If we're creating a zone file from scratch, and we don't remember all the details about the syntax, we can take a look at some of the sample files in the /usr/share/doc/bind-9.7.3/sample directory. In fact, the /usr/share/doc folder is always very helpful when we try to configure or tune a service, as we can find there plenty of sample configuration files for almost all the software installed in the server.

The zone file should be something like this:

```
1   ;
2   ;Data file for olimpus.local
3   ;
4   $TTL 2D
5   olimpus.local.    IN SOA olimpus.local. root.olimpus.local. (
6                     2014082701;      Serial
7                     1D;              Refresh
8                     2H;              Retry
9                     1W;              Expire
10                    2D);             Default TTL
11
12          IN NS delphos.olimpus.local.
13          IN MX 10 prometheus.olimpus.local.
14
15   delphos       IN A    192.168.1.20
16   prometheus    IN A    192.168.1.21
17   aphrodite     IN A    192.168.1.22
```

```
18   delphos          IN AAAA fe80::20c:29ff:fe78:4cb1
19   dns              IN CNAME      delphos
20   mail             IN CNAME      prometheus
```

The lines beginning with ; are comments used to clarify the content of the file. After that, we define the parameters associated with the zone file, such as the refresh and retry rates, the expiration time, and the default TTL. Every zone file must have an associated serial number. This number will be used when replicating information between DNS servers, to determine whether there is a newer version of a zone file.

```
1   IN NS delphos.olimpus.local.
```

This is an NS register. It identifies what the name servers of olimpus.local are. This is a mandatory register. In this case, the only name server is delphos.olimpus.local, but we could have many of them.

```
1   IN MX 10 prometheus.olimpus.local.
```

Similarly, we define here the mail server for the olimpus.local domain and the associated priority (10). In this case, we have only a mail server, but we could have two, or even more, and assign different priorities to every one of them, according to their processing power. We'll see this again when I discuss mail service.

```
1   delphos      IN A      192.168.1.20
2   prometheus   IN A      192.168.1.21
3   aphrodite    IN A      192.168.1.22
```

Now we have a list with all the machines in the zone and their associated IP addresses. These are called type A registers.

```
1   delphos              IN AAAA fe80::20c:29ff:fe78:4cb1
```

In addition, we can associate names and IPv6 addresses; that's what AAAA registers are for.

```
1   dns      IN CNAME      delphos
2   mail     IN CNAME      prometheus
```

And finally, we have a couple of CNAME registers, which work as an alias. That is, the client will be able to ping delphos.olimpus.local or dns.olimpus.local indistinctly.

Once we're done, we can check the syntax with the named-checkzone command.

```
1   [root@delphos named]# named-checkzone olimpus.local olimpus.local.zone
2   zone olimpus.local/IN: loaded serial 20140827
3   OK
```

We now restart the named service.

In CentOS 6:

```
1  [root@delphos named]# service named restart
2  Stopping named:                              [ OK ]
3  Starting named:                              [ OK ]
```

In CentOS 7:

```
1  [root@Centos7 ~]# systemctl restart named
```

Apparently, everything is fine, but to make sure, we'll query the DNS server for the address of the delphos.olimpus.local machine. You'll see later in more detail some of the tools we can use to check the DNS service, but to make sure our name server is working, I'll introduce the dig command here.

dig allows us to query the DNS server we choose. To check our new name server, we could type the following:

```
1  [root@delphos named]# dig @192.168.1.20 delphos.olimpus.local
2  -bash: dig: command not found
```

As I have mentioned several times before, if the utility is not installed by default you'll have to find out the package it belongs to and install it. From now on I will no longer mention this.

```
1   [root@delphos named]# yum provides dig
2   Loaded plugins: fastestmirror
3   Loading mirror speeds from cached hostfile
4   * c6-media:
5   Warning: 3.0.x versions of yum would erroneously match against
    filenames.
6   You can use "*/dig" and/or "*bin/dig" to get that behaviour
7   No Matches found
8   [root@delphos named]# yum provides */dig
9   Loaded plugins: fastestmirror
10  Loading mirror speeds from cached hostfile
11  * c6-media:
12  32:bind-utils-9.7.3-8.P3.el6.i686 : Utilities for querying DNS name
    servers
13  Repo        : c6-media
14  Matched from:
15  Filename    : /usr/bin/dig
16
17  [root@delphos named]# yum install bind-utils
18  Loaded plugins: fastestmirror
19  Loading mirror speeds from cached hostfile
20  * c6-media:
21  Setting up Install Process
22  Resolving Dependencies
```

```
23   --> Running transaction check
24   ---> Package bind-utils.i686 32:9.7.3-8.P3.el6 will be installed
25   --> Finished Dependency Resolution
26
27   Dependencies Resolved
28
29   =======================================================================
30   Package          Arch        Version              Repository      Size
31   =======================================================================
32   Installing:
33    bind-utils      i686        32:9.7.3-8.P3.el6    c6-media        177 k
34
35   Transaction Summary
36   =======================================================================
37   Install        1 Package(s)
38
39   Total download size: 177 k
40   Installed size: 423 k
41   Is this ok [y/N]: y
42   Downloading Packages:
43   Running rpm_check_debug
44   Running Transaction Test
45   Transaction Test Succeeded
46   Running Transaction
47     Installing : 32:bind-utils-9.7.3-8.P3.el6.i686          1/1
48
49   Installed:
50     bind-utils.i686 32:9.7.3-8.P3.el6
51
52   Complete!
53   [root@delphos named]#
```

Now we can actually perform the query.

```
1    [root@delphos named]# dig @192.168.1.20 delphos.olimpus.local
2    ; <<>> DiG 9.7.3-P3-RedHat-9.7.3-8.P3.el6 <<>> @192.168.1.20 delphos.
     olimpus.loc\
3    al
4    ; (1 server found)
5    ;; global options: +cmd
6    ;; Got answer:
7    ;; ->>HEADER<<- opcode: QUERY, status: NOERROR, id: 27770
8    ;; flags: qr aa rd ra; QUERY: 1, ANSWER: 1, AUTHORITY: 1, ADDITIONAL: 1
9
10   ;; QUESTION SECTION:
11   ;delphos.olimpus.local.          IN     A
12
13   ;; ANSWER SECTION:
```

```
14    delphos.olimpus.local.   172800    IN    A    192.168.1.20
15
16    ;; AUTHORITY SECTION:
17    olimpus.local.           172800    IN    NS   delphos.olimpus.local.
18
19    ;; ADDITIONAL SECTION:
20    delphos.olimpus.local.   172800    IN    AAAA    fe80::20c:29ff:fe78:4cb1
21
22    ;; Query time: 7 msec
23    ;; SERVER: 192.168.1.20#53(192.168.1.20)
24    ;; WHEN: Sat Aug     2 10:42:07 2014
25    ;; MSG SIZE  rcvd: 97
26
27    [root@delphos named]#
```

We want to query the 192.168.1.20 server, so we pass it as a parameter (@192.168.1.20). We can see that the query executed correctly (status: NOERROR). In addition, the server reports that delphos.olimpus.local has the IPv4 address 192.168.1.20 and the IPv6 address fe80::20c:29ff:fe78:4cb1, which is correct.

It looks like we have a working DNS server, but, unfortunately, this is not completely true. So far, we have a way to translate names into IP addresses. This is what is called direct lookup, but we should also have a way to translate IP addresses into machine names (reverse lookup). To achieve this, the procedure is quite similar to that which we have seen before.

In the /etc/named.conf, file we'll define the new zone that provides the reverse lookup. We'll type it just below the olimpus.local zone.

```
1    zone "1.168.192.in-addr.arpa" IN {
2            type master;
3            file "192.168.1.zone";
4    };
```

The format x.x.x.in-addr.arpa, where x.x.x is the network address in reverse order, is a standard way of naming reverse zones.

Now we create the /var/named/192.168.1.zone file. The syntax is quite similar to the one used in the olimpus.local.zone file.

```
1    $TTL 2D;
2    1.168.192.in-addr.arpa. IN SOA delphos.olimpus.local. root.olimpus.
     local. (
3                            2014082701      ;serial
4                            259200          ;refresh(3 days)
5                            14400           ;retry(4 hours)
6                            18140           ;expire(3 weeks)
7                            604800          ;minimum(1 week)
8                            )
9                    NS delphos.olimpus.local.
10
11    20              PTR delphos.olimpus.local.
```

And we check it.

```
1  [root@delphos named]# named-checkzone 1.168.192.in-addr.arpa
   192.168.1.zone
2  zone 1.168.192.in-addr.arpa/IN: loaded serial 2014082701
3  OK
```

We restart the service.
In CentOS 6:

```
1  [root@delphos named]# service named restart
2  Stopping named:                              [  OK  ]
3  Starting named:                              [  OK  ]
```

In CentOS 7:

```
1  [root@Centos7 ~]# systemctl restart named
```

And we query the server with dig.

```
1   [root@delphos named]# dig @192.168.1.20 -x 192.168.1.20
2
3   ; <<>> DiG 9.7.3-P3-RedHat-9.7.3-8.P3.el6 <<>> @192.168.1.20 -x
    192.168.1.20
4   ; (1 server found)
5   ;; global options: +cmd
6   ;; Got answer:
7   ;; ->>HEADER<<- opcode: QUERY, status: NOERROR, id: 62275
8   ;; flags: qr aa rd ra; QUERY: 1, ANSWER: 1, AUTHORITY: 1, ADDITIONAL: 2
9
10  ;; QUESTION SECTION:
11  ;20.1.168.192.in-addr.arpa.      IN      PTR
12
13  ;; ANSWER SECTION:
14  20.1.168.192.in-addr.arpa. 172800 IN  PTR  delphos.olimpus.local.
15
16  ;; AUTHORITY SECTION:
17  1.168.192.in-addr.arpa. 172800  IN   NS   delphos.olimpus.local.
18
19  ;; ADDITIONAL SECTION:
20  delphos.olimpus.local.  172800  IN   A    192.168.1.20
21  delphos.olimpus.local.  172800  IN   AAAA fe80::20c:29ff:fe78:4cb1
22
23  ;; Query time: 2 msec
24  ;; SERVER: 192.168.1.20#53(192.168.1.20)
25  ;; WHEN: Sat Aug 2 11:28:31 2014
26  ;; MSG SIZE rcvd: 136
```

As happened before, we see that the query has executed without errors (status: NOERROR), and the server has answered that the IPv4 address 192.168.1.20 is assigned to the server delphos.olimpus.local.

Finally, we'll create the reverse zone for IPv6. We open the /etc/named.conf file again and add the following lines:

```
1    zone "0.0.0.0.0.0.0.0.0.0.0.0.0.0.8.e.f.ip6.arpa" IN {
2            type master;
3            file "fe80.0.0.0.zone";
4    };
```

As we see, the standard name is similar to the one used with IPv4 zones. It also consists of the network address in reverse order, but now the suffix is ip6.arpa.

As for the /var/named/fe80.0.0.0.zone, the following is what we'll type:

```
1    $TTL 172800 ; 2 days
2    0.0.0.0.0.0.0.0.0.0.0.0.0.0.8.e.f.ip6.arpa. IN SOA delphos.olimpus.local.
     root.oli\
3    mpus.local. (
4                        2014082701          ;serial
5                        259200              ;refresh(3 days)
6                        14400               ;retry(4 hours)
7                        18140               ;expire(3 weeks)
8                        604800              ;minimum(1 week)
9                        )
10
11                              NS delphos.olimpus.local.
12   1.b.c.4.8.7.e.f.f.f.9.2.c.0.2.0 IN PTR delphos
```

And we check the result.

```
1    [root@delphos named]# named-checkzone 0.0.0.0.0.0.0.0.0.0.0.0.0.0.8.e.f.
     ip6.arpa f\
2    e80.0.0.0.zone
3    zone 0.0.0.0.0.0.0.0.0.0.0.0.0.0.8.e.f.ip6.arpa/IN: loaded serial
     2014082701
4    OK
```

We restart the named service and query the server again.

```
1    [root@delphos named]# dig @192.168.1.20 -x fe80::20c:29ff:fe78:4cb1
2
3    ; <<>> DiG 9.7.3-P3-RedHat-9.7.3-8.P3.el6 <<>> @192.168.1.20 -x
     fe80::20c:29ff:f\
4    e78:4cb1
5    ; (1 server found)
6    ;; global options: +cmd
7    ;; Got answer:
```

```
8   ;; ->>HEADER<<- opcode: QUERY, status: NOERROR, id: 29346
9   ;; flags: qr aa rd ra; QUERY: 1, ANSWER: 1, AUTHORITY: 1, ADDITIONAL: 2
10
11  ;; QUESTION SECTION:
12  ;1.b.c.4.8.7.e.f.f.f.9.2.c.0.2.0.0.0.0.0.0.0.0.0.0.0.0.0.8.e.f.ip6.
    arpa. IN PT\
13  R
14
15  ;; ANSWER SECTION:
16  1.b.c.4.8.7.e.f.f.f.9.2.c.0.2.0.0.0.0.0.0.0.0.0.0.0.0.0.8.e.f.ip6.
    arpa. 172800\
17  IN PTR delphos.0.0.0.0.0.0.0.0.0.0.0.0.0.8.e.f.ip6.arpa.
18
19  ;; AUTHORITY SECTION:
20  0.0.0.0.0.0.0.0.0.0.0.0.0.8.e.f.ip6.arpa. 172800 IN NS delphos.olimpus.
    local.
21
22  ;; ADDITIONAL SECTION:
23  delphos.olimpus.local.    172800        IN      A      192.168.1.20
24  delphos.olimpus.local.    172800        IN      AAAA
    fe80::20c:29ff:fe78:4cb1
25
26  ;; Query time: 1 msec
27  ;; SERVER: 192.168.1.20#53(192.168.1.20)
28  ;; WHEN: Sat Aug    2 11:58:03 2014
29  ;; MSG SIZE  rcvd: 191
```

Everything is working fine now, so we'll configure it to start automatically after a reboot. There are different ways of doing this. For example, in CentOS 6, we can use chkconfig.

```
1   [root@delphos ~]# chkconfig named on
2   [root@delphos ~]# chkconfig --list named
3   named           0:off   1:off   2:on   3:on   4:on   5:on   6:off
```

In CentOS 7, we should use the systemctl command.

```
1   [root@Centos7 ~]# systemctl enable named
```

From now on, every time we restart the server, the named service will be activated.

Now we'll be able to resolve the domain names we have defined in our zones, but if we want our server to resolve internet domain names such as www.google.com, we'll have to forward those requests to an external DNS server. If the external DNS server IP address is 192.168.1.1, we will have to include the following lines in the /etc/named.conf file:

```
1   forwarders {
2               192.168.1.1;
3           };
```

These preceding lines should be included in the general options section, so that the configuration file remains like this:

```
1   options {
2           listen-on port 53 { any; };
3           listen-on-v6 port 53 { any; };
4   .
5   .
6   .
7   forwarders {
8                   192.168.1.1;
9           };
10  .
11  .
12  .
13  };
```

Besides, in order to properly resolve external domain names, we'll need to activate recursion, by adding the option (if it's not already included) recursion yes in the /etc/named.conf file:

```
1   options {
2   .
3   .
4   .
5   recursion yes
6   .
7   .
8   .
9   };
```

4.4. Client Configuration

In Linux, we can see the current DNS client configuration in the /etc/resolv.conf file.

```
1   [root@delphos ~]# cat /etc/resolv.conf
2   nameserver 192.168.1.20
3   search olimpus.local
```

In this example, the client will send the DNS requests to the server at 192.168.1.20. If no DNS suffix is provided, it will automatically add olimpus.local.

We can edit this file manually, but it is usually more convenient to use one of the administrative tools every Linux distribution has at its disposal. For example, in CentOS 6, we can use the system-config-network program. In CentOS 7, there isn't a system-config-network program, but there is a similar one called nmtui. In SUSE, we can do the same thing with YaST. In Ubuntu, we can open System Settings, and then go to network.

On the other hand, in Windows, we have to edit the LAN connection and then edit the properties of TCP/IP (Figures 4-2 and 4-3).

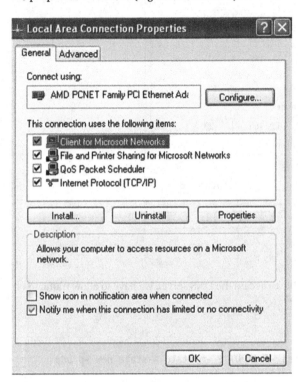

Figure 4-2. *LAN connection properties*

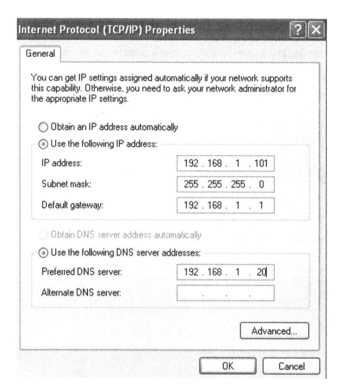

Figure 4-3. *IP configuration*

Of course, for clients to be able to access the DNS server, we have to allow traffic to port 53 UDP in the firewall.

In CentOS 6:

```
1   [root@delphos ~]# iptables -I INPUT 2 -m state --state new -p udp
    --dport 53 -j \
2   ACCEPT
```

In CentOS 7:

```
1   [root@CentOS7 ~]# firewall-cmd --add-service=dns
2   success
```

In the case of CentOS 7, with the previous command, we have allowed traffic to port 53 for both protocols UDP and TCP. You can see more details about the firewall included in CentOS 7 in Chapter 10 of this book.

4.5. Slave Servers and Zone Transfers

At this point, we have a name server that holds all of the information related to `olimpus.local.zone`. As we will see throughout this book, the DNS is of utmost importance, as it affects many other services. Needless to say, a shutdown of the service can be a complete disaster for our network. To try to minimize this risk, we could install another server, to provide the name service too. This new server would be a slave server, that is, a server with a read-only copy of the zone files. It would be able to answer queries, but it wouldn't be able to update the information. Thus, we have two servers to share the load. In addition, if the master server becomes completely unusable, we could easily transform the slave server into a master server.

So, in order to try and balance the load between the different name servers in our network, we'll have to configure the clients accordingly. For example, if we have a master server (192.168.1.20) and a slave server (192.168.1.40), we should configure half the clients with the master server as the "preferred server," and the slave server as the "alternate server." In the other half, we should do just the opposite and configure the slave server as the "preferred server" and the master server as the "alternate server." This way, we are not only distributing the workload across the two servers but are also protecting ourselves against the failure of one of the name servers, because if the client can't contact its primary server, it will connect to the secondary server.

You have seen in a previous chapter how to install CentOS, so I'll assume you have a working CentOS server. We'll install the bind package as we saw before. The named.conf file will have to be modified to add the following lines:

```
1    zone "olimpus.local" IN {
2    type slave;
3    file "slaves/olimpus.local.zone";
4    masters {
5                    192.168.1.20;
6            };
7    };
8
9    zone "1.168.192.in-addr.arpa" IN {
10           type slave;
11           file "slaves/192.168.1.zone";
12           masters {
13                   192.168.1.20;
14           };
15
16   };
17
18   zone "0.0.0.0.0.0.0.0.0.0.0.0.0.0.8.e.f.ip6.arpa" IN {
19           type slave;
20           file "slaves/fe80.0.0.0.zone";
21           masters {
22                   192.168.1.20;
23           };
24
25   };
```

Basically, we name our zones, declare them to be slave zones, and tell the server about the master servers, 192.168.1.20, in this case.

Of course, we'll have to make the same changes we made in the master server, to make sure that the server listens in all the network addresses and can be queried by anybody.

```
1   listen-on port 53 { any; };
2   listen-on-v6 port 53 { any; };
3   allow-query    { any; };
```

We'll also have to make some minor changes in the zone files of the master server. We'll create another NS register for the slave server. If the new server is prometheus, the new line would be like the following:

```
1   .
2   .
3   .
4   IN NS delphos.olimpus.local.
5   IN NS prometheus.olimpus.local.
6   .
7   .
8   .
```

This should be done in olimpus.local.zone, 192.168.1.zone, and fe80.0.0.0.zone files. In addition, we should also notify the slave server whenever the zone file is updated. For that, we use the notify yes directive in the zone definition of the named.conf file:

```
1   zone "olimpus.local" IN {
2           type master;
3           file "olimpus.local.zone";
4           notify yes;
5   };
6
7   zone "1.168.192.in-addr.arpa" IN {
8           type master;
9           file "192.168.1.zone";
10          notify yes;
11  };
12
13  zone "0.0.0.0.0.0.0.0.0.0.0.0.0.0.8.e.f.ip6.arpa" IN {
14          type master;
15          file "fe80.0.0.0.zone";
16          notify yes;
17  };
```

In the slave server, the named service should be able to create the zone files in the /var/named/slaves folder, so we'll make sure the user named has the rights to write into that directory.

```
1   [root@delphos named]# ls -ld slaves/
2   drwxrwx---. 2 named named 4096 Dec   8   2011 slaves/
```

I have already reviewed SELinux briefly. It could be described as a security mechanism that creates another layer of protection against unauthorized access and limits the damage a hacker could do to the system. SELinux limits what a process can do, which includes, of course, the named service. We'll see how to make named work with it.

First, we check if SELinux is active:

```
1   [root@delphos named]# sestatus
2   SELinux status:                 enabled
3   SELinuxfs mount:                /selinux
4   Current mode:                   enforcing
5   Mode from config file:          enforcing
6   Policy version:                 24
7   Policy from config file:        targeted
```

We also have to check the SELinux Booleans associated with the DNS service.

```
1   [root@delphos named]# getsebool -a | grep named
2   named_write_master_zones --> off
```

This parameter implies that named won't be allowed to write the zone files. Obviously, this would make the zone transfer fail, so we have to change the value to on.

```
1   [root@delphos named]# setsebool named_write_master_zones on
2   [root@delphos named]# getsebool -a | grep named
3   named_write_master_zones --> on
```

We'll make the change permanent with -P.

```
1   [root@delphos ~]# setsebool -P named_write_master_zones 1
```

When transferring zones, the slave server will have to connect to port 53 on the master server. Obviously, this port has to be accessible from the slave server. To check this, we can execute the nmap program from the slave server.

```
1   [root@delphos named]# nmap -p 53 192.168.1.20
2   Starting Nmap 5.21 ( http://nmap.org ) at 2013-11-12 01:12 CET
3   mass_dns: warning: Unable to determine any DNS servers. Reverse DNS is
    disabled.\
4   Try using --system-dns or specify valid servers with --dns-servers
5   Nmap scan report for 192.168.1.20
6   Host is up (0.00026s latency).
```

```
7   PORT     STATE         SERVICE
8   53/tcp filtered domain
9   MAC Address: 00:0C:29:78:4C:B1 (VMware)
10
11  Nmap done: 1 IP address (1 host up) scanned in 0.06 seconds
```

As we see, the port is being filtered. We'll have to open the port in the firewall in the master server. You'll also see the use of the firewall in more detail later in this book. For now, I'll just explain how to open the port. Depending on whether we are using CentOS 6 or CentOS 7, the way to do this will be different.

In CentOS 6, we can list the firewall configuration by typing iptables -L in the master server.

```
1   [root@delphos named]# iptables -L
2   Chain INPUT (policy ACCEPT)
3   target       prot opt source         destination
4   ACCEPT       all  --  anywhere       anywhere           state RELATED,ESTAB\
5   LISHED
6   ACCEPT       icmp --  anywhere       anywhere
7   ACCEPT       all  --  anywhere       anywhere
8   ACCEPT       tcp  --  anywhere       anywhere           state NEW tcp dpt:s\
9   sh
10  REJECT       all  --  anywhere       anywhere           reject-with icmp-ho\
11  st-prohibited
12
13  Chain FORWARD (policy ACCEPT)
14  target       prot opt source         destination
15  REJECT       all --  anywhere        anywhere           reject-with icmp-ho\
16  st-prohibited
17
18  Chain OUTPUT (policy ACCEPT)
19  target       prot opt source         destination
```

By default, only connections to the ssh port are allowed. We'll have to add the following line to permit access to port 53.

```
1   [root@delphos named]# iptables -I INPUT 5 -m state --state NEW -m tcp -p
    tcp --d\
2   port 53 -j ACCEPT
```

We insert a new input rule in the fifth position. We specify that new connections to port 53 should be allowed. Once the new connection is established, further traffic will be allowed too, as specified in the following line:

```
1   ACCEPT all -- anywhere        anywhere             state RELATED,ESTAB\
2   LISHED
```

The complete set of firewall rules could be similar to this:

```
 1  [root@delphos named]# iptables -L
 2  Chain INPUT (policy ACCEPT)
 3  target     prot opt source        destination
 4  ACCEPT     all  -- anywhere       anywhere       state RELATED,ESTAB\
 5  LISHED
 6  ACCEPT     icmp -- anywhere       anywhere
 7  ACCEPT     all  -- anywhere       anywhere
 8  ACCEPT     tcp  -- anywhere       anywhere       state NEW tcp dpt:s\
 9  sh
10  ACCEPT     tcp  -- anywhere       anywhere       state NEW tcp dpt:d\
11  omain
12  REJECT     all  -- anywhere       anywhere       reject-with icmp-ho\
13  st-prohibited
14
15  Chain FORWARD (policy ACCEPT)
16  target     prot opt source        destination
17  REJECT     all -- anywhere        anywhere       reject-with icmp-ho\
18  st-prohibited
19
20  Chain OUTPUT (policy ACCEPT)
21  target     prot opt source        destination
```

In CentOS 7, it is also possible to use iptables, but it is recommended that the firewall-cmd command be used instead. First of all, we have to find out the default zone.

```
1  [root@delphos ~]# firewall-cmd --get-default-zone
2  public
```

Then, we list the services allowed.

```
1  [root@delphos ~]# firewall-cmd --zone=internal --list-services
2  ssh
```

In this case, only the ssh service is allowed, so we'll have to add the dns service.

```
1  [root@delphos ~]# firewall-cmd --zone=internal --add-service=dns
2  success
```

If now we repeat the test with nmap from the slave server, we'll see that the port is open.

```
1  [root@delphos named]# nmap -p 53 192.168.1.20
2
3  Starting Nmap 5.21 ( http://nmap.org ) at 2013-11-12 01:31 CET
4  mass_dns: warning: Unable to determine any DNS servers. Reverse DNS is
   disabled.\
5   Try using --system-dns or specify valid servers with --dns-servers
6  Nmap scan report for 192.168.1.20
```

```
7    Host is up (0.0020s latency).
8    PORT     STATE  SERVICE
9    53/tcp open         domain
10   MAC Address: 00:0C:29:78:4C:B1 (VMware)
11
12   Nmap done: 1 IP address (1 host up) scanned in 0.07 seconds
```

We'll do the same in the slave server, so that zone transfers can take place in both directions.

Now we can check if the transfer zone actually works, by restarting the named service on the slave server.

In CentOS 6:

```
1    [root@delphos named]# service named restart
2    Stopping named:                              [ OK ]
3    Starting named:                              [ OK ]
4    [root@delphos named]#
```

In CentOS 7:

```
1    [root@Centos7 ~]# systemctl restart named
```

If everything is OK, we should now have three files in the /var/named/slaves folder.

```
1    [root@delphos named]# ls /var/named/slaves/
2    192.168.1.zone  fe80.0.0.0.zone  olimpus.local.zone
```

Now every time we modify a zone in the master server, we'll update the serial number, thus the change should be replicated to the slave server. For example, let's say we add a new server vulcan with IPv4 192.168.1.23 and IPv6 fe80::20c:29ff:fedf:d786/64.

We add the new A and AAAA registers in the zone file.

```
1    .
2    .
3    .
4    delphos      IN A     192.168.1.20
5    prometheus   IN A     192.168.1.21
6    aphrodite    IN A     192.168.1.22
7    vulcan       IN A     192.168.1.23
8
9    delphos      IN AAAA  fe80::20c:29ff:fe78:4cb1
10   prometheus   IN AAAA  fe80::20c:29ff:feeb:4443
11   vulcan       IN AAAA  fe80::20c:29ff:fedf:d786
12   .
13   .
14   .
```

Then we add the PTR registers in the reverse zone files.

```
1   .
2   .
3   .
4   22              PTR vulcan.olimpus.local.
5   .
6   .
7   .
8   6.8.7.d.f.d.e.f.f.f.9.2.c.0.2.0 IN PTR vulcan
```

Finally, we update the serial number in all the three files.

```
1   2014090102;          Serial
```

The update of the zone files should take place at one moment or another, depending on the parameters defined in the zones themselves. But, in any case, we can force the zone transfer with the rndc command. (See the following section, "DNSSEC and TSIG," on how to install it.) We execute it from the slave server.

```
1   rndc retransfer olimpus.local
```

After a few seconds, master and slave will have the same information. We can check this by querying both servers with the dig command. From the slave server, we can query both servers. First, we query the slave server itself.

```
1   [root@delphos ~]# dig @192.168.1.21 prometheus.olimpus.local
2
3   ; <<>> DiG 9.7.3-P3-RedHat-9.7.3-8.P3.el6 <<>> @192.168.1.21
    prometheus.olimpus.\
4   local
5   ; (1 server found)
6   ;; global options: +cmd
7   ;; Got answer:
8   ;; ->>HEADER<<- opcode: QUERY, status: NOERROR, id: 18441
9   ;; flags: qr aa rd ra; QUERY: 1, ANSWER: 1, AUTHORITY: 2, ADDITIONAL: 3
10
11  ;; QUESTION SECTION:
12  ;prometheus.olimpus.local.            IN      A
13
14  ;; ANSWER SECTION:
15  prometheus.olimpus.local. 172800     IN      A      192.168.1.21
16
17  ;; AUTHORITY SECTION:
18  olimpus.local.          172800       IN      NS     prometheus.
    olimpus.local.
19  olimpus.local.          172800       IN      NS     delphos.olimpus.
    local.
```

```
20
21    ;; ADDITIONAL SECTION:
22    delphos.olimpus.local.      172800         IN      A       192.168.1.20
23    delphos.olimpus.local.      172800         IN      AAAA
      fe80::20c:29ff:fe78:4cb1
24    prometheus.olimpus.local 172800            IN      AAAA
      fe80::20c:29ff:feeb:4443
25
26    ;; Query time: 1 msec
27    ;; SERVER: 192.168.1.21#53(192.168.1.21)
28    ;; WHEN: Sun Aug       3 04:40:00 2014
29    ;; MSG SIZE  rcvd: 166
```

Then we query the master server, to see if the two answers are the same. We must take into account that the firewall might be blocking the query. In order to allow zone transfers, we opened before the firewall for connections to TCP port 53. Nevertheless, DNS queries don't use TCP port 53, but UDP port 53. If this is the case, we'll have to open UDP port 53 in the firewall.

In CentOS 6:

```
1    [root@delphos ~]# iptables -I INPUT 4 -p udp --dport 53 -j ACCEPT
```

In CentOS 7:

The same command we used to allow zone transfers will permit both transfers and queries.

```
1    [root@Centos7 ~]# firewall-cmd --zone=internal --add-service=dns
2    success
```

Now we can perform the query.

```
 1    [root@delphos ~]# dig @192.168.1.20 prometheus.olimpus.local
 2
 3    ; <<>> DiG 9.7.3-P3-RedHat-9.7.3-8.P3.el6 <<>> @192.168.1.20
      prometheus.olimpus.\
 4    local
 5    ; (1 server found)
 6    ;; global options: +cmd
 7    ;; Got answer:
 8    ;; ->>HEADER<<- opcode: QUERY, status: NOERROR, id: 57417
 9    ;; flags: qr aa rd ra; QUERY: 1, ANSWER: 1, AUTHORITY: 2, ADDITIONAL: 3
10
11    ;; QUESTION SECTION:
12    ;prometheus.olimpus.local.          IN      A
13
14    ;; ANSWER SECTION:
15    prometheus.olimpus.local. 172800 IN        A       192.168.1.21
16
```

```
17   ;; AUTHORITY SECTION:
18   olimpus.local.              172800 IN         NS          prometheus.
     olimpus.local.
19   olimpus.local.              172800 IN         NS          delphos.olimpus.
     local.
20
21   ;; ADDITIONAL SECTION:
22   delphos.olimpus.local.      172800 IN         A           192.168.1.20
23   delphos.olimpus.local.      172800 IN         AAAA
     fe80::20c:29ff:fe78:4cb1
24   prometheus.olimpus.local.   172800 IN         AAAA
     fe80::20c:29ff:feeb:4443
25
26   ;; Query time: 2 msec
27   ;; SERVER: 192.168.1.20#53(192.168.1.20)
28   ;; WHEN: Sun Aug   3 05:42:05 2014
29   ;; MSG SIZE  rcvd: 166
```

As we can see, the result is the same in both cases.

Now that we have a working DNS infrastructure, we must pay attention to some of the security implications. In order for the slave servers to have the same information as the master server, the zones must be transferred from the master to the slave. By default, bind allows zone transfer to any computer. This might be a risk, because a malicious user might get the list of computers in the network and even identify some of them, such as the mail server. With that information in hand, an attack would be easier. For this reason, it is recommended that zone transfers be limited only to certain IP addresses. In fact, it would be even better to limit the transfer of zones by using keys, but we'll see this in the next section ("DNSSEC and TSIG").

So, if the slave server has the 192.168.1.21 IP address, in the master server, we should change the definition of the zone in the /etc/named.conf file.

```
1    .
2    .
3    .
4    zone "olimpus.local" IN {
5            type master;
6            file "olimpus.local.zone.signed";
7            notify yes;
8            allow-transfer {
9                    192.168.1.21;
10           };
11   };
12   .
13   .
14   .
```

If we now try to perform a zone transfer from a different computer, we'll get the following error:

```
1   antonio@antonio-i7:~$ dig axfr @192.168.1.20 olimpus.local
2
3   ; <<>> DiG 9.9.5-3ubuntu0.8-Ubuntu <<>> axfr @192.168.1.218
    olimpus.local
4   ; (1 server found)
5   ;; global options: +cmd
6   ; Transfer failed.
```

Of course, if we launch this same command from a slave server, the zone transfer will be executed without any problem.

We should repeat this operation in all the name servers and zones, allowing the transfer only to certain IP addresses.

4.6. DNSSEC and TSIG

The domain name service is of utmost importance in any network infrastructure, but, unfortunately, it is quite vulnerable to attacks. If a malicious hacker manages to inject wrong DNS answers in a network, he or she would be able to control the traffic. For example, let's say a user wants to check her mail and so tries to access http://gmail.com. If an attacker can send a DNS reply for the domain gmail.com, the user's computer will attempt to access the wrong gmail.com.

To minimize this risk, there are two complementary approaches: TSIG (Transaction Signatures) and DNSSEC (Domain Name System Security Extensions).

TSIG is a networking protocol whose aim is to provide a means of authenticating updates to a DNS database. It works by using keys. First, we generate a key with the dnssec command, then we configure the slave server (or the DHCP server) with the key. This is mainly used in Dynamic DNS and in slave servers. In the section of Chapter 5 entitled "DHCP and DNS Dynamic Update," you'll see a complete example of the use of TSIG.

The second approach to protect our DNS infrastructure against tampering of the zones is DNSSEC. DNSSEC doesn't actually avoid these attacks, but it makes their detection possible. It works by signing the zone files, so that we know if an unauthorized change has taken place. To use DNSSEC, we must first generate two keys for our zone.

All these steps will take place in the master server.

We'll have to generate two sets of keys: the Zone Signing Keys (ZSK) and the Key Signing Keys (KSK). First, we create the ZSK.

```
1   [root@delphos named]# dnssec-keygen -a RSASHA1 -b 512 -n ZONE
    olimpus.local
2   Generating key pair.....++++++++++++ ....++++++++++++
3   Kolimpus.local.+005+08586
```

The process of generating the keys can be very, very long, up to several hours. If we want to speed up the process, we can install haveged, which acts as a random number generator. Currently, haveged is not included as part of the CentOS 6 software package, but it can be installed from the Internet.[1] On the other hand, if we're working with CentOS 7, we can download it from the EPEL repository. This repository is not part of the default repositories for CentOS 7, but it can be configured very easily by executing the following command:

```
1    [root@CentOS7 ~]# yum install epel-release
```

Next, we generate the KSK. As I said before, it can take quite a long time, but if we execute the haveged service before, the execution will be considerably faster.

```
1    [root@delphos named]# dnssec-keygen -f KSK -a RSASHA1 -b 4096 -n ZONE
     olimpus.lo\
2    cal
3    Generating key pair..............++.................................
     .........\
4    ....................................++
5    Kolimpus.local.+005+35116
```

Now we'll have to add to the zone file the key files that we created previously.

```
1    [root@delphos named]# cat Kolimpus.local.*.key >> olimpus.local.zone
```

And sign the zone file, as follows:

```
1    [root@delphos named]# dnssec-signzone -N increment -o olimpus.local
     olimpus.loca\
2    l.zone
3    Verifying the zone using the following algorithms: RSASHA1.
4    Zone signing complete:
5    Algorithm: RSASHA1: KSKs: 1 active, 0 stand-by, 0 revoked
6                        ZSKs: 1 active, 0 stand-by, 0 revoked
7    olimpus.local.zone.signed
```

Now we have a new olimpus.local.zone.signed file. We'll have to change the definition of the olimpus.local zone in /etc/named.conf to point to this new file.

```
1    .
2    .
3    .
4    zone "olimpus.local" IN {
5            type master;
```

---

[1]"haveged—A simple entropy daemon," http://www.issihosts.com/haveged, 2014.

```
6              file "olimpus.local.zone.signed";
7              notify yes;
8    };
9    .
10   .
11   .
```

And we restart the named service. In CentOS 6:

```
1    [root@delphos named]# service named restart
2    Stopping named:                               [ OK ]
3    Starting named:                               [ OK ]
```

In CentOS 7:

```
1    [root@CentOS7 named]# systemctl restart named
```

To make sure that DNSSEC is actually working, we can query for the DNSKEY record of the domain, like this:

```
1    [root@delphos ~]# dig @192.168.1.20 DNSKEY olimpus.local. +multiline
2    ;; Truncated, retrying in TCP mode.
3
4    ; <<>> DiG 9.7.3-P3-RedHat-9.7.3-8.P3.el6 <<>> @192.168.1.20 DNSKEY
     olimpus.loca\
5    l. +multiline
6    ; (1 server found)
7    ;; global options: +cmd
8    ;; Got answer:
9    ;; ->>HEADER<<- opcode: QUERY, status: NOERROR, id: 48176
10   ;; flags: qr aa rd ra; QUERY: 1, ANSWER: 2, AUTHORITY: 0, ADDITIONAL: 0
11
12   ;; QUESTION SECTION:
13   ;olimpus.local.            IN DNSKEY
14
15   ;; ANSWER SECTION:
16   olimpus.local.            172800   IN DNSKEY 257 3 5 (
17   AwEAAeGilVrj9hxnmjRY9Yd9SqrBMwtiqKwfSda3wXhn
18   d3koFZQzVI129xRVxEhaXpQvcH4tZG724hE/NF/zq6jI
19   H2q6OtUOposlWLnRTE4CteOEMP/Q4dSpSzLqjT4+cPrw
20   Fyfgvv7q+dHBHJOTiWJjeSffFDFcACPfqY3KIFHNxgD3
21   bBwdO/GXgLDACBVoH7qVCNRBosuji24lmxwYu9qOoqX5
22   sTF1mhmKpOm4uO2CEVhSnTeXlER4XermehqLhOLlodWl
23   R75EmAYc13SvMS9CoFc66eXEOpSLOl7F9eZQ/RHh/Wob
24   x74moN1uSwP32fTYhJZr3GXOTey+kfnpvhBIxXRa6nbB
25   2jfLsNOPMb4ZEYTAXOICtevRDYptuM3ytakPd3elNfrm
26   px9vxkFMye1/18diS/VWXD7RBc8wpbKOaQBMYV94dKhB
27   a3F6SV9tbXF7nTadG7kOI+USOkUSfppCjWr+TTwdfvGR
```

```
28    e/M7XPM1riBv/zUgSp7XzOKWdYT2mQjPR4xl21FcsSwy
29    tehCWoS+xGEd3y9AaW7RHAwPjeexMR30458/h1cqQcEs
30    QCQltl3uboqjFon3s4iHcHIqtpnBUC/TaonMA39pBTXt
31    VFPO+EV3YJBKFgGf1qZRW9aFAU+BHAnaRt2svPmBId7n
32    40778a14Jgaco4b64Y6Ij3Mx8as5
33    ) ; key id = 9187
34    olimpus.local.           172800 IN DNSKEY 256 3 5 (
35    AwEAAb386KgB7QrWAWBZ9+uSaHjHmpW+3TpcGkCfh9T4
36    Znl6BJVb/kPp6DmfeTRzjFUQSbAGRiI3yvzJ9+iEUhra
37         dME=
38        ) ; key id = 28332
39
40    ;; Query time: 2 msec
41    ;; SERVER: 192.168.1.20#53(192.168.1.20)
42    ;; WHEN: Sun Aug   3 20:11:10 2014
43    ;; MSG SIZE   rcvd: 647
```

As you see, the query was answered correctly.

Now, to perform a very simple test, we should save this key in the /etc/trusted-key.key file.

```
1    [root@centos7 ~]# dig +noall +answer -t dnskey @192.168.1.20 olimpus.
     local > /et\
2    c/trusted-key.key
```

We activate the use of dnssec, and we add the trusted-keys entry in the /etc/named.conf file. We include the key value we obtained previously.

```
1    options{
2    .
3    .
4    .
5    dnssec-enable yes
6    dnssec-validation yes
7    .
8    .
9    .
10   };
11   .
12   .
13   .
14   trusted-keys {
15   olimpus.local.         256 3 5 "AwEAAatIDOYQB6awuS3A8SDMaPdVuVHkNjzvwy
     RePG+gD/zyerAmpO9\
16   w X7o8yqXotVbsS6OCU5q3gBHqMwgAMjzzJxk=";
17   olimpus.local.        257 3 5 "AwEAAcdLMSqlh3e/m3vYm38+IOHJ45S7cC8o8Ie9s6
     eN+6XPVpMO/vM\
```

```
18    j N7azRBsoutLvOIrOHd556KYjiH5MzDTdcgQx4RD/hHI6HLshtmaW//HK
      3MTDfPp1wLX2KEHS/vOHI\
19    7jZuatmpNViAoDRso16GlRk3kQJGmpdHZ8g AwoPns3zep5JB3CJLAipKbSh4kPJOmPuR9
      n3jLfs4H+H\
20    148rhfEOao8+ f64Ut1viACzro3b1sWHs5YWlBu2C1ZYG8fF6sI5NLLedfCDLYiyzbD6D
      94dnv4Wgjj\
21    AfJBiuFEPkXvZrD6vF/KxHqSTyV8lVuTOXdIi7oyXQCYv4 2MMj//
      nZSTmOwLgXiREEzQO2VbuL+OHLl\
22    9Oe66BXqmEH+F4HVADGAo68 4UXuSvZyJXnW7TPZ6pjyGHZLJ+eXfMuJgrN7OOkFYhX93Q
      gh9Dw9e9yt\
23    TnIuHoyCSTeXMYOrCmarjUJVgDOMihl6dklcwx/NZrj/VPE9cizasxsx
      IZiavb5xhcfbXXOXqjQC94\
24    Bzt6526UE1w+qGkfBUze+NWpixz8WgLkua
      MXaJNAY7NxDvGpz1ridarJwe3zHnGT4RvaySZhTJKNUAe\
25    HDUnxitF6wR QpzXK9ZbGRnRMaFDII87c5WEIqSJXOkto8FKRxEuQDJTwTdyVlqPXBfH
      KJLMYExg2XV\
26    mVtXN";
27    };
28    .
29    .
30    .
```

After restarting the named service, we check whether we can resolve names in the olimpus.local zone successfully.

```
1    [root@Centos7 ~]# dig +noall +answer @192.168.1.20 delphos.olimpus.
     local
2    delphos.olimpus.local.          172800          IN          A
     192.168.1.218
```

If we try to resolve names in other domains, we get an error.

```
1    [root@Centos7 ~]# dig +noall +answer @192.168.1.20 www.linuxaholics.com
2    [root@Centos7 ~]# dig @192.168.1.218 www.linuxaholics.com
3
4    ; <<>> DiG 9.9.4-RedHat-9.9.4-29.el7_2.3 <<>> @192.168.1.20
     www.linuxaholics.com
5    ; (1 server found)
6    ;; global options: +cmd
7    ;; Got answer:
8    ;; ->>HEADER<<- opcode: QUERY, status: SERVFAIL, id: 8646
9    ;; flags: qr rd ra; QUERY: 1, ANSWER: 0, AUTHORITY: 0, ADDITIONAL: 1
10
11   ;; OPT PSEUDOSECTION:
12   ; EDNS: version: 0, flags:; udp: 4096
13   ;; QUESTION SECTION:
14   ;www.apress.com.                          IN          A
15
```

```
16   ;; Query time: 4 msec
17   ;; SERVER: 192.168.1.218#53(192.168.1.20)
18   ;; WHEN: dom sep 25 16:21:06 CEST 2016
19   ;; MSG SIZE   rcvd: 43
```

In the test we've just performed, this is completely normal. We created a key for our zone, olimpus.local, and saved that key in the /etc/trusted-key.key file. So, from now on, our server trusts itself, but as it doesn't have the key for the .com zone, it can check whether the information received is correct or not and fails.

We can also test the dnssec configuration using the +sigchase flag with the dig command.

```
1    [root@centos7 named]# dig +sigchase @192.168.1.20 olimpus.local
2    .
3    .
4    .
5    Launch a query to find a RRset of type DNSKEY for  zone: olimpus.local.
6
7    ;; DNSKEYset that signs the RRset to chase:
8    olimpus.local.          172800            IN          DNSKEY
     257 3 5 AwEAAcdLMSqlh3e/m3vYm38+I
9    .
10   .
11   .
12   ;; WE HAVE MATERIAL, WE NOW DO VALIDATION
13   ;; VERIFYING NSEC RRset for olimpus.local. with DNSKEY:4578: success
14   ;; OK We found DNSKEY (or more) to validate the RRset
15   ;; Ok, find a Trusted Key in the DNSKEY RRset: 10921
16   ;; VERIFYING DNSKEY RRset for olimpus.local. with DNSKEY:10921: success
17
18   ;; Ok this DNSKEY is a Trusted Key, DNSSEC validation is ok: SUCCESS
```

In real life, DNSSEC is based on the concepts of keys, signatures, and hierarchy. When the admin of a certain DNS domain wants to use DNSSEC, he creates the keys (as we did), signs the zone (as we did), and publishes the public key of the domain, so that everybody can check the signature of the zones. Obviously, as we are working on a local domain, we haven't published the key.

DNSSEC is a big improvement in the security of the DNS protocol, and it should be implemented in every name server on the Internet. Nevertheless, in our case, we can disable it, in order to make its operation easier for the rest of the exercises in the book.

4.7. Chroot

Another further step in protecting our name server is working in a chroot environment. To better understand this, let's see briefly what a chroot environment is.

107

A chroot is an operation that changes the apparent root directory of the current process, so that this program can't access files that reside below its working directory. Let's see an example.

We log on to our server and create a new folder. Later, this folder will become the apparent root directory.

```
1   [root@delphos ~]# mkdir -p /new/root
```

We can try to chroot the user session with the chroot command.

```
1   [root@delphos ~]# chroot /new/root/
2   chroot: failed to run command /bin/bash: No such file or directory
```

As we see, we have to access /bin/bash to chroot the user session. So we create a bin subfolder and copy the bash file in it.

```
1   [root@delphos ~]# mkdir /new/root/bin
2   [root@delphos ~]# cp /bin/bash /new/root/bin/
```

However, we're not done yet. If we try to run chroot again, we get the same error.

```
1   [root@delphos ~]# chroot /new/root/
2   chroot: failed to run command /bin/bash: No such file or directory
```

This is due to the fact that the bash executable file is dynamically linked and has to access a series of libraries. We can find out what libraries it needs by using the ldd command. **Note:** Libraries will vary, depending on the exact version of the operating system.

```
1   [root@delphos ~]# ldd /bin/bash
2           linux-vdso.so.1 =>           (0x00007fffc57fe000)
3           libtinfo.so.5 => /lib64/libtinfo.so.5 (0x00007f76faeb3000)
4           libdl.so.2 => /lib64/libdl.so.2 (0x00007f76facaf000)
5           libc.so.6 => /lib64/libc.so.6 (0x00007f76fa8ed000)
6           /lib64/ld-linux-x86-64.so.2 (0x00007f76fb0f1000)
```

So, we create a new subfolder and copy the required files.

```
1   [root@delphos ~]# mkdir /new/root/lib64
2   [root@delphos ~]# cp /lib64/libtinfo.so.5 /new/root/lib64/
3   [root@delphos ~]# cp /lib64/libdl.so.2 /new/root/lib64/
4   [root@delphos ~]# cp /lib64/libc.so.6 /new/root/lib64/
5   [root@delphos ~]# cp /lib64/ld-linux-x86-64.so.2 /new/root/lib64/
```

Now we can execute chroot.

```
1   [root@delphos ~]# chroot /new/root/
2   bash-4.2#
```

If we type "pwd," the system will tell us that we are already at the root directory, and we won't be able to access other folders outside of the chroot environment.

```
1   bash-4.2# pwd
2   /
3   bash-4.2# cd ..
4   bash-4.2# pwd
5   /
```

This is an extremely simple chroot environment meant only as a proof of concept. If we try, for example, to list the directory contents with the ls command, we'll get an error, because we haven't copied the ls file and the libraries it depends on to run. Besides, we should also have created some other folders, such as a dev subfolder, etc.

Once we've completed this little experiment, we leave the chroot environment and remove the folder we created.

```
1   bash-4.2# exit
2   exit
3   [root@delphos ~]# rm -rf /new/root/
```

As a chrooted service can't access folders or files outside of its home directory, it is considered a good practice. Thus, if the named service gets compromised, it will only be able to access the content of its home directory.

If we want the named service to execute in a chroot environment, we could do it manually, as we have done before with our "proof of concept." But, fortunately, there is a much easier way. We only need to install the bind-root package.

```
1   [root@delphos ~]# yum install bind-chroot
```

Right after installing the package, we see that a new subfolder has been created below /var/named. This subfolder contains all the necessary files and folders for named to work properly.

```
1   [root@delphos ~]# ls -l /var/named/chroot/
2   total 0
3   drwxr-x---. 2 root  named 41 Sep 26 12:02 dev
4   drwxr-x---. 4 root  named 44 Sep 26 12:02 etc
5   drwxr-x---. 3 root  named 18 Sep 26 12:02 run
6   drwxrwx---. 3 named named 18 Sep 26 12:02 usr
7   drwxr-x---. 5 root  named 48 Sep 26 12:02 var
```

Right after installing bind-root, the named service will already be running in a chroot environment in CentOS 6.

However, in CentOS 7, we still have to start this service.

```
1   [root@delphos ~]# systemctl start named-chroot
```

We must make sure that the service starts automatically every time the system boots.

```
1  [root@delphos ~]# systemctl enable named-chroot
2  ln -s '/usr/lib/systemd/system/named-chroot.service' '/etc/systemd/
   system/multi-\
3  user.target.wants/named-chroot.service'
```

4.8. Diagnostic Tools
4.8.1. rndc

rndc is a great tool to manage the name server. Remember: When we checked the status of the named service, we saw a message saying "rndc: neither /etc/rndc.conf nor /etc/rndc.key was found." These two files are required in order for the rndc command to work. rndc is a front end to control the DNS server, so we'll have to modify /etc/named.conf to allow rndc to manage the server. We can do it by hand, but it is much easier to do by typing rndc-confgen. This command will show a sample rndc.key and rndc.conf file that we can use.

rndc-confgen will have to generate keys, so it can take as long as a few minutes to complete. A bit of patience is required.

```
1   [root@delphos ~]# rndc-confgen
2   # Start of rndc.conf
3   key "rndc-key" {
4          algorithm hmac-md5;
5          secret "Yg1R5vvMWBu/+P9RxCKm8g==";
6   };
7
8   options {
9          default-key "rndc-key";
10         default-server 127.0.0.1;
11         default-port 953;
12  };
13  # End of rndc.conf
14
15  # Use with the following in named.conf, adjusting the allow list as
    needed:
16  # key "rndc-key" {
17  #        algorithm hmac-md5;
18  #        secret "Yg1R5vvMWBu/+P9RxCKm8g==";
19  # };
20  #
21  # controls {
22  #        inet 127.0.0.1 port 953
23  #        allow { 127.0.0.1; } keys { "rndc-key"; };
24  # };
25  # End of named.conf
```

So, we create a file named /etc/rnc.conf, as follows:

```
1   # Start of rndc.conf
2   key "rndc-key" {
3           algorithm hmac-md5;
4           secret "Yg1R5vvMWBu/+P9RxCKm8g==";
5   };
6
7   options {
8           default-key "rndc-key";
9           default-server 127.0.0.1;
10          default-port 953;
11  };
12  # End of rndc.conf
```

Then we modify the /etc/named.conf file, as instructed. Adding the lines generated by rndc-confgen, we restart the service and try to execute rndc.

```
1   [root@delphos named]# rndc status
2   version: 9.7.3-P3-RedHat-9.7.3-8.P3.el6
3   CPUs found: 1
4   worker threads: 1
5   number of zones: 22
6   debug level: 0
7   xfers running: 0
8   xfers deferred: 0
9   soa queries in progress: 0
10  query logging is OFF
11  recursive clients: 0/0/1000
12  tcp clients: 0/100
13  server is up and running
```

To see the options available, we can use the -h option.

```
1   [root@delphos named]# rndc -h
2   Usage: rndc [-b address] [-c config] [-s server] [-p port]
3           [-k key-file ] [-y key] [-V] command
4
5   command is one of the following:
6
7   reload          Reload configuration file and zones.
8   reload zone [class [view]]
9                   Reload a single zone.
10  refresh zone [class [view]]
11                  Schedule immediate maintenance for a zone.
12  retransfer zone [class [view]]
13                  Retransfer a single zone without checking serial number.
14  freeze          Suspend updates to all dynamic zones.
```

```
15  freeze zone [class [view]]
16                  Suspend updates to a dynamic zone.
17  thaw            Enable updates to all dynamic zones and reload them.
18  thaw zone [class [view]]
19                  Enable updates to a frozen dynamic zone and reload it.
20  notify zone [class [view]]
21                  Resend NOTIFY messages for the zone.
22  reconfig        Reload configuration file and new zones only.
23  sign zone [class [view]]
24                  Update zone keys, and sign as needed.
25  loadkeys zone [class [view]]
26                  Update keys without signing immediately.
27  stats           Write server statistics to the statistics file.
28  querylog        Toggle query logging.
29  dumpdb [-all|-cache|-zones] [view ...]
30                  Dump cache(s) to the dump file (named_dump.db).
31  secroots [view ...]
32                  Write security roots to the secroots file.
33  stop            Save pending updates to master files and stop the server.
34  stop -p         Save pending updates to master files and stop the server
35                  reporting process id.
36  halt            Stop the server without saving pending updates.
37  halt -p         Stop the server without saving pending updates reporting
38                  process id.
39  trace           Increment debugging level by one.
40  trace level     Change the debugging level.
41  notrace         Set debugging level to 0.
42  flush           Flushes all of the server's caches.
43  flush [view]    Flushes the server's cache for a view.
44  flushname name [view]
45                  Flush the given name from the server's cache(s)
46  status          Display status of the server.
47  recursing       Dump the queries that are currently recursing
                    (named.recursing)
48  validation newstate [view]
49                  Enable / disable DNSSEC validation.
50  *restart        Restart the server.
51  addzone ["file"] zone [class [view]] { zone-options }
52                      Add zone to given view. Requires new-zone-file
                        option.
53  delzone ["file"] zone [class [view]]
54                      Removes zone from given view. Requires new-zone-file
                        option.
55
56  * == not yet implemented
57  Version: 9.7.3-P3-RedHat-9.7.3-8.P3.el6
```

4.8.2. dig

We have already seen this tool, and we can use it to query a DNS server and specify the type of register we want to know about. For example, to know the mail server of the domain olimpus.local, we'd type the following:

```
1   [root@delphos ~]# dig mx @192.168.1.21 olimpus.local
2
3   ; <<>> DiG 9.7.3-P3-RedHat-9.7.3-8.P3.el6 <<>> mx @192.168.1.21
    olimpus.local
4   ; (1 server found)
5   ;; global options: +cmd
6   ;; Got answer:
7   ;; ->>HEADER<<- opcode: QUERY, status: NOERROR, id: 3247
8   ;; flags: qr aa rd ra; QUERY: 1, ANSWER: 1, AUTHORITY: 2, ADDITIONAL: 4
9
10  ;; QUESTION SECTION:
11  ;olimpus.local.                    IN      MX
12
13  ;; ANSWER SECTION:
14  olimpus.local.          172800   IN      MX           10 prometheus.
    olimpus.local.
15
16  ;; AUTHORITY SECTION:
17  olimpus.local.          172800   IN      NS           prometheus.
    olimpus.local.
18  olimpus.local.          172800   IN      NS           delphos.
    olimpus.local.
19
20  ;; ADDITIONAL SECTION:
21  prometheus.olimpus.local. 172800  IN      A            192.168.1.21
22  prometheus.olimpus.local. 172800  IN      AAAA
    fe80::20c:29ff:feeb:4443
23  delphos.olimpus.local.    172800  IN      A            192.168.1.20
24  delphos.olimpus.local.    172800  IN      AAAA
    fe80::20c:29ff:fe78:4cb1
25
26  ;; Query time: 12 msec
27  ;; SERVER: 192.168.1.21#53(192.168.1.21)
28  ;; WHEN: Sun Aug   3 04:37:03 2014
29  ;; MSG SIZE  rcvd: 182
```

If we don't want to be overwhelmed with so much information, we can tell dig not to show all the details of the query (+noall) and include only the answer itself (+answer).

```
1   [root@delphos ~]# dig +noall +answer mx @192.168.1.21 olimpus.local
2   olimpus.local.          172800 IN     MX        10
    prometheus.olimpus.local.
```

113

We can also ask for a complete zone transfer.

```
1    [root@delphos ~]# dig axfr @192.168.1.20 olimpus.local
2
3    ; <<>> DiG 9.7.3-P3-RedHat-9.7.3-8.P3.el6 <<>> axfr @192.168.1.20
     olimpus.local
4    ; (1 server found)
5    ;; global options: +cmd
6    olimpus.local.          172800    IN    SOA    olimpus.local.
     root.olimpus.loca\
7    l. 2014090103 60 7200 604800 172800
8    olimpus.local.          172800    IN    NS     delphos.olimpus.
                                                    local.
9    olimpus.local.          172800    IN    NS     prometheus.olimpus.
                                                    local.
10   olimpus.local.          172800    IN    MX     10 prometheus.
     olimpus.local.
11   aphrodite.olimpus.local. 172800   IN    A      192.168.1.22
12   delphos.olimpus.local.   172800   IN    AAAA
     fe80::20c:29ff:fe78:4cb1
13   delphos.olimpus.local.   172800   IN    A      192.168.1.20
14   dns.olimpus.local.       172800   IN    CNAME  delphos.olimpus.
                                                    local.
15   mail.olimpus.local.      172800   IN    CNAME  prometheus.olimpus.
                                                    local.
16   prometheus.olimpus.local.  172800  IN   AAAA
     fe80::20c:29ff:feeb:4443
17   prometheus.olimpus.local.  172800  IN   A      192.168.1.21
18   vulcan.olimpus.local.    172800   IN    AAAA
     fe80::20c:29ff:fedf:d786
19   vulcan.olimpus.local.    172800   IN    A      192.168.1.23
20   olimpus.local.           172800   IN    SOA    olimpus.local.
     root.olimpus.loca\
21   l. 2014090103 60 7200 604800 172800
22   ;; Query time: 6 msec
23   ;; SERVER: 192.168.1.20#53(192.168.1.20)
24   ;; WHEN: Sun Aug 3 05:46:46 2014
25   ;; XFR size: 14 records (messages 1, bytes 373)
```

4.8.3. host

host is a tool quite similar to dig. The syntax is slightly different, however.

```
1    [root@delphos ~]# host prometheus.olimpus.local 192.168.1.20
2    Using domain server:
3    Name: 192.168.1.20
4    Address: 192.168.1.20#53
```

```
5   Aliases:
6
7   prometheus.olimpus.local has address 192.168.1.21
8   prometheus.olimpus.local has IPv6 address fe80::20c:29ff:feeb:4443
```

4.9. Troubleshooting

As every systems administrator knows, unfortunately, incidents happen, and sometimes things don't work as expected, or don't work at all. In the following subsections, we'll take a look at some of the most common scenarios we could encounter. But before proceeding, I'll make a quick review of the name resolution process.

I already briefly discussed /etc/hosts and how it can be used to resolve names. And, of course, we have reviewed many details of the named service too. But there is also a file that plays an important role when troubleshooting name resolution problems. This is the /etc/nsswitch.conf file.

This file is used by the system to identify the sources from which it can obtain name-services related information, such as hostnames, usernames, etc. If we open this file with a text editor, we'll see a line beginning with "hosts:".

```
1   #
2   # /etc/nsswitch.conf
3   #
4   # An example Name Service Switch config file. This file should be
5   # sorted with the most-used services at the beginning.
6   #
7   .
8   .
9   .
10  hosts:          files dns
```

This means that the server will try to resolve names based on the contents of the /etc/hosts file, and if the name can't be resolved in this manner, it will query the DNS server. This is the default behavior after a fresh installation, but if problems occur, you should check this file, to make sure the values associated with the hosts option are the right ones. The installation of some additional software could alter the contents of this file.

4.9.1. A Computer Can't Resolve Names

If there is only a small percentage of computers that cannot resolve names, that is probably a problem with the client computers themselves. You'll have to check that the computer has set the address of the DNS server in the network correctly. In the case of a Linux, this is configured in the /etc/resolv.conf file. For example, if the DNS server is 192.168.1.20, the /etc/resolv.conf file should be something like this:

```
1   [root@delphos ~]# cat /etc/resolv.conf
2   nameserver 192.168.1.20
```

If the file is correct we'd also have to check the network configuration and the physical connection to the network.

4.9.2. Many Computers Can't Resolve Names

If there are many computers unable to resolve names, there might be some problem with the DNS server itself. First of all, you'll have to check that the service is running.

```
1   [root@delphos ~]# service named status
2   version: 9.7.3-P3-RedHat-9.7.3-8.P3.el6
3   CPUs found: 1
4   worker threads: 1
5   number of zones: 22
6   debug level: 0
7   xfers running: 0
8   xfers deferred: 0
9   soa queries in progress: 0
10  query logging is OFF
11  recursive clients: 0/0/1000
12  tcp clients: 0/100
13  server is up and running
14  named (pid    8616) is running...
```

If the service is up and running, the next step is to make sure that the service can be accessed from the network. As I said before, the DNS queries are addressed to UDP port 53 in the server, so we can use nmap from a client computer to check whether or not the port is open.

```
1   [root@delphos ~]# nmap -sU -p 53 192.168.1.20
2
3   Starting Nmap 5.21 ( http://nmap.org ) at 2014-08-03 05:40 CEST
4   Nmap scan report for delphos.olimpus.local (192.168.1.20)
5   Host is up (0.00085s latency).
6   PORT    STATE    SERVICE
7   53/udp filtered domain
8   MAC Address: 00:0C:29:78:4C:B1 (VMware)
```

In this case, the port is filtered. That's the reason the clients can't resolve names. They're unable to contact the name server.

```
1   [root@delphos ~]# nmap -sU -p 53 192.168.1.20
2
3   Starting Nmap 5.21 ( http://nmap.org ) at 2014-08-03 06:23 CEST
4   Nmap scan report for delphos.olimpus.local (192.168.1.20)
5   Host is up (0.00033s latency).
6   PORT    STATE   SERVICE
7   53/udp open      domain
```

```
8    MAC Address: 00:0C:29:78:4C:B1 (VMware)
9
10   Nmap done: 1 IP address (1 host up) scanned in 0.07 seconds
```

Now that the port is open, we should perform a query from the client computer, by using dig or host.

```
1    [root@delphos ~]# dig @192.168.1.20 delphos.olimpus.local
2
3    ; <<>> DiG 9.7.3-P3-RedHat-9.7.3-8.P3.el6 <<>> @192.168.1.20 delphos.
     olimpus.loc\
4    al
5    ; (1 server found)
6    ;; global options: +cmd
7    ;; Got answer:
8    ;; ->>HEADER<<- opcode: QUERY, status: NOERROR, id: 51991
9    ;; flags: qr aa rd ra; QUERY: 1, ANSWER: 1, AUTHORITY: 2, ADDITIONAL: 3
10
11   ;; QUESTION SECTION:
12   ;delphos.olimpus.local.          IN      A
13
14   ;; ANSWER SECTION:
15   delphos.olimpus.local.   172800 IN      A       192.168.1.20
16
17   ;; AUTHORITY SECTION:
18   olimpus.local.           172800 IN      NS      delphos.olimpus.local.
19   olimpus.local.           172800 IN      NS      prometheus.olimpus.
                                                     local.
20
21   ;; ADDITIONAL SECTION:
22   delphos.olimpus.local.   172800 IN      AAAA
     fe80::20c:29ff:fe78:4cb1
23   prometheus.olimpus.local. 172800 IN     A       192.168.1.21
24   prometheus.olimpus.local. 172800 IN     AAAA
     fe80::20c:29ff:feeb:4443
25
26   ;; Query time: 2 msec
27   ;; SERVER: 192.168.1.20#53(192.168.1.20)
28   ;; WHEN: Sun Aug 3 06:26:04 2014
29   ;; MSG SIZE rcvd: 166
```

In this case, the DNS server seems to be working fine. The client made a query and got an answer.

```
1    [root@delphos ~]# dig @192.168.1.20 neptune.olimpus.local
2
3    ; <<>> DiG 9.7.3-P3-RedHat-9.7.3-8.P3.el6 <<>> @192.168.1.20 neptune.
     olimpus.loc\
```

```
4    al
5    ; (1 server found)
6    ;; global options: +cmd
7    ;; Got answer:
8    ;; ->>HEADER<<- opcode: QUERY, status: NXDOMAIN, id: 60601
9    ;; flags: qr aa rd ra; QUERY: 1, ANSWER: 0, AUTHORITY: 1, ADDITIONAL: 0
10
11   ;; QUESTION SECTION:
12   ;neptune.olimpus.local.           IN     A
13
14   ;; AUTHORITY SECTION:
15   olimpus.local.          172800      IN     SOA      olimpus.local. root.
     olimpus.loca\
16   1. 2014090103 60 7200 604800 172800
17
18   ;; Query time: 2 msec
19   ;; SERVER: 192.168.1.20#53(192.168.1.20)
20   ;; WHEN: Sun Aug   3 06:26:21 2014
21   ;; MSG SIZE   rcvd: 80
```

On the other hand, also in this case, the server answered the query, but it couldn't find any neptune.olimpus.local register. It might not exist in the zone, or maybe the server has an outdated zone file.

4.9.3. Master and Slave Servers Don't Have the Same Information

If the slave server has outdated information, we have to know whether there is a problem with zone transfers. As we have seen, we can use dig on the slave server, to request a zone transfer.

```
1    [root@delphos ~]# dig axfr @192.168.1.20 olimpus.local
2    ;; Connection to 192.168.1.20#53(192.168.1.20) for olimpus.local failed:
     host un\
3    reachable.
```

In this case, we couldn't perform the zone transfer. The TCP port 53 on the master server is probably closed or filtered.

```
1    [root@delphos ~]# dig axfr @192.168.1.20 olimpus.local
2
3    ; <<>> DiG 9.7.3-P3-RedHat-9.7.3-8.P3.el6 <<>> axfr @192.168.1.20
     olimpus.local
4    ; (1 server found)
5    ;; global options: +cmd
6    olimpus.local.          172800      IN     SOA      olimpus.local.
     root.olimpus.loca\
```

```
 7    1. 2014090103 60 7200 604800 172800
 8    olimpus.local.              172800    IN    NS      delphos.olimpus.
                                                          local.
 9    olimpus.local.              172800    IN    NS      prometheus.olimpus.
                                                          local.
10    olimpus.local.              172800    IN    MX      10 prometheus.
      olimpus.local.
11    aphrodite.olimpus.local.    172800    IN    A       192.168.1.22
12    delphos.olimpus.local.      172800    IN    AAAA
      fe80::20c:29ff:fe78:4cb1
13    delphos.olimpus.local.      172800    IN    A       192.168.1.20
14    dns.olimpus.local.          172800    IN    CNAME   delphos.olimpus.
                                                          local.
15    mail.olimpus.local.         172800    IN    CNAME   prometheus.olimpus.
                                                          local.
16    prometheus.olimpus.local.   172800    IN    AAAA
      fe80::20c:29ff:feeb:4443
17    prometheus.olimpus.local.   172800    IN    A       192.168.1.21
18    vulcan.olimpus.local.       172800    IN    AAAA
      fe80::20c:29ff:fedf:d786
19    vulcan.olimpus.local.       172800    IN    A       192.168.1.23
20    olimpus.local.              172800    IN    SOA     olimpus.local.
      root.olimpus.loca\
21    l. 2014090103 60 7200 604800 172800
22    ;; Query time: 6 msec
23    ;; SERVER: 192.168.1.20#53(192.168.1.20)
24    ;; WHEN: Sun Aug   3 05:46:46 2014
25    ;; XFR size: 14 records (messages 1, bytes 373)
```

Now the transfer zone is correct. We can use rndc to request a zone transfer on the slave server.

```
1    [root@delphos ~]# rndc retransfer olimpus.local
2    [root@delphos ~]#
```

4.10. Log Files

Log files are perhaps the most important tools when troubleshooting. In a default installation of bind, the log file will be /var/named/data/named.run. This is defined in the following lines of the /etc/named.conf file.

```
1    logging {
2            channel default_debug {
3                    file "data/named.run";
4                    severity dynamic;
5            };
6    };
```

By watching this file, we can monitor the state of the server. For instance, this could be part of the log file.

```
1   .
2   .
3   .
4   received control channel command 'stop'
5   shutting down: flushing changes
6   stopping command channel on 127.0.0.1#953
7   no longer listening on ::#53
8   no longer listening on 127.0.0.1#53
9   no longer listening on 192.168.1.20#53
10  exiting
11  zone 0.in-addr.arpa/IN: loaded serial 0
12  zone 1.0.0.127.in-addr.arpa/IN: loaded serial 0
13  zone 1.168.192.in-addr.arpa/IN: loaded serial 2014090102
14  zone 1.0.0.0.0.0.0.0.0.0.0.0.0.0.0.0.0.0.0.0.0.0.0.0.0.0.0.0.0.0.0.0.i
    p6.arpa/IN\
15  : loaded serial 0
16  zone 0.0.0.0.0.0.0.0.0.0.0.0.0.0.8.e.f.ip6.arpa/IN: loaded serial
    2014090102
17  zone olimpus.local/IN: loaded serial 2014090103
18  zone localhost.localdomain/IN: loaded serial 0
19  zone localhost/IN: loaded serial 0
20  .
21  .
22  .
```

In the preceding, we can see that the name server stopped and started to load the zone files again.

4.10.1. journalctl (only in CentOS 7)

In addition to logging into the usual syslog files (/var/log/messages/, etc.), CentOS 7 also logs important information into the systemd journal. The contents of this journal can be seen with the journalctl command.

```
1   -- Logs begin at Thu 2016-06-02 12:48:52 CEST, end at Sat 2016-09-03
    06:11:04 CE
2   Jun 02 12:48:52 localhost.localdomain systemd-journal[335]: Runtime
    journal is u
3   Jun 02 12:48:52 localhost.localdomain systemd-journal[335]: Runtime
    journal is u
4   Jun 02 12:48:52 localhost.localdomain kernel: Initializing cgroup subsys
    cpuset
```

```
5    Jun 02 12:48:52 localhost.localdomain kernel: Initializing cgroup subsys
     cpu
6    .
7    .
8    .
```

The amount of information might be overwhelming, but to refine the search, there are some parameters we can pass to the journalctl command. For example, we can pass the _COMM=named parameter to see only information about the named service.

```
1    [root@Centos7 ~]# journalctl _COMM=named
2
3    -- Logs begin at Tue 2016-09-20 13:40:32 CEST, end at Mon 2016-09-26
     14:20:01 CE\
4    ST. --
5    Sep 26 09:59:55 delphos.olimpus.local named[18896]: starting BIND
     9.9.4-RedHat-9\
6    .9.4-14.el7 -u named
7    Sep 26 09:59:55 delphos.olimpus.local named[18896]: built with
     '--build=x86_64-r\
8    edhat-linux-gnu' '--host=x86_64-redhat-linux-gnu' '--program-prefix='
     '--disa
9    Sep 26 09:59:55 delphos.olimpus.local named[18896]: -------------------
     ----------\
10   -----------------------
11   Sep 26 09:59:55 delphos.olimpus.local named[18896]: BIND 9 is
     maintained by Inte\
12   rnet Systems Consortium,
13   .
14   .
15   .
```

We can also confine the search to a certain period of time, with the –since and -until options.

```
1    [root@Centos7 ~]# journalctl _COMM=named --since="2016-09-26 10:00:00"
     --until="\
2    2016-09-26 11:00:00"
3
4    Sep 26 10:12:53 delphos.olimpus.local named[19185]: starting BIND
     9.9.4-RedHat-9\
5    .9.4-14.el7 -u named
6    Sep 26 10:12:53 delphos.olimpus.local named[19185]: built with
     '--build=x86_64-r\
7    edhat-linux-gnu' '--host=x86_64-redhat-linux-gnu' '--program-prefix='
     '--disa
8    Sep 26 10:12:53 delphos.olimpus.local named[19185]: -------------------
     ---------\
```

121

```
 9    -----------------------
10    Sep 26 10:12:53 delphos.olimpus.local named[19185]: BIND 9 is
      maintained by Inte\
11    rnet Systems Consortium,
12    Sep 26 10:12:53 delphos.olimpus.local named[19185]: Inc. (ISC), a non-
      profit 501\
13    (c)(3) public-benefit
14    .
15    .
16    .
```

One thing we must take into account is the fact that the contents of the systemd journal are volatile by default, so every time the system restarts, the information it contains will be lost. If we want to make the contents permanent, we need to create the following folder:

```
1    [root@Centos7 ~]# mkdir /var/log/journal
```

We must also make the systemd-journal group the owner of the folder.

```
1    [root@Centos7 ~]# chown .systemd-journal /var/log/journal/
```

Finally, we restart the systemd service, and the contents of the journal will be permanent.

CHAPTER 5

■ ■ ■

DHCP

As we all know, to connect to a network, every computer requires an IP address. In small networks, it is not a problem to assign manually a different IP address to every computer, but when working with tens or hundreds of network devices, one has to be very careful, in order not to make mistakes.

To make things easier, we could delegate this task to the DHCP service. What DHCP does is essentially provide IP addresses to all network devices.

In fact, not only can it provide IP addresses, but also parameters, such as default gateway, dns server, etc.

The way the DHCP protocol works is quite simple (Figure 5-1). In the case of DHCPv4, the DHCP version that works with IPv4, when the DHCP client boots up, it sends a DHCP discover message to the network. By this means, it tries to find an available DHCP server. If there is one (or more) DHCP servers in the network, it will answer back with a DHCP offer message. When the client receives one of these DHCP offer messages, it will send back a DHCP request to the server. The server, in turn, replies with a DHCP ack message, and the address is assigned.

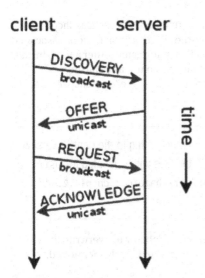

Figure 5-1. DHCP protocol

© Antonio Vazquez 2016

A. Vazquez, *Learn CentOS Linux Network Services*, DOI 10.1007/978-1-4842-2379-6_5

In the case of DHCPv6, the procedure is not the same, but it doesn't differ too much from that for DHCPv4. Here, the client sends a DHCP solicitation message, to which the server replies with an advertise message. Once the client receives the advertise message, it sends a request back to the server, and the server answers with a reply, completing the process.

5.1. Installing a DHCP Server

To convert our CentOS server into a DHCP server, we have only to install the dhcp package.

```
1   [root@CentOS7 ~]# yum install dhcp
```

This will create a new service in /etc/init.d called dhcpd. As we did when we installed the DNS service, we configure the dhcpd service to start automatically with every reboot.

In CentOS 6:

```
1   [root@delphos ~]# chkconfig dhcpd on
```

In CentOS 7:

```
1   [root@CentOS7 ~]# systemctl enable dhcpd
2   ln -s '/usr/lib/systemd/system/dhcpd.service' '/etc/systemd/system/
    multi-user.ta\
3   rget.wants/dhcpd.service'
```

The server configuration will be stored in two different files: /etc/dhcp/dhcpd.conf and /etc/dhcpd/dhcpd6.conf. The first file will have the configuration options associated with IPv4, whereas the second will do the same with IPv6 parameters. After a fresh install, both files are empty, but there are two sample files that we can use as a starting point: /usr/share/doc/dhcp-4.1.1/dhcpd.conf.example and /usr/share/doc/dhcp-4.1.1/dhcpd6.conf.example.

Note The exact location of the sample files will differ according to the CentOS version you are using. For example, if you are using CentOS 7, the files will be located in /usr/share/doc/dhcp- 4.2.5/dhcpd.conf.example and /usr/share/doc/dhcp-4.2.5/dhcpd6.conf.example.

The easiest way to configure the new DHCP server is probably to overwrite the default (empty) configuration files with the two sample files previously mentioned.

```
1   [root@localhost ~]# cp /usr/share/doc/dhcp-4.1.1/dhcpd.conf.sample /etc/
    dhcp/dhc\
```

```
2  pd.conf
3  cp: overwrite `/etc/dhcp/dhcpd.conf'? y
4  [root@localhost ~]# cp /usr/share/doc/dhcp-4.1.1/dhcpd6.conf.sample /
   etc/dhcp/dh\
5  cpd6.conf
6  cp: overwrite `/etc/dhcp/dhcpd6.conf'? y
```

We'll comment out all the lines in both files to start adding our directives one by one. We can do this easily with the sed and tee commands, as follows:

```
1  [root@localhost ~]# sed s/^/#/ /etc/dhcp/dhcpd.conf | tee /etc/dhcp/
   dhcpd.conf
2  [root@localhost ~]# sed s/^/#/ /etc/dhcp/dhcpd6.conf | tee /etc/dhcp/
   dhcpd6.conf
```

Now we're ready to start configuring our DHCP server.

5.1.1. DHCPv4

If we take a look at the /etc/dhcp/dhcpd.conf file, we can see the many parameters that we can assign to the DHCP clients, such as domain-name, domain-servers, etc.

To start with a very basic configuration, we can create the following subnet:

```
1  subnet 192.168.1.0 netmask 255.255.255.0 {
2  range 192.168.1.40 192.168.1.43;
3  }
```

We have defined a range of addresses from 192.168.1.40 to 192.168.1.43 that will be assigned to the DHCP clients. Of course, the DHCP server should have at least one IP address belonging to the 192.168.1.0/24 network. We can check that the syntax of the file is correct with the following command:

```
1  [root@localhost ~]# dhcpd -t /etc/dhcp/dhcpd.conf
2  Internet Systems Consortium DHCP Server 4.1.1-P1
3  Copyright 2004-2010 Internet Systems Consortium.
4  All rights reserved.
5  For info, please visit https://www.isc.org/software/dhcp/
6  Not searching LDAP since ldap-server, ldap-port and ldap-base-dn were
   not specif\
7  ied in the config file
```

In CentOS 7, the interface names are longer than they used to be in CentOS 6, so when checking the dhcpd.conf file syntax, we might receive this warning:

```
1  [root@CentOS7 ~]# dhcpd -t /etc/dhcp/dhcpd.conf
2  /etc/dhcp/dhcpd.conf: interface name too long (is 20)
3  ...
```

```
 4   This version of ISC DHCP is based on the release available
 5   on ftp.isc.org. Features have been added and other changes
 6   have been made to the base software release in order to make
 7   it work better with this distribution.
 8
 9   Please report for this software via the CentOS Bugs Database:
10   http://bugs.centos.org/
11
12   exiting.
```

But this shouldn't prevent the dhcpd service from working properly.

We start the service, and the clients will be able to receive the addresses specified in the pool.

```
1   [root@localhost ~]# service dhcpd start
2   Starting dhcpd: [ OK ]
3   [root@localhost ~]#
```

If the client is a Windows computer, we can force it to renew its IP address, as shown in Figure 5-2.

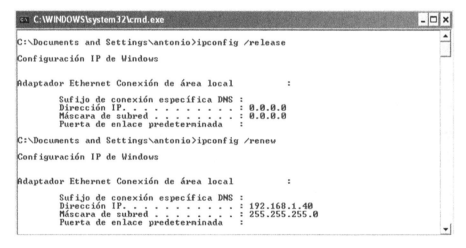

Figure 5-2. *Obtaining an IP address*

As we can see, the IP assigned is 192.168.1.40.

We can also see it in the server itself, by looking at the /var/lib/dhcpd/dhcpd. leases file.

```
1   .
2   .
3   .
4   lease 192.168.1.40 {
```

```
 5    starts 5 2013/09/13 08:49:48;
 6    ends 5 2013/09/13 20:49:48;
 7    cltt 5 2013/09/13 08:49:48;
 8    binding state active;
 9    next binding state free;
10    hardware ethernet 00:0c:29:fe:08:d4;
11    uid "\001\000\014)\376\010\324";
12    clienthostname
13    "windowscli";
14    }
15    .
16    .
17    .
```

We have seen before that the server can provide more parameters to the client through DHCP. A slightly more advanced example could be this one:

```
1    subnet 192.168.1.0 netmask 255.255.255.0 {
2    range 192.168.1.40 192.168.1.43;
3    option domain-name-servers 192.168.1.133;
4    option routers 192.168.1.20;
5    }
```

In this case, we supply the default gateway and the name server address. If we force the client to renew the lease, this is what we'll see (Figure 5-3).

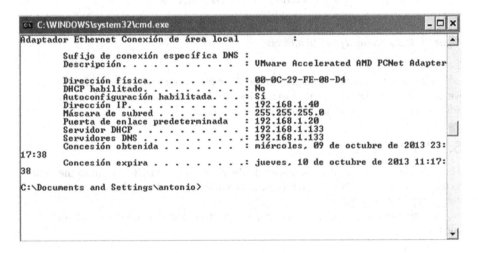

Figure 5-3. *Renewing the IP lease*

Dynamically assigned IPs could change through time, but the DHCP always allows us to assign the same IP to a certain client. To do this, we just add the following directive:

```
1  host windowscli {
2  hardware ethernet 00:0C:29:FE:08:D4;
3  fixedaddress 192.168.1.55;
4  }
```

Once the dhcpd service is restarted, the client with the 00:0C:29:FE:08:D4 MAC address will always be assigned the IP 192.168.1.55 (Figure 5-4).

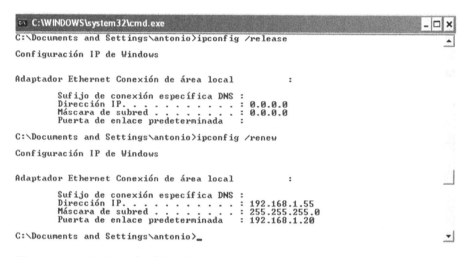

Figure 5-4. *Assigning a fixed IP address*

Of course, the address specified shouldn't be included in any range such as the one we defined earlier. Otherwise, we run the risk of having two computers with the same IP address in the network, which is not a good idea at all!

5.1.2. DHCPv6

The procedure to assign IPv6 parameters to the client through DHCP is almost the same as the one we saw for IPv4. But in this case, the configuration file we have to modify is /etc/dhcp/dhcpd6.conf.

The options are quite similar. For example, to assign a single IPv6 address, we should add this:

```
1  subnet6 fe80::/64 {
2          range6 fe80::4321 fe80::4322;
3  }
```

And when we're done, we start the dhcpd6 service.

In CentOS 6:

```
1    [root@delphos dhcp]# service dhcpd6 restart
2    Starting dhcpd (DHCPv6): [ OK ]
```

In CentOS 7:

```
1    [root@CentOS7 ~]# systemctl restart dhcpd6
```

We'll also have to permit in the firewall the traffic to udpv6 port 547.
In CentOS 6:

```
1    [root@delphos dhcp]# ip6tables -I INPUT 2 -m state --state NEW -m udp -p
     udp --d\
2    port 547 -j ACCEPT
```

In CentOS 7:

```
1    [root@CentOS7 ~]# firewall-cmd --add-service=dhcpv6
2    success
```

Now we force the client to ask for a lease. If the client is a Linux computer, we use the dhclient command with the parameter (-6) to specify IPv6.

```
1    [root@delphos dhcp]# dhclient -6 eth0 -v
```

If everything goes as expected, we'll see onscreen something similar to Figure 5-5.

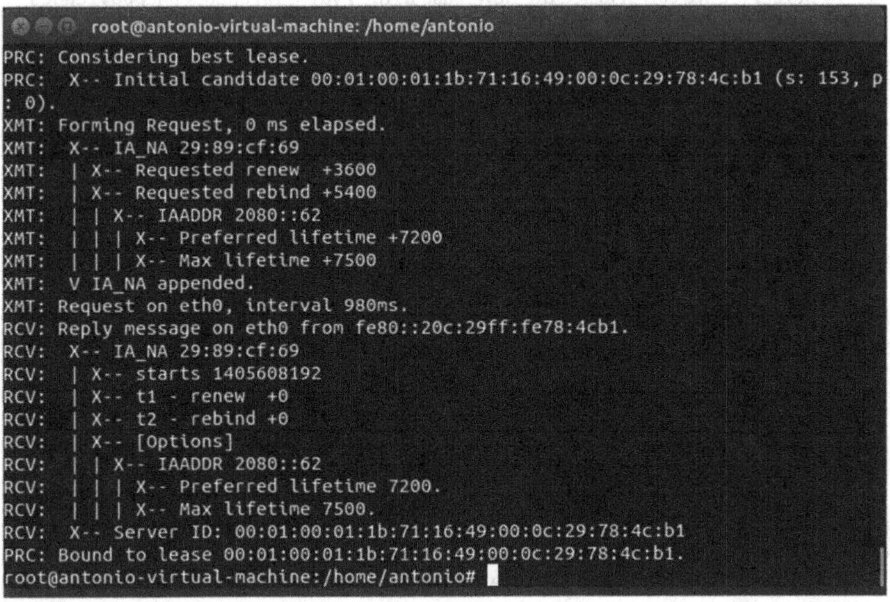

Figure 5-5. Getting an IP address in Linux

As we can see, the computer now has the new IPv6 address assigned (Figure 5-6).

```
RCV:   X-- Server ID: 00:01:00:01:1b:71:16:49:00:0c:29:78:4c:b1
PRC: Bound to lease 00:01:00:01:1b:71:16:49:00:0c:29:78:4c:b1.
root@antonio-virtual-machine:/home/antonio# ifconfig
eth0      Link encap:Ethernet  HWaddr 00:0c:29:89:cf:69
          inet addr:192.168.1.22  Bcast:192.168.1.255  Mask:255.255.255.0
          inet6 addr: 2080::62/64 Scope:Global
          inet6 addr: fe80::20c:29ff:fe89:cf69/64 Scope:Link
          UP BROADCAST RUNNING MULTICAST  MTU:1500  Metric:1
          RX packets:11602 errors:0 dropped:53 overruns:0 frame:0
          TX packets:1494 errors:0 dropped:0 overruns:0 carrier:0
          collisions:0 txqueuelen:1000
          RX bytes:912743 (912.7 KB)  TX bytes:135153 (135.1 KB)
          Interrupt:19 Base address:0x2000

lo        Link encap:Local Loopback
          inet addr:127.0.0.1  Mask:255.0.0.0
          inet6 addr: ::1/128 Scope:Host
          UP LOOPBACK RUNNING  MTU:65536  Metric:1
          RX packets:178 errors:0 dropped:0 overruns:0 frame:0
          TX packets:178 errors:0 dropped:0 overruns:0 carrier:0
          collisions:0 txqueuelen:0
          RX bytes:13203 (13.2 KB)  TX bytes:13203 (13.2 KB)

root@antonio-virtual-machine:/home/antonio#
```

Figure 5-6. *Showing the IP address assigned*

In the server, we can also see the new lease in the /var/lib/dhcpd/dhcpd6.leases file.

```
1   ia-na "\376\017\000\016\000\001\000\001\030\210p\377\000\017\376\343\35
    0]" {
2     cltt 0 2014/08/03 17:34:39;
3     iaaddr 2080::61 {
4       binding state active;
5       preferred-life 27000;
6       max-life 43200;
7       ends 1 2014/08/04 05:34:39;
8     }
9   }
```

5.2. Troubleshooting and Diagnostic Tools

As the interaction between the DHCP server and the client takes place before a real TCP connection is established, the tools available to detect errors are somewhat limited.

One thing that can be done is to use the OS tools to force the renewal of an IP address.

In Windows:

```
1   ipconfig /release
2   ipconfig /renew
```

In Linux:
For DHCPv4:

```
1   dhclient -r
2   dhclient -s direccion_IP_del_servidor_dhcp
```

For DHCPv6:

```
1   dhclient -6 -r
2   dhclient -6
```

We can go an additional step and monitor the DHCP network traffic. We can easily do that with the following command:

```
1   [root@CentOS ~]# tcpdump -w salida.dump -s 1500 -vv port bootps or port
    bootpc
2   tcpdump: listening on eth0, link-type EN10MB (Ethernet), capture size
    1500 bytes
```

In CentOS 7, we'll probably have to specify the interface name. As we saw previously, we can list the interfaces with `ip address show`.

```
1    [root@CentOS7 ~]# ip address show
2    1: lo: <LOOPBACK,UP,LOWER_UP> mtu 65536 qdisc noqueue state UNKNOWN
3        link/loopback 00:00:00:00:00:00 brd 00:00:00:00:00:00
4        inet 127.0.0.1/8 scope host lo
5           valid_lft forever preferred_lft forever
6        inet6 ::1/128 scope host
7           valid_lft forever preferred_lft forever
8    2: eno16777736: <BROADCAST,MULTICAST,UP,LOWER_UP> mtu 1500 qdisc pfifo_
     fast stat\
9    e UP qlen 1000
10       link/ether 00:0c:29:c4:f2:f2 brd ff:ff:ff:ff:ff:ff
11       inet 192.168.10.23/24 brd 192.168.10.255 scope global eno16777736
12          valid_lft forever preferred_lft forever
13       inet6 fe80::20c:29ff:fec4:f2f2/64 scope link
14          valid_lft forever preferred_lft forever
```

So, in this example, we have to specify the interface eno16777736.

```
1   [root@CentOS7 ~]# tcpdump -i eno16777736 -w salida.dump -s 1500 -vv port
    bootps \
2   or port bootpc
```

```
3    tcpdump: listening on eno16777736, link-type EN10MB (Ethernet), capture
     size 150\
4    0 bytes
```

Of course, we'll have to substitute eno16777736 for the name of the interface in our server.

This way, we tell tcpdump to record all traffic related with DHCPv4 (ports bootps and bootpc) in the salida.dump file. If we want to capture the DHCPv6 traffic, the command will be similar:

```
1    [root@localhost ~]# tcpdump -w salidav6.dump -s 1500 -vv -i eth0 ip6
```

When we want to finish the capture, we can do it at any time, by pressing Ctrl+C. The file generated can be read by tcpdump itself.

```
1    [root@localhost ~]# tcpdump -r salidav6.dump -vv
2    reading from file salidav6_2.dump, link-type EN10MB (Ethernet)
3    21:08:00.663163 IP6 (hlim 1, next-header Options (0) payload length:
     36) fe80::2\
4    0c:29ff:fe78:4cb1 > ff02::16: HBH (rtalert: 0x0000) (padn)[icmp6 sum
     ok] ICMP6, \
5    multicast listener report v2, length 28, 1 group record(s) [gaddr
     ff05::1:3 to_e\
6    x { }]
7    21:08:01.355955 IP6 (hlim 1, next-header UDP (17) payload length: 113)
     fe80::f97\
8    8:3ba9:55c5:1d38.dhcpv6-client > ff02::1:2.dhcpv6-server: [udp sum ok]
     dhcp6 sol\
9    icit (xid=5dbf1f (elapsed-time 1500) (client-ID hwaddr/time type 1 time
     43447933\
10   9 000ffee3c6cf) (IA_NA IAID:234885118 T1:0 T2:0) (Client-FQDN) (vendor-
     class) (o\
11   ption-request DNS-name DNS vendor-specific-info Client-FQDN))
12   21:08:01.357247 IP6 (hlim 64, next-header UDP (17) payload length: 96)
     fe80::20c\
13   :29ff:fe78:4cb1.dhcpv6-server > fe80::f978:3ba9:55c5:1d38.dhcpv6-
     client: [udp su\
14   m ok] dhcp6 advertise (xid=5dbf1f (client-ID hwaddr/time type 1 time
     434479339 0\
15   00ffee3c6cf) (server-ID hwaddr/time type 1 time 460396105 000c29784cb1)
     (status-\
16   code no addresses))
17   21:08:01.957120 IP6 (hlim 255, next-header ICMPv6 (58) payload length:
     32) fe80:\
```

```
18    :fd53:b4bf:a082:24ab > fe80::20c:29ff:fe78:4cb1: [icmp6 sum ok] ICMP6,
      neighbor \
19    solicitation, length 32, who has fe80::20c:29ff:fe78:4cb1
20            source link-address option (1), length 8 (1):
              24:be:05:05:4f:a9
21            0x0000: 24be 0505 4fa9
22    21:08:01.957160 IP6 (hlim 255, next-header ICMPv6 (58) payload length:
      24) fe80:\
23    :20c:29ff:fe78:4cb1 > fe80::fd53:b4bf:a082:24ab: [icmp6 sum ok] ICMP6,
      neighbor \
24    advertisement, length 24, tgt is fe80::20c:29ff:fe78:4cb1, Flags
      [solicited]
25    21:08:01.960569 IP6 (hlim 1, next-header UDP (17) payload length: 115)
      fe80::3cf\
26    8:8ec6:71e3:61b8.dhcpv6-client > ff02::1:2.dhcpv6-server: [udp sum ok]
      dhcp6 sol\
27    icit (xid=73811e (elapsed-time 6300) (client-ID hwaddr/time type 1 time
      42188220\
28    2 000ffee3de6f) (IA_NA IAID:234885118 T1:0 T2:0) (Client-FQDN)
      (vendor-class) (o\
29    ption-request DNS-name DNS vendor-specific-info Client-FQDN))
30    21:08:01.963141 IP6 (hlim 255, next-header ICMPv6 (58) payload length:
      32) fe80:\
31    :20c:29ff:fe78:4cb1 > ff02::1:ffe3:61b8: [icmp6 sum ok] ICMP6, neighbor
      solicita\
32    tion, length 32, who has fe80::3cf8:8ec6:71e3:61b8
33            source link-address option (1), length 8 (1):
              00:0c:29:78:4c:b1
34            0x0000: 000c 2978 4cb1
35    21:08:01.963671 IP6 (hlim 255, next-header ICMPv6 (58) payload length:
      32) fe80:\
36    :3cf8:8ec6:71e3:61b8 > fe80::20c:29ff:fe78:4cb1: [icmp6 sum ok] ICMP6,
      neighbor \
37    advertisement, length 32, tgt is fe80::3cf8:8ec6:71e3:61b8, Flags
      [solicited, ov\
38    erride]
39            destination link-address option (2), length 8 (1):
              00:0f:fe:e3:de:6f
40    .
41    .
42    .
```

But it is probably much clearer to open the file in Wireshark. Wireshark is a graphic network protocol analyzer currently available for Linux, MacOS X, and Windows. It can be installed in CentOS with yum (`yum install wireshark`), or it can be directly downloaded from www.wireshark.org and installed in Windows or MacOS X.

Wireshark is a graphic application, so it requires a graphic environment in order to run. This is not a problem in Windows and MacOS X, but in the case of Linux, the graphic environment might not be installed by default. If that's the case, you should install it with yum `groupinstall desktop` (in CentOS). Another possible solution is to export the X11 protocol to another computer with X windows, but that's something you'll see later when I discuss remote access (Chapter 6).

In any case, if we want to open the files in a different machine, we should transfer them. If the destination computer is a Linux box, we can use scp. (See Chapter 6 for further details.) Or, if we want to copy the file to a Windows machine, we can use a program such as WinSCP.[1]

Once the file is transferred, we can open it in Wireshark through File ➤ Open, and we'll see something similar to Figures 5-7 and 5-8.

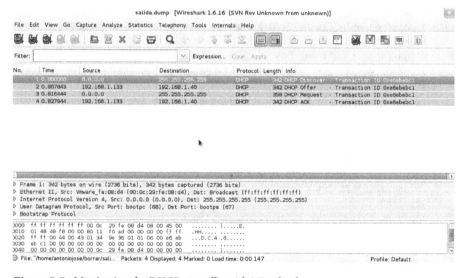

Figure 5-7. *Monitoring the DHCPv4 traffic with Wireshark*

---

[1]WinSCP: Free SFTP, SCP and FTP client for Windows http://winscp.net/eng/index.php, 2016.

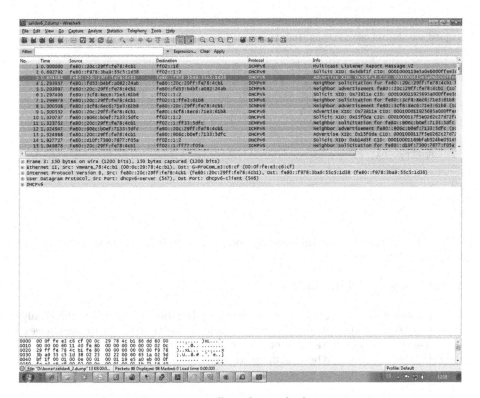

Figure 5-8. *Monitoring the DHCPv6 traffic with Wireshark*

In both cases, we can see the interaction between the server and DHCP client. By clicking any packet, we can see more details, such as the address offered, the lease time, etc.

5.3. DHCP and DNS Dynamic Update

As we have seen, the Domain Name System (DNS) states that a name corresponds to a certain IP address. On the other hand, the DHCP service is in charge of assigning IP addresses to the clients.

So, if we have in our network a DNS and DHCP server, clients will be assigned IP addresses that could change in time, so the list of names and associated IPs has to be updated accordingly every time a change takes place. In order to ensure that, we can use the DNS Dynamic Update. This requires some changes in the configuration of both DNS and DHCP servers. From now on, I'll presume that you have a working DNS server with at least a master zone. We'll assume that DNSSEC is not activated, so we require the following parameters in /etc/named.conf:

```
1    dnssec-enable no;
2    dnssec-validation no;
```

In addition, the zone files shouldn't be signed, so instead of olimpus.local.zone. signed, we should use olimpus.local.zone.

```
1   .
2   .
3   .
4   zone "olimpus.local" IN {
5   type master;
6   file "olimpus.local.zone";
7   notify yes;
8   };
9   .
10  .
11  .
```

To allow for the dynamic updating of a zone file, we must add the following directive in the zone definition:

```
1   allow-update { localhost; };
```

This means that the localhost is authorized to update the zone. Of course, this is only valid if the DHCP server and the DNS server are actually the same; otherwise, we'll have to change localhost with the address of the DHCP server. The corresponding section of the /etc/named.conf would be something like this:

```
1    .
2    .
3    .
4    zone "olimpus.local" IN {
5            type master;
6            file "olimpus.local.zone";
7            notify yes;
8            allow-update { localhost; };
9    };
10
11   zone "1.168.192.in-addr.arpa" IN {
12           type master;
13           file "192.168.1.zone";
14           notify yes;
15           allow-update { localhost; };
16   };
17
18   zone "0.0.0.0.0.0.0.0.0.0.0.0.0.0.8.e.f.ip6.arpa" IN {
19           type master;
20           file "fe80.0.0.0.zone";
21           notify yes;
22           allow-update { localhost; };
23   };
```

```
24
25 .
26 .
27 .
```

After checking that there are no errors, we restart the service.

```
1  [root@centosv6 ~]# namedcheckconf
2  [root@centosv6 ~]# service named restart
3  Stopping named: . [ OK ]
4  Starting named: [ OK ]
```

When activating this characteristic, bind doesn't change the zone files immediately. Instead, it maintains a jnl file for each zone in which it stores the changes. Because of this, we have to be sure that the directory in which the zone files are stored has the appropriate permissions.

```
1  [root@localhost named]# ls -ld /var/named/
2  drwxr-x---. 5 root named 4096 Aug 3 16:25 /var/named/
```

In this case, we must add write permission to the group named.

```
1  [root@localhost named]# chmod g+w /var/named/
2  [root@localhost named]# ls -ld /var/named/
3  drwxrwx---. 5 root named 4096 Aug 3 16:25 /var/named/
```

We'll have to check SELinux too, as there is a value that could be affected.

```
1  [root@centosv6 ~]# getsebool named_write_master_zones
2  named_write_master_zones > off
```

If this value is set to "off," bind won't be able to create the necessary files, so we'd have to change it with the following command:

```
1  [root@centosv6 ~]# setsebool -P named_write_master_zones on
2  [root@localhost ~]# getsebool named_write_master_zones
3  named_write_master_zones --> on
```

Now we'll run a little test to check that everything is working as expected. First of all, we see the registers in the zone.

```
1  [root@localhost ~]# dig @192.168.1.20 axfr olimpus.local
2
3  ; <<>> DiG 9.7.3-P3-RedHat-9.7.3-8.P3.el6 <<>> @192.168.1.20 axfr
   olimpus.local
4  ; (1 server found)
5  ;; global options: +cmd
```

```
6    olimpus.local. 172800 IN SOA olimpus.local. root.olimpus.loca\
7    l. 2014090103 60 7200 604800 172800
8    olimpus.local. 172800 IN DNSKEY 256 3 5 AwEAAb386KgB7QrWAWBZ9+uS\
9    aHjHmpW+3TpcGkCfh9T4Znl6BJVb/kPp 6DmfeTRzjFUQSbAGRiI3yvzJ9+iEUhradME=
10   olimpus.local. 172800 IN DNSKEY 257 3 5 AwEAAeGilVrj9hxnmjRY9Yd9\
11   SqrBMwtiqKwfSda3wXhnd3koFZQzVI12 9xRVxEhaXpQvcH4tZG724hE/NF/
     zq6jIH2q6OtUOposlWLn\
12   RTE4CteOE MP/Q4dSpSzLqjT4+cPrwFyfgvv7q+dHBHJOTiWJjeSffFDFcACPfqY3K
     IFHNxgD3bBwdO\
13   /GXgLDACBVoH7qVCNRBosuji24lmxwYu9qOOqX5sTF1
     mhmKpOm4uO2CEVhSnTeXlER4XermehqLhOLl\
14   odWlR75EmAYc13SvMS9C oFc66eXEOpSLOl7F9eZQ/RHh/
     Wobx74moN1uSwP32fTYhJZr3GXOTey+ kf\
15   npvhBIxXRa6nbB2jfLsNOPMb4ZEYTAXOICtevRDYptuM3ytakPd3el
     Nfrmpx9vxkFMye1/18diS/VWX\
16   D7RBc8wpbKOaQBMYV94dKhBa3F6SV9t bXF7nTadG7kOI+USOkUSfppCjWr+TTwdfvGRe/
     M7XPM1riBv\
17   /zUgSp7X zOKWdYT2mQjPR4xl21FcsSwytehCWoS+xGEd3y9AaW7RHAwPjeexMR3O 458/
     h1cqQcEsQC\
18   Qltl3uboqjFon3s4iHcHIqtpnBUC/TaonMA39pBTXt VFPO+EV3YJBKFgGf1qZRW9aFAU+
     BHAnaRt2sv\
19   PmBId7n40778a14Jgac o4b64Y6Ij3Mx8as5
20   olimpus.local.           172800  IN    NS      delphos.olimpus.local.
21   olimpus.local.           172800  IN    NS      prometheus.olimpus.
     local.
22   olimpus.local.           172800  IN    MX      10 prometheus.olimpus.
     local.
23   aphrodite.olimpus.local. 172800  IN    A       192.168.1.22
24   delphos.olimpus.local.   172800  IN    AAAA    fe80::20c:29ff:fe78:4cb1
25   delphos.olimpus.local.   172800  IN    A       192.168.1.20
26   dns.olimpus.local.       172800  IN    CNAME   delphos.olimpus.local.
27   mail.olimpus.local.      172800  IN    CNAME   prometheus.olimpus.
     local.
28   prometheus.olimpus.local. 172800 IN    AAAA    fe80::20c:29ff:feeb:4443
29   prometheus.olimpus.local. 172800 IN    A       192.168.1.21
30   vulcan.olimpus.local.    172800  IN    AAAA    fe80::20c:29ff:fedf:d786
31   vulcan.olimpus.local.    172800  IN    A       192.168.1.23
32   olimpus.local.           172800  IN    SOA     olimpus.local. root.
     olimpus.loca\
33   l. 2014090103 60 7200 604800 172800
34   ;; Query time: 4 msec
35   ;; SERVER: 192.168.1.20#53(192.168.1.20)
36   ;; WHEN: Mon Aug 4 06:49:34 2014
37   ;; XFR size: 16 records (messages 1, bytes 989)
```

We'll try to add the register neptune.olimpus.local and delete the register vulcan.
olimpus.local. To do this, we'll use the nsupdate tool. When typing nsupdate, we enter
a new shell in which we can indicate the server we want to update, as well as the type of
update. Let's see an example.

```
1  [root@localhost named]# nsupdate
2  > server 192.168.1.20
3  > update delete vulcan.olimpus.local
4  >
5  > ^C[root@localhost named]#
```

We connect to the server 192.168.1.20, and we try to delete the record vulcan.
olimpus.local with the command update delete. After that, we can type "send," to
actually execute the command sequence, but pressing the Enter key has the same effect.
Once completed, we press Ctrl+C.

As we don't see any error message, we can assume that everything worked, but we
can check with the dig command.

```
1   [root@localhost named]# dig @192.168.1.20 axfr olimpus.local
2
3   ; <<>> DiG 9.7.3-P3-RedHat-9.7.3-8.P3.el6 <<>> @192.168.1.20 axfr
    olimpus.local
4   ; (1 server found)
5   ;; global options: +cmd
6   olimpus.local.          172800  IN    SOA    olimpus.local. root.
    olimpus.loca\
7   l. 2014090104 60 7200 604800 172800
8   olimpus.local.          172800  IN    DNSKEY 256 3 5
    AwEAAb386KgB7QrWAWBZ9+uS\
9   aHjHmpW+3TpcGkCfh9T4Znl6BJVb/kPp 6DmfeTRzjFUQSbAGRiI3yvzJ9+iEUhradME=
10  olimpus.local. 172800 IN DNSKEY 257 3 5 AwEAAeGilVrj9hxnmjRY9Yd9\
11  SqrBMwtiqKwfSda3wXhnd3koFZQzVI12 9xRVxEhaXpQvcH4tZG724hE/NF/
    zq6jIH2q60tUOposlWLn\
12  RTE4CteOE MP/Q4dSpSzLqjT4+cPrwFyfgvv7q+dHBHJOTiWJjeSffFDFcACPfqY3K
    IFHNxgD3bBwdO\
13  /GXgLDACBVoH7qVCNRBosuji24lmxwYu9qOOqX5sTF1
    mhmKpOm4uO2CEVhSnTeXlER4XermehqLhOLl\
14  odWlR75EmAYc13SvMS9C oFc66eXEOpSLOl7F9eZQ/RHh/
    Wobx74moN1uSwP32fTYhJZr3GXOTey+ kf\
15  npvhBIxXRa6nbB2jfLsNOPMb4ZEYTAXOICtevRDYptuM3ytakPd3el
    Nfrmpx9vxkFMye1/18diS/VWX\
16  D7RBc8wpbKOaQBMYV94dKhBa3F6SV9t bXF7nTadG7kOI+USOkUSfppCjWr+TTwdfvGRe/
    M7XPM1riBv\
17  /zUgSp7X zOKWdYT2mQjPR4xl21FcsSwytehCWoS+xGEd3y9AaW7RHAwPjeexMR30 458/
    h1cqQcEsQC\
18  Qltl3uboqjFon3s4iHcHIqtpnBUC/TaonMA39pBTXt VFPO+EV3YJBKFgGf1qZRW9aFAU+
    BHAnaRt2sv\
19  PmBId7n40778a14Jgac o4b64Y6Ij3Mx8as5
20  olimpus.local.          172800  IN    NS     delphos.olimpus.local.
21  olimpus.local.          172800  IN    NS     prometheus.olimpus.local.
22  olimpus.local.          172800  IN    MX     10 prometheus.olimpus.local.
23  aphrodite.olimpus.local. 172800 IN    A      192.168.1.22
24  delphos.olimpus.local.  172800  IN    AAAA   fe80::20c:29ff:fe78:4cb1
```

```
25   delphos.olimpus.local.      172800   IN   A      192.168.1.20
26   dns.olimpus.local.          172800   IN   CNAME  delphos.olimpus.local.
27   mail.olimpus.local.         172800   IN   CNAME  prometheus.olimpus.local.
28   prometheus.olimpus.local. 172800   IN   AAAA   fe80::20c:29ff:feeb:4443
29   prometheus.olimpus.local. 172800   IN   A      192.168.1.21
30   olimpus.local.              172800   IN   SOA    olimpus.local. root.
     olimpus.loca\
31   l. 2014090104 60 7200 604800 172800
32   ;; Query time: 4 msec
33   ;; SERVER: 192.168.1.20#53(192.168.1.20)
34   ;; WHEN: Mon Aug 4 07:27:58 2014
35   ;; XFR size: 14 records (messages 1, bytes 938)
```

As expected, there is no longer a vulcan.olimpus.local. Now we'll try to add the new record.

```
1    [root@localhost named]# nsupdate
2    > server 192.168.1.20
3    > update add neptune.olimpus.local 172800 A 192.168.1.240
4    > update add neptune.olimpus.local 172800 AAAA fe80::20c:29ff:fe78:abcd
5    > send
6    >
7    > ^C[root@localhost named]#
8
9    [root@localhost named]# dig @192.168.1.20 axfr olimpus.local
10
11   ; <<>> DiG 9.7.3-P3-RedHat-9.7.3-8.P3.el6 <<>> @192.168.1.20 axfr
     olimpus.local
12   ; (1 server found)
13   ;; global options: +cmd
14   olimpus.local.           172800 IN   SOA olimpus.local. root.olimpus.
     loca\
15   l. 2014090106 60 7200 604800 172800
16   olimpus.local.           172800 IN   DNSKEY 256 3 5
     AwEAAb386KgB7QrWAWBZ9+uS\
17   aHjHmpW+3TpcGkCfh9T4Znl6BJVb/kPp 6DmfeTRzjFUQSbAGRiI3yvzJ9+iEUhradME=
18   olimpus.local.           172800 IN   DNSKEY 257 3 5
     AwEAAeGilVrj9hxnmjRY9Yd9\
19   SqrBMwtiqKwfSda3wXhnd3koFZQzVI12 9xRVxEhaXpQvcH4tZG724hE/NF/
     zq6jIH2q6OtUOposlWLn\
20   RTE4CteOE MP/Q4dSpSzLqjT4+cPrwFyfgvv7q+dHBHJOTiWJjeSffFDFcACPfqY3K
     IFHNxgD3bBwdO\
21   /GXgLDACBVoH7qVCNRBosuji24lmxwYu9qOOqX5sTF1
     mhmKpOm4uO2CEVhSnTeXlER4XermehqLhOLl\
22   odWlR75EmAYc13SvMS9C oFc66eXEOpSLOl7F9eZQ/RHh/
     Wobx74moN1uSwP32fTYhJZr3GXOTey+ kf\
23   npvhBIxXRa6nbB2jfLsNOPMb4ZEYTAXOICtevRDYptuM3ytakPd3el
     Nfrmpx9vxkFMye1/18diS/VWX\
```

```
24   D7RBc8wpbKOaQBMYV94dKhBa3F6SV9t bXF7nTadG7kOI+USOkUSfppCjWr+TTwdfvGRe/
     M7XPM1riBv\
25   /zUgSp7X zOKWdYT2mQjPR4xl21FcsSwytehCWoS+xGEd3y9AaW7RHAwPjeexMR30 458/
     h1cqQcEsQC\
26   Qlt13uboqjFon3s4iHcHIqtpnBUC/TaonMA39pBTXt VFPO+EV3YJBKFgGf1qZRW9aFAU+
     BHAnaRt2sv\
27   PmBId7n40778a14Jgac o4b64Y6Ij3Mx8as5
28   olimpus.local.            172800  IN  NS    delphos.olimpus.local.
29   olimpus.local.            172800  IN  NS    prometheus.olimpus.local.
30   olimpus.local.            172800  IN  MX    10 prometheus.olimpus.
     local.
31   aphrodite.olimpus.local.  172800  IN  A     192.168.1.22
32   delphos.olimpus.local.    172800  IN  AAAA  fe80::20c:29ff:fe78:4cb1
33   delphos.olimpus.local.    172800  IN  A     192.168.1.20
34   dns.olimpus.local.        172800  IN  CNAME delphos.olimpus.local.
35   mail.olimpus.local.       172800  IN  CNAME prometheus.olimpus.local.
36   neptune.olimpus.local.    172800  IN  AAAA  fe80::20c:29ff:fe78:abcd
37   neptune.olimpus.local.    172800  IN  A     192.168.1.240
38   prometheus.olimpus.local. 172800  IN  AAAA  fe80::20c:29ff:feeb:4443
39   prometheus.olimpus.local. 172800  IN  A     192.168.1.21
40   olimpus.local.            172800  IN  SOA   olimpus.local. root.
     olimpus.loca\
41   l. 2014090106 60 7200 604800 172800
42   ;; Query time: 3 msec
43   ;; SERVER: 192.168.1.20#53(192.168.1.20)
44   ;; WHEN: Mon Aug 4 07:33:30 2014
45   ;; XFR size: 16 records (messages 1, bytes 990)
```

The record was created successfully. The DNS server is ready to receive the updates from the DHCP. But before that, we have to make some changes to the DHCP configuration.

In the /etc/dhcpd/dhcpd.conf file, we'll have to add the following lines:

```
1   .
2   .
3   .
4   ddns-update-style interim;
5   ignore client-updates;
6   .
7   .
8   .
```

This way, we activate the DNS dynamic updates. Because some clients might themselves try to update their information in the DNS, we tell the server to ignore them, so that it is only the DHCP that updates that information. We should also specify the zones we are updating.

```
1   zone olimpus.local. {
2           primary 192.168.1.20;
```

```
3              }
4
5
6    zone 1.168.192.in-addr.arpa. {
7              primary 192.168.1.20;
8              }
```

And, of course, we also have to update the pool definition with the required parameters:

```
1    .
2    .
3    .
4    subnet 192.168.1.0 netmask 255.255.255.0 {
5              range 192.168.1.40 192.168.1.43;
6              option domain-name-servers 192.168.1.20;
7              option routers 192.168.1.1;
8              option domain-name "olimpus.local";
9    }
10   .
11   .
12   .
```

Now we restart the service and force the address renewal in the client (Figure 5-9).

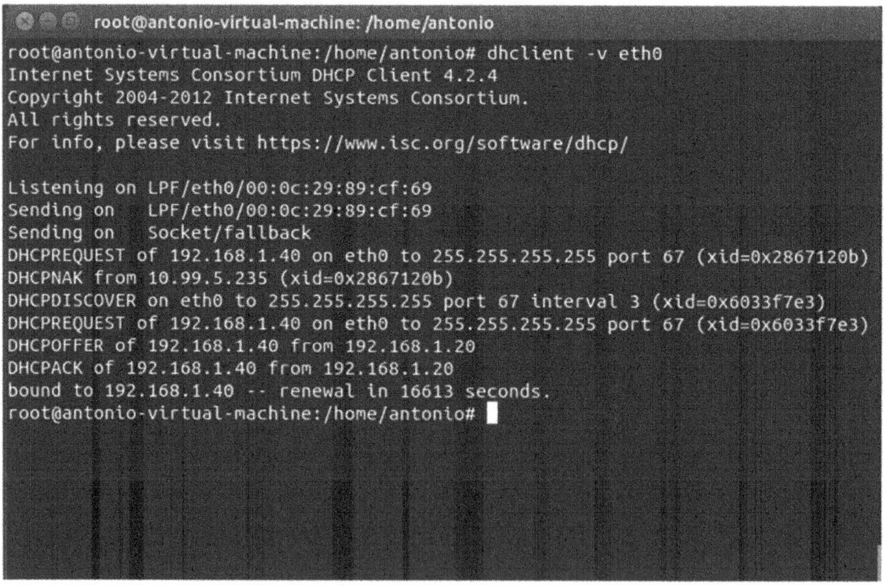

```
root@antonio-virtual-machine: /home/antonio
root@antonio-virtual-machine:/home/antonio# dhclient -v eth0
Internet Systems Consortium DHCP Client 4.2.4
Copyright 2004-2012 Internet Systems Consortium.
All rights reserved.
For info, please visit https://www.isc.org/software/dhcp/

Listening on LPF/eth0/00:0c:29:89:cf:69
Sending on   LPF/eth0/00:0c:29:89:cf:69
Sending on   Socket/fallback
DHCPREQUEST of 192.168.1.40 on eth0 to 255.255.255.255 port 67 (xid=0x2867120b)
DHCPNAK from 10.99.5.235 (xid=0x2867120b)
DHCPDISCOVER on eth0 to 255.255.255.255 port 67 interval 3 (xid=0x6033f7e3)
DHCPREQUEST of 192.168.1.40 on eth0 to 255.255.255.255 port 67 (xid=0x6033f7e3)
DHCPOFFER of 192.168.1.40 from 192.168.1.20
DHCPACK of 192.168.1.40 from 192.168.1.20
bound to 192.168.1.40 -- renewal in 16613 seconds.
root@antonio-virtual-machine:/home/antonio# █
```

Figure 5-9. Renewing the IP address

We see that the client received the IP address, gateway, and DNS server from the DHCP server (Figure 5-10). Let's see whether the DNS zone was updated accordingly.

```
root@antonio-virtual-machine: /home/antonio
root@antonio-virtual-machine:/home/antonio# ifconfig eth0
eth0      Link encap:Ethernet  HWaddr 00:0c:29:89:cf:69
          inet addr:192.168.1.40  Bcast:192.168.1.255  Mask:255.255.255.0
          inet6 addr: fe80::20c:29ff:fe89:cf69/64 Scope:Link
          UP BROADCAST RUNNING MULTICAST  MTU:1500  Metric:1
          RX packets:128397 errors:1 dropped:53 overruns:0 frame:0
          TX packets:2339 errors:0 dropped:0 overruns:0 carrier:0
          collisions:0 txqueuelen:1000
          RX bytes:12028290 (12.0 MB)  TX bytes:234452 (234.4 KB)
          Interrupt:19 Base address:0x2000

root@antonio-virtual-machine:/home/antonio# netstat -nr
Kernel IP routing table
Destination     Gateway         Genmask         Flags   MSS Window  irtt Iface
0.0.0.0         192.168.1.1     0.0.0.0         UG        0 0          0 eth0
192.168.1.0     0.0.0.0         255.255.255.0   U         0 0          0 eth0
root@antonio-virtual-machine:/home/antonio# cat /etc/resolv.conf
# Dynamic resolv.conf(5) file for glibc resolver(3) generated by resolvconf(8)
#      DO NOT EDIT THIS FILE BY HAND -- YOUR CHANGES WILL BE OVERWRITTEN
nameserver 192.168.1.20
search olimpus.local
root@antonio-virtual-machine:/home/antonio#
```

Figure 5-10. Renewing the IP address

```
1   [root@localhost named]# dig @192.168.1.20 axfr olimpus.local
2
3   ; <<>> DiG 9.7.3-P3-RedHat-9.7.3-8.P3.el6 <<>> @192.168.1.20 axfr
    olimpus.local
4   ; (1 server found)
5   ;; global options: +cmd
6   olimpus.local. 172800 IN SOA olimpus.local. root.olimpus.loca\
7   l. 2014090107 60 7200 604800 172800
8   olimpus.local. 172800 IN DNSKEY 256 3 5 AwEAAb386KgB7QrWAWBZ9+uS\
9   aHjHmpW+3TpcGkCfh9T4Znl6BJVb/kPp 6DmfeTRzjFUQSbAGRiI3yvzJ9+iEUhradME=
10  olimpus.local. 172800 IN DNSKEY 257 3 5 AwEAAeGilVrj9hxnmjRY9Yd9\
11  SqrBMwtiqKwfSda3wXhnd3koFZQzVI12 9xRVxEhaXpQvcH4tZG724hE/NF/
    zq6jIH2q6OtUOposlWLn\
12  RTE4CteOE MP/Q4dSpSzLqjT4+cPrwFyfgvv7q+dHBHJOTiWJjeSffFDFcACPfqY3K
    IFHNxgD3bBwdO\
13  /GXgLDACBVoH7qVCNRBosuji24lmxwYu9qOOqX5sTF1
    mhmKpOm4uO2CEVhSnTeXlER4XermehqLhOLl\
14  odWlR75EmAYc13SvMS9C oFc66eXEOpSLOl7F9eZQ/RHh/
    Wobx74moN1uSwP32fTYhJZr3GXOTey+ kf\
15  npvhBIxXRa6nbB2jfLsNOPMb4ZEYTAXOICtevRDYptuM3ytakPd3el
    Nfrmpx9vxkFMye1/18diS/VWX\
```

```
16    D7RBc8wpbKOaQBMYV94dKhBa3F6SV9t bXF7nTadG7kOI+USOkUSfppCjWr+TTwdfvGRe/
      M7XPM1riBv\
17    /zUgSp7X zOKWdYT2mQjPR4xl21FcsSwytehCWoS+xGEd3y9AaW7RHAwPjeexMR3O 458/
      h1cqQcEsQC\
18    Qltl3uboqjFon3s4iHcHIqtpnBUC/TaonMA39pBTXt VFPO+EV3YJBKFgGf1qZRW9aFAU+
      BHAnaRt2sv\
19    PmBId7n4O778a14Jgac o4b64Y6Ij3Mx8as5
20    olimpus.local. 172800 IN NS delphos.olimpus.local.
21    olimpus.local. 172800 IN NS prometheus.olimpus.local.
22    olimpus.local. 172800 IN MX 10 prometheus.olimpus.local.
23    antonio-virtual-machine.olimpus.local. 21600 IN TXT
      "0020ebba00f97540d54b8850290\
24    bf1ecb7"
25    antonio-virtual-machine.olimpus.local. 21600 IN A 192.168.1.40
26    aphrodite.olimpus.local. 172800 IN A 192.168.1.22
27    delphos.olimpus.local. 172800 IN AAAA fe80::20c:29ff:fe78:4cb1
28    delphos.olimpus.local. 172800 IN A 192.168.1.20
29    dns.olimpus.local. 172800 IN CNAME delphos.olimpus.local.
30    mail.olimpus.local. 172800 IN CNAME prometheus.olimpus.local.
31    neptune.olimpus.local. 172800 IN AAAA fe80::20c:29ff:fe78:abcd
32    neptune.olimpus.local. 172800 IN A 192.168.1.240
33    prometheus.olimpus.local. 172800 IN AAAA fe80::20c:29ff:feeb:4443
34    prometheus.olimpus.local. 172800 IN A 192.168.1.21
35    olimpus.local. 172800 IN SOA olimpus.local. root.olimpus.loca\
36    l. 2014090107 60 7200 604800 172800
37    ;; Query time: 2 msec
38    ;; SERVER: 192.168.1.20#53(192.168.1.20)
39    ;; WHEN: Mon Aug 4 14:00:23 2014
40    ;; XFR size: 18 records (messages 1, bytes 1077)
```

Exactly! A new record antonio-virtual-machine.olimpus.local was added. If we
check the reverse zone now, we'll see that it has been updated too.

```
1     [root@delphos named]# dig -x 192.168.1.40 @192.168.1.20
2
3     ; <<>> DiG 9.7.3-P3-RedHat-9.7.3-8.P3.el6 <<>> -x 192.168.1.40
      @192.168.1.20
4     ;; global options: +cmd
5     ;; Got answer:
6     ;; ->>HEADER<<- opcode: QUERY, status: NOERROR, id: 2528
7     ;; flags: qr aa rd ra; QUERY: 1, ANSWER: 1, AUTHORITY: 2, ADDITIONAL: 4
8
9     ;; QUESTION SECTION:
10    ;40.1.168.192.in-addr.arpa.    IN    PTR
11
12    ;; ANSWER SECTION:
13    40.1.168.192.in-addr.arpa. 21600 IN  PTR antonio-virtual-machine.
      olimpus.\
```

```
14    local.
15
16    ;; AUTHORITY SECTION:
17    1.168.192.in-addr.arpa. 172800  IN   NS    prometheus.olimpus.local.
18    1.168.192.in-addr.arpa. 172800  IN   NS    delphos.olimpus.local.
19
20    ;; ADDITIONAL SECTION:
21    delphos.olimpus.local.   172800  IN   A     192.168.1.20
22    delphos.olimpus.local.   172800  IN   AAAA  fe80::20c:29ff:fe78:4cb1
23    prometheus.olimpus.local. 172800 IN   A     192.168.1.21
24    prometheus.olimpus.local. 172800 IN   AAAA  fe80::20c:29ff:feeb:4443
25
26    ;; Query time: 0 msec
27    ;; SERVER: 192.168.1.20#53(192.168.1.20)
28    ;; WHEN: Mon Aug 4 14:40:14 2014
29    ;; MSG SIZE rcvd: 229
```

5.3.1. Use of Keys

Previously, we have used the directive allow-update{localhost;}; in order to allow updates. Nevertheless, it is far more common and more appropriate to use keys for this.

That way, we can be sure that the only DHCP server to update the DNS zones is the official server and not a rogue DHCP server that might exist in the network, because the right DHCP server will be the only one with the right key.

To generate the key, we can use the dnssec-keygen command that we saw already when talking about DNSSEC.

```
1    [root@delphos ~]# dnssec-keygen -a HMAC-MD5 -b 128 -n HOST dhcp-dns
2    Kdhcp-dns.+157+29271
```

In this example, we use the algorithm (-a) HMAC-MD5 to generate a key with a length (-b) of 128 bytes. This key will be associated to a machine (-n HOST), to the DHCP server, to be exact.

Once executed, two files are generated in the working directory.

```
1    Kdhcp-dns.+157+29271.key Kdhcp-dns.+157+29271.private.
```

If we see the contents of the .private file, we see the value of the key.

```
1    [root@localhost ~]# cat Kdhcp-dns.+157+48018.private
2    Private-key-format: v1.3
3    Algorithm: 157 (HMAC_MD5)
4    Key: N4+TL8rf+DqJMX8WlZGKQg==
5    Bits: AAA=
6    Created: 20140805052812
7    Publish: 20140805052812
8    Activate: 20140805052812
```

Now we add a new entry in the /etc/named.conf file to define the key we just created.

```
 1   .
 2   .
 3   .
 4   key dhcp-dns
 5   {
 6   algorithm HMAC-MD5;
 7   secret N4+TL8rf+DqJMX8WlZGKQg==;
 8   };
 9   .
10   .
11   .
```

Obviously, we have to change the definition of the zones and substitute the allow-update{ localhost; }; directive.

```
 1   .
 2   .
 3   .
 4   zone "olimpus.local" IN {
 5           type master;
 6           file "olimpus.local.zone";
 7           notify yes;
 8           allow-update { key dhcp-dns; };
 9   };
10
11   zone "1.168.192.in-addr.arpa" IN {
12           type master;
13           file "192.168.1.zone";
14           notify yes;
15           allow-update { key dhcp-dns; };
16   };
17
18   zone "0.0.0.0.0.0.0.0.0.0.0.0.0.8.e.f.ip6.arpa" IN {
19           type master;
20           file "fe80.0.0.0.zone";
21           notify yes;
22           allow-update { key dhcp-dns; };
23   };
24   .
25   .
26   .
```

We restart the service to apply the changes, and we begin to configure the DHCP server. As we did on the DNS server, we also have to add a key entry in the /etc/dhcp/dhcpd.conf file.

```
1   .
2   .
3   .
4   key dhcp-dns
5   {
6           algorithm HMAC-MD5;
7           secret N4+TL8rf+DqJMX8WlZGKQg==;
8   }
9   .
10  .
11  .
```

Next, we change the corresponding zone definitions in the same dhcpd.conf file.

```
1   .
2   .
3   .
4   zone olimpus.local. {
5           primary 192.168.1.20;
6           key dhcp-dns;
7           }
8
9
10  zone 1.168.192.in-addr.arpa. {
11          primary 192.168.1.20;
12          key dhcp-dns;
13          }
14  .
15  .
16  .
```

We restart the DHCP server and force the renewal of the IP address in the client (Figure 5-11).

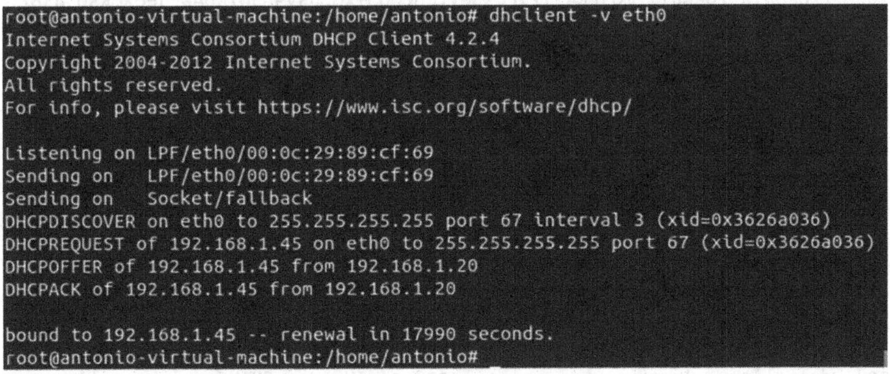

```
root@antonio-virtual-machine:/home/antonio# dhclient -v eth0
Internet Systems Consortium DHCP Client 4.2.4
Copyright 2004-2012 Internet Systems Consortium.
All rights reserved.
For info, please visit https://www.isc.org/software/dhcp/

Listening on LPF/eth0/00:0c:29:89:cf:69
Sending on   LPF/eth0/00:0c:29:89:cf:69
Sending on   Socket/fallback
DHCPDISCOVER on eth0 to 255.255.255.255 port 67 interval 3 (xid=0x3626a036)
DHCPREQUEST of 192.168.1.45 on eth0 to 255.255.255.255 port 67 (xid=0x3626a036)
DHCPOFFER of 192.168.1.45 from 192.168.1.20
DHCPACK of 192.168.1.45 from 192.168.1.20

bound to 192.168.1.45 -- renewal in 17990 seconds.
root@antonio-virtual-machine:/home/antonio#
```

Figure 5-11. Renewing the IP address

We can see that the client has been assigned a new IP. Let's see whether the DNS record has been updated.

```
1    [root@localhost ~]# dig @localhost olimpus.local axfr
2
3    ; <<>> DiG 9.7.3-P3-RedHat-9.7.3-8.P3.el6 <<>> @localhost olimpus.local
     axfr
4    ; (2 servers found)
5    ;; global options: +cmd
6    olimpus.local.           172800  IN     SOA    olimpus.local. root.
                                                     olimpus.loca\
7    l. 2014090111 60 7200 604800 172800
8    olimpus.local.           172800  IN     NS     delphos.olimpus.local.
9    olimpus.local.           172800  IN     NS     prometheus.olimpus.local.
10   olimpus.local.           172800  IN     MX     10 prometheus.olimpus.
                                                     local.
11   olimpus.local.           172800  IN     DNSKEY 256 3 5
     AwEAAb386KgB7QrWAWBZ9+uS\
12   aHjHmpW+3TpcGkCfh9T4Znl6BJVb/kPp 6DmfeTRzjFUQSbAGRiI3yvzJ9+iEUhradME=
13   olimpus.local.           172800  IN     DNSKEY 257 3 5
     AwEAAeGilVrj9hxnmjRY9Yd9\
14   SqrBMwtiqKwfSda3wXhnd3koFZQzVI12 9xRVxEhaXpQvcH4tZG724hE/NF/
     zq6jIH2q6OtUOposlWLn\
15   RTE4CteOE MP/Q4dSpSzLqjT4+cPrwFyfgvv7q+dHBHJOTiWJjeSffFDFcACPfqY3K
     IFHNxgD3bBwdO\
16   /GXglDACBVoH7qVCNRBosuji24lmxwYu9qOOqX5sTF1
     mhmKpOm4uO2CEVhSnTeXlER4XermehqLhOLl\
17   odWlR75EmAYc13SvMS9C oFc66eXEOpSLOl7F9eZQ/RHh/
     Wobx74moN1uSwP32fTYhJZr3GXOTey+ kf\
18   npvhBIxXRa6nbB2jfLsNOPMb4ZEYTAXOICtevRDYptuM3ytakPd3el
     Nfrmpx9vxkFMye1/18diS/VWX\
19   D7RBc8wpbKOaQBMYV94dKhBa3F6SV9t bXF7nTadG7kOI+USOkUSfppCjWr+TTwdfvGRe/
     M7XPM1riBv\
20   /zUgSp7X zOKWdYT2mQjPR4xl21FcsSwytehCWoS+xGEd3y9AaW7RHAwPjeexMR3O 458/
     h1cqQcEsQC\
21   Qltl3uboqjFon3s4iHcHIqtpnBUC/TaonMA39pBTXt VFPO+EV3YJBKFgGf1qZRW9aFAU+
     BHAnaRt2sv\
22   PmBId7n40778a14Jgac o4b64Y6Ij3Mx8as5
23   antonio-virtual-machine.olimpus.local. 21600 IN TXT
     "0020ebba00f97540d54b8850290\
24   bf1ecb7"
25   antonio-virtual-machine.olimpus.local. 21600 IN A      192.168.1.45
26   aphrodite.olimpus.local.     172800  IN     A      192.168.1.22
27   delphos.olimpus.local.       172800  IN     A      192.168.1.20
28   delphos.olimpus.local.       172800  IN     AAAA
     fe80::20c:29ff:fe78:4cb1
29   dns.olimpus.local.           172800  IN     CNAME delphos.olimpus.
     local.
```

```
30  G99D02467402cor.olimpus.local. 21600 IN TXT
    "31cd0178098b2d89febcf6fb6c86a02\
31  352"
32  G99D02467402cor.olimpus.local. 21600 IN A      192.168.1.40
33  mail.olimpus.local.      172800  IN     CNAME prometheus.olimpus.local.
34  neptune.olimpus.local.   172800  IN     A     192.168.1.240
35  neptune.olimpus.local.   172800  IN     AAAA  fe80::20c:29ff:fe78:abcd
36  prometheus.olimpus.local. 172800 IN     A     192.168.1.21
37  prometheus.olimpus.local. 172800 IN     AAAA  fe80::20c:29ff:feeb:4443
38  olimpus.local.           172800  IN     SOA   olimpus.local. root.
    olimpus.loca\
39  l. 2014090111 60 7200 604800 172800
40  ;; Query time: 1 msec
41  ;; SERVER: ::1#53(::1)
42  ;; WHEN: Tue Aug 5 04:49:47 2014
43  ;; XFR size: 20 records (messages 1, bytes 1156)
```

The IP address for the machine antonio-virtual-machine.olimpus.local has indeed been updated.

CHAPTER 6

Remote Access

A systems administrator can sit in front of the console of a server and perform any administrative task, but this is not always possible or desirable, because there could be servers in other countries, or even on other continents, that should be administered too. So, it is almost mandatory to be able to administer servers remotely.

6.1. Telnet

Today, the most usual way to connect to a remote Linux server is by using the ssh protocol. Years ago, admins used the Telnet protocol, but the latter has a great disadvantage: it transmits information in clear text, so an attacker can access sensitive information, such as usernames or passwords. We'll observe this in practice.

As the Telnet server isn't installed by default, the first thing we have to do is actually install it.

```
1   [root@delphos ~]# yum install telnet-server
```

Once installed, we have to start the associated services. As we saw earlier, services such as named and dhcpd have corresponding script files in /etc/init.d that are used to start, stop, and check the status of the service. But sometimes, a group of services is bundled in a superservice called xinetd.

In CentOS 6, Telnet is one of the services that uses this approach by default.

After installing the Telnet server, we have several files inside the /etc/xinetd.d folder.

```
1   [root@CentOS ~]# ls /etc/xinetd.d/
2   chargendgram      daytimestream     echodgram      telnet
3   chargenstream     discarddgram      echostream     timedgram
4   daytimedgram      discardstream     tcpmuxserver   timestream
```

© Antonio Vazquez 2016
A. Vazquez, *Learn CentOS Linux Network Services*, DOI 10.1007/978-1-4842-2379-6_6

If we open the telnet file, we'll see this:

```
1   # default: on
2   # description: The telnet server serves telnet sessions; it uses \
3   # unencrypted username/password pairs for authentication.
4   service telnet
5   {
6           flags = REUSE
7           socket_type = stream
8           wait = no
9           user = root
10          server = /usr/sbin/in.telnetd
11          log_on_failure += USERID
12          disable = yes
13  }
```

These parameters will be passed to the xinetd superservice. To actually start the service, we'll have to change the line disable = yes to disable = no, and restart the xinetd service.

```
1   [root@CentOS ~]# service xinetd restart
2   Stopping xinetd: [ OK ]
3   Starting xinetd: [ OK ]
```

On the other hand, in CentOS 7, the Telnet service doesn't depend on xinetd. So, we'll start it like this:

```
1   [root@Centos7 ~]# systemctl start telnet.socket
```

Of course, we have to allow access to port 23 through the firewall.
In CentOS 6:

```
1   [root@delphos ~]# iptables -I INPUT 2 -p tcp --dport 23 -j ACCEPT
```

In CentOS 7:

```
1   [root@Centos7 ~]# firewall-cmd --add-service=telnet
2   success
```

As it happens, Telnet is an inherently insecure protocol. By default, the root user is not allowed to log in to the system through a Telnet connection. So, in order to connect to the server, we'll have to log in as a normal user and then switch to the root user (Figure 6-1).

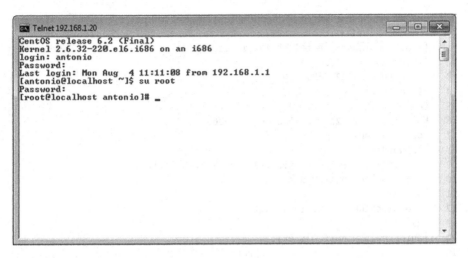

```
Telnet 192.168.1.20
CentOS release 6.2 (Final)
Kernel 2.6.32-220.el6.i686 on an i686
login: antonio
Password:
Last login: Mon Aug  4 11:11:08 from 192.168.1.1
[antonio@localhost ~]$ su root
Password:
[root@localhost antonio]#
```

Figure 6-1. *Telneting to a server*

If we connect from another CentOS computer, perhaps we'll have to install the telnet client too.

```
1  [root@localhost ~]# yum install telnet
```

If we wanted to connect directly as the root user, we could do it by editing the PAM configuration of the server. The PAM configuration determines how to authenticate and authorize users into the system. It consists of a series of libraries in /lib/security and a series of configuration files in /etc/pam.d/. These files establish how to handle user access through ssh, telnet, local console, etc. In the case of telnet, we'll have to edit the /etc/pam.d/remote file and comment out the following line:

```
1  auth required pam_securetty.so
```

so that it looks like this:

```
1  #auth required pam_securetty.so
```

After this change, the root user will be able to log in directly to the server through a telnet connection. To demonstrate that the Telnet protocol transmits all the information in clear text, we will capture the network traffic with tcpdump. In the Telnet server, we type the following command.

```
1  [root@localhost ~]# tcpdump -X -vvv -w salida.dump -p tcp "port 23"
```

Next, we establish a `telnet` connection from another computer.

```
1   [root@localhost ~]# telnet 192.168.1.20
2   Trying 192.168.1.20...
3   Connected to 192.168.1.20.
4   Escape character is '^]'.
5   CentOS release 6.2 (Final)
6   Kernel 2.6.32-220.el6.i686 on an i686
7   login: antonio
8   Password:
9   Last login: Tue Aug 5 05:27:37 from 192.168.1.21
10  [antonio@localhost ~]$ su root
11  Password:
12  [root@localhost antonio]# exit
13  exit
14  [antonio@localhost ~]$ exit
15                              logout
16  Connection closed by foreign host.
```

Now, if we open the file with Wireshark, we can see the packets exchanged between the server and the client. To see it more clearly, we can place the cursor over one of the packets, click the right button, and choose "Follow TCP stream" (Figure 6-2).

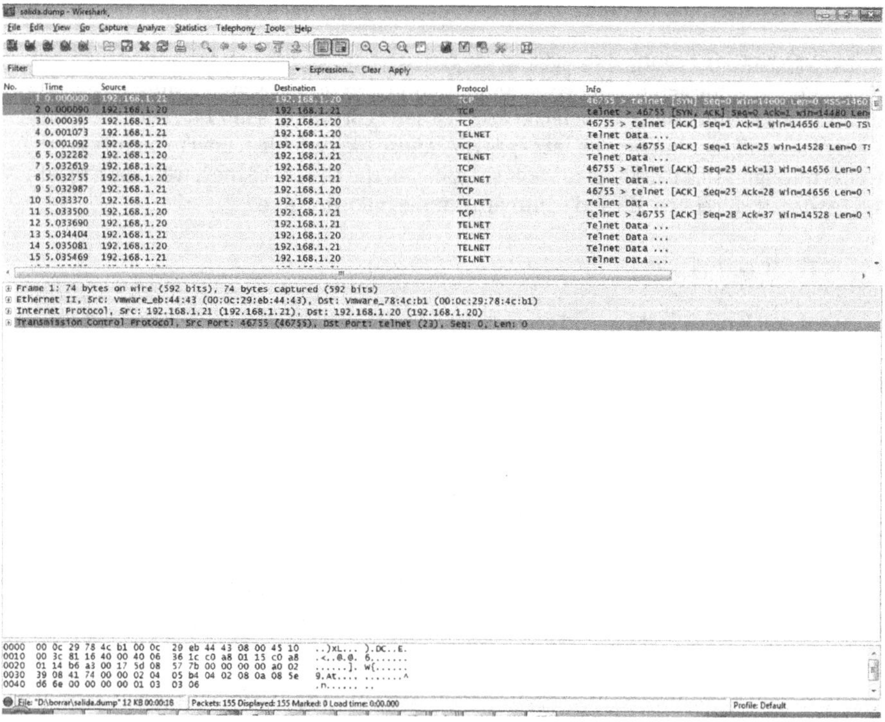

***Figure 6-2.** Sniffing the Telnet traffic*

We can see clearly the passwords of the users antonio and root (Figure 6-3).

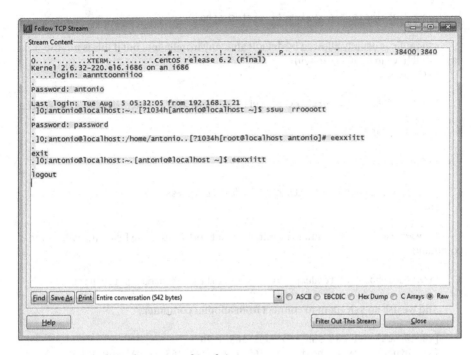

Figure 6-3. *Watching the password in plain text*

After this little experiment, we can uninstall the telnet server, as there is a much better solution.

```
1   [root@delphos ~]# yum remove telnet-server
```

Next, we remove the rules in the firewall, allowing incoming traffic to port 23 (see Chapter 10 for more details).

6.2. ssh

The sshd service is usually installed by default. If for some reason it hasn't been installed, we can install it the usual way.

```
1   [root@delphos ~]# yum install openssh-server
```

We must ensure that the service is running. if it is not, we launch it.

```
1   [root@delphos ~]# service sshd status
2   openssh-daemon (pid 1342) is running...
```

In CentOS 7:

```
1  [root@localhost ~]# systemctl status sshd
```

ssh traffic is usually allowed by default after any installation, but if this is not the case, we'll have to allow it explicitly.

In CentOS 6:

```
1  [root@delphos ~]# iptables -I INPUT 2 -m state --state NEW -m tcp -p tcp
   --dport\
2    53 -j ACCEPT
```

In CentOS 7:

```
1  [root@Centos7 ~]# firewall-cmd --add-service=ssh
2  success
```

Now we use tcpdump again, to monitor the network traffic. The following will be the command:

```
1  [root@delphos ~]# tcpdump -vvv -X -w salidassh.dump -p tcp port 22
```

And we use an ssh client to connect from another computer.

```
1  [root@localhost ~]# ssh root@192.168.1.20
2  The authenticity of host '192.168.1.20 (192.168.1.20)' can't be
   established.
3  RSA key fingerprint is 7f:c2:7e:6f:23:7d:e9:0c:cc:58:9e:5d:14:3c:57:d9.
4  Are you sure you want to continue connecting (yes/no)? yes
5  Warning: Permanently added '192.168.1.20' (RSA) to the list of known
   hosts.
6  root@192.168.1.20's password:
7  Last login: Tue Aug 5 12:45:11 2014 from 192.168.1.1
8  [root@localhost ~]#
```

As we did before, we open the salidassh.dump file with wireshark, and we use the option "Follow TCP stream," but now what we see is shown in Figure 6-4.

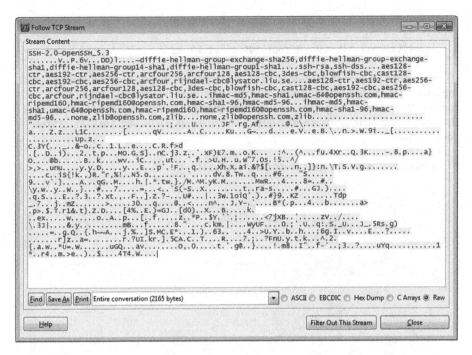

Figure 6-4. *Where is the password?*

We can no longer see the username and password in plain text.

6.2.1. X11 Forwarding

This is a really useful characteristic of the sshd service. Let's imagine we have a Linux server without a graphic environment. If we connect from any Linux workstation with a working graphic environment, we can actually execute graphical applications in the server, and the result will be shown in the workstation. We'll see a couple of examples in a moment.

To start with, the server we are connecting to must have the sshd service installed and running. In addition, in the configuration file /etc/ssh/sshd_config, there should be a line such as the following:

```
1    X11Forwarding yes
```

We have to install an additional package (xorg-x11-xauth) to allow X11 forwarding. Also, in order for the windows to show the correct fonts, we'll have to install at least the following font packages: xorg-x11-fonts-misc.noarch, dejavu-fonts-common.noarch, dejavu-sans-fonts.noarch.

```
1    [root@Centos7 ~]$ yum install xorg-x11-xauth xorg-x11-fonts-misc.noarch, dejavu\
2    -fonts-common.noarch, dejavu-sans-fonts.noarch
```

Now we connect from the client computer like this:

```
1    [root@Centos7 ~]$ ssh -X root@192.168.1.20
```

From now on, we can execute any graphical application installed on the server, and the associated window will appear in the client computer. For example, in CentOS 6, we can launch system-config-firewall, a graphical front end to manage the Linux firewall (Figure 6-5). If this program is not installed, we can install it with yum install system-config-firewall.

```
1    [root@centosv6 ~]# system-config-firewall
```

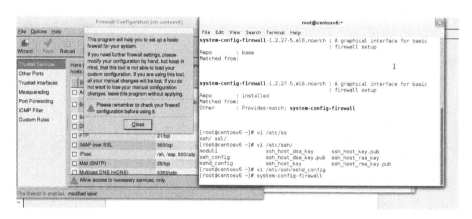

Figure 6-5. *Launching a graphic app*

In CentOS 7, the equivalent graphical application would be firewall-config, but the procedure is exactly the same.

We've done this from a Linux box, but we can also do it from a Windows workstation. However, as Windows computers have no ssh client or X server installed by default, we have to install them first. As an X server, we can use Xming, which is free and can be downloaded from the SourceForge site.[1]

---

[1]SourceForge, http://sourceforge.net/projects/xming/, 2006.

The installation process is the typical in Windows (next, next,...). Once installed, we launch it by clicking the corresponding icon (Figure 6-6).

Figure 6-6. *Launching Xming*

The X server will continue to execute in the background, awaiting connections.

As far as the ssh client is concerned, there are many choices available. One of the best is PuTTY, also freely available from the Internet.[2] Once having launched this, by clicking putty.exe, we'll have to activate the option "Enable X11 Forwarding" under Connection ➤ SSH ➤ X11 (Figure 6-7). After that, we can connect to the CentOS server and execute any graphical utility (Figure 6-8).

---

[2]PuTTY Download Page, http://www.chiark.greenend.org.uk/~sgtatham/putty/download.html, 2016.

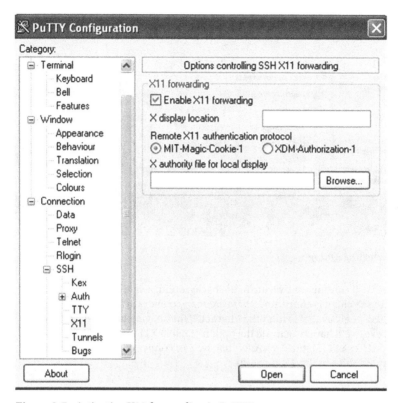

Figure 6-7. *Activating X11 forwarding in PuTTY*

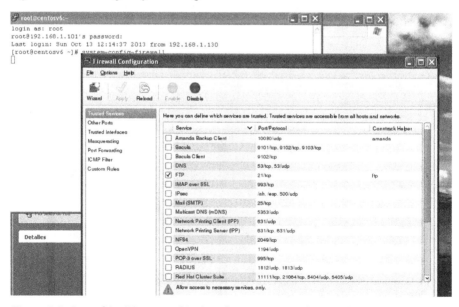

Figure 6-8. *Launching Linux graphical applications in Windows with Xming*

Of course, until now, we have connected to the server by using a, IPv4 address, but we can also connect with an IPv6 address, although, given the nature of IPv6 addresses, it would be much easier to connect by using the computer name.

6.2.2. File Transfer

When the first computer networks appeared, one of the first things these networks were used for was to transfer files. For this purpose, the FTP protocol was developed, and it is still widely used today. However, the FTP protocol has the same security problems as the Telnet protocol, as both transmit information in plain text. Obviously, this poses a big problem, because a hacker could easily access a username and password.

In order to solve this, SFTP was developed. It executes over an SSH connection and works in a way similar to the traditional FTP, but all connections are encrypted. To use it, you must have installed the openssh-clients package. Let's see some examples.

Obviously, the first thing to do is to check that the sshd service is running.

```
1  [root@centosv6 ~]# service sshd status
2  openssh-daemon (pid 1432) is running...
```

Now you can connect from the client like this.

```
1  [root@localhost ~]# sftp 192.168.1.20
2  Connecting to 192.168.1.20...
3  root@192.168.1.20's password:
4  sftp>
```

You can employ exactly the same commands used in the old FTP protocol.

```
1   sftp> ls
2   Kdhcp-dns.+157+48018.key           Kdhcp-dns.+157+48018.private
3   Kolimpus.local.+005+43902.key      Kolimpus.local.+005+43902.
    private
4   anaconda-ks.cfg                    borrar
5   docs                               install.log
6   install.log.syslog                 new_file
7   salida.dump                        salidassh.dump
8   salidav6.dump                      salidav6_2.dump
9   soft                               sshd_config
10  sftp> get salida.dump
11  Fetching /root/salida.dump to salida.dump
12  /root/salida.dump                       100%   13KB   13.0KB/s
    00:00
13  sftp> put example.txt
14  Uploading example.txt to /root/example.txt
15  example.txt                             100%   25     0.0KB/s
    00:00
16  sftp>
```

Another way to transfer files is by using the scp command, which uses an ssh connection too. The syntax is quite simple. If you want to copy the datos.txt file from one computer to another, here is what you'd have to type:

```
1  [cliente@localhost ~]$ scp datos.txt root@192.168.1.101:/root
2  root@192.168.1.101's password:
3  datos.txt 100% 6 0.0KB/s 00:00
```

In this case, you copy a file from the client to the server, but copying from the server to the client is also possible.

```
1  [cliente@localhost ~]$ scp root@192.168.1.101:/root/install.log ./
2  root@192.168.1.101's password:
3  install.log 100% 10KB 10.0KB/s 00:00
```

6.2.3. Authenticating with Keys

Until now, whenever you wanted to establish an ssh connection, you had to indicate the user you wanted to connect as and type the password of that user. This is the means the server employs to authenticate you as a legitimate user. However, it is also possible to use keys for authentication, so that you don't have to type your password every time you try to connect to a server.

To enable this type of authentication, the first thing you have to do is to create a pair of keys, public and private. You do this in your client computer.

```
1   [root@localhost ~]# ssh-keygen -t dsa
2   Generating public/private dsa key pair.
3   Enter file in which to save the key (/root/.ssh/id_dsa):
4   Enter passphrase (empty for no passphrase):
5   Enter same passphrase again:
6   Your identification has been saved in /root/.ssh/id_dsa.
7   Your public key has been saved in /root/.ssh/id_dsa.pub.
8   The key fingerprint is:
9   cf:fc:47:9e:2c:f9:ac:e6:c5:3e:01:66:5c:1f:9b:09 root@localhost.
    localdomain
10  The key's randomart image is:
11  +--[ DSA 1024]----+
12  |                 |
13  |          E..    |
14  |         . ...=  |
15  |          = +.   |
16  |         S o .   |
17  |          + .o   |
18  |          + =oo  |
19  |           .++*  |
20  |          o+=+.  |
21  +-----------------+
22  [root@localhost ~]#
```

A private and a public DSA key have been generated and stored (by default) in /root/.ssh/.

```
1   [root@localhost ~]# ls /root/.ssh/
2   id_dsa id_dsa.pub known_hosts
```

You can associate the key with a passphrase, if you want to.

Execute the ssh-agent now. The agent will handle the keys, using them to authenticate you without prompting for a password. Once the ssh-agent is running, you add the key you created a moment ago. If you chose to associate the key with a passphrase, you'll have to enter this passphrase too.

```
1   [root@localhost ~]# ssh-agent /bin/bash
2   [root@localhost ~]# ssh-add /root/.ssh/id_dsa
3   Identity added: /root/.ssh/id_dsa (/root/.ssh/id_dsa)
```

Copy the key to the server.

```
1   [root@localhost ~]# ssh-copy-id root@192.168.1.20
2   root@192.168.1.20's password:
3   Now try logging into the machine, with "ssh 'root@192.168.1.20'", and
    check in:
4
5     .ssh/authorized_keys
6
7   to make sure we haven't added extra keys that you weren't expecting.
```

You'll be asked for the password, but from now on, you can connect directly to the server without typing the password again.

```
1   [root@localhost ~]# ssh root@192.168.1.20
2   Last login: Tue Aug 5 18:56:20 2014 from 192.168.1.1
3   [root@localhost ~]
```

You can use sftp and scp too.

```
1   [root@localhost ~]# scp root@192.168.1.20:/root/anaconda-ks.cfg /root/
    borrar/
2   anaconda-ks.cfg 100% 1117 1.1KB/s 00:00
3   [root@localhost ~]#
```

6.3. VNC

Another remote access program widely used in Linux, as well as in Windows, is VNC. Through VNC, the server can be accessed in graphical mode. Obviously, the server must be executing in a graphical environment.

In the CentOS server we want to connect to through VNC, we'll have to install a series of software packages.

```
1   [root@localhost ~]# yum install vinagre tigervnc tigervnc-server
```

In CentOS 6:
Once the software is installed, we'll have to edit the /etc/sysconfig/vncservers file. At the bottom of the file, we'll see these two lines:

```
1   # VNCSERVERS="2:myusername"
2   # VNCSERVERARGS[2]="-geometry 800x600 -nolisten tcp -localhost"
```

We uncomment and edit the two lines; we substitute myusername for the user we want to use for this connection; and we delete the -nolisten and -localhost options, as we want to be able to connect with other computers.

```
1   VNCSERVERS="2:root"
2   VNCSERVERARGS[2]="-geometry 800x600"
```

After that, we assign a password with vncpasswd.

```
1   [root@localhost ~]# vncpasswd
2   Password:
3   Verify:
4   [root@localhost ~]#
```

We can now restart the service.

```
1   [root@localhost ~]# service vncserver restart
2   Shutting down VNC server:                              [ OK ]
3   Starting VNC server: 2:root
4   New 'localhost.localdomain:2 (root)' desktop is localhost.localdomain:2
5
6   Creating default startup script /root/.vnc/xstartup
7   Starting applications specified in /root/.vnc/xstartup
8   Log file is /root/.vnc/localhost.localdomain:2.log
```

In CentOS 7:
CentOS 7 no longer uses the /etc/sysconfig/vncservers file. Instead, we'll have to copy the /lib/sys- temd/system/vncserver@.service file to /etc/systemd/system/vncserver@:[display].service, and edit the file according to our needs.

```
1   [root@CentOS7 named]# cp /lib/systemd/system/vncserver@.service /etc/
    systemd/sys\
2   tem/vncserver@:2.service
```

We substitute the [USER] tag appropriately. In this instance, we employ the username "antonio."

```
1   .
2   .
3   .
4   ExecStart=/sbin/runuser -l antonio -c "/usr/bin/vncserver %i"
5   PIDFile=/home/antonio/.vnc/%H%i.pid
6   .
7   .
8   .
```

We restart the daemon service.

```
1   [root@CentOS7 ~]# systemctl daemon-reload
```

Next, we enable the VNC service we just configured.

```
1   [root@CentOS7 ~]# systemctl enable vncserver@:2.service
2   ln -s '/etc/systemd/system/vncserver@:2.service' '/etc/systemd/system/
    multi-user\
3   .target.wants/vncserver@:2.service'
```

Logged in locally as "antonio," we assign a password with the vncpasswd command.

```
1   [antonio@CentOS7 ~]$ vncpasswd
2   Password:
3   Verify:
```

Now we can start the VNC service.

```
1   [root@CentOS7 ~]# systemctl start vncserver@:2
```

The VNC server will listen for incoming connections in the port 5902 by default. We can check it with the netstat command.

```
1   [root@localhost ~]# netstat -patne | grep -i vnc
2   tcp 0 0 0.0.0.0:5902 0.0.0.0:* LIST\
3   EN 0 37441 8984/Xvnc
4   tcp 0 0 0.0.0.0:6002 0.0.0.0:* LIST\
5   EN 0 37435 8984/Xvnc
6   tcp 0 0 :::6002 :::* LIST\
7   EN 0 37434 8984/Xvnc
```

We see that it opened two ports, 5902 and 6002, but the one it uses to listen to the client connections is the first one. So, we'll have to open this port in the firewall.

In CentOS 6:

```
1   [root@localhost ~]# iptables -I INPUT 5 -m state --state NEW -m tcp -p
    tcp --dpo\
2   rt 5902 -j ACCEPT
```

165

In CentOS 7:

```
1   [root@CentOS7 ~]# firewall-cmd --add-service=vnc-server
2   success
```

Now, from the client computer, we execute the vncviewer command (Figure 6-9). This command is part of the tigervnc package, so we have to install it in the client.

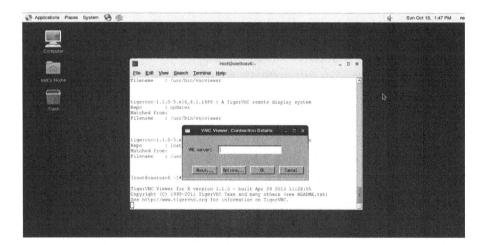

Figure 6-9. *Connecting to a remote server with VNC*

In the pop-up window, we have to type the IP address of the server, as well as the display. If we follow the instructions, the display will be the number 2, as established in the following line in /etc/sysconfig/vncserver (in CentOS 6):

```
1   VNCSERVERS="2:root"
```

or in the name of the /etc/systemd/system/vncserver@:2.service file.

So, the full address will be something like 192.168.1.21:2. Now a new window appears, asking for the password we just created a moment ago (Figure 6-10).

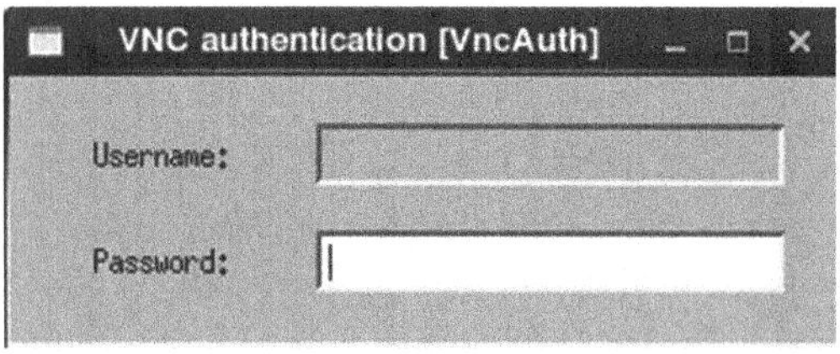

Figure 6-10. *Authenticating to the VNC server*

And, finally, we have access to the graphical desktop (Figure 6-11).

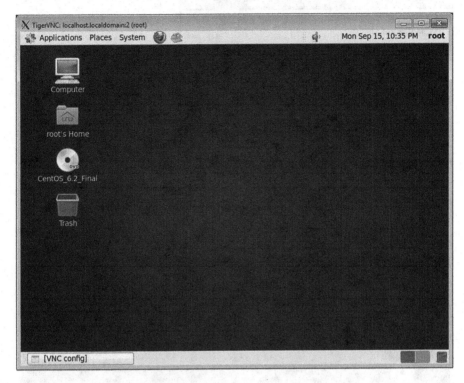

Figure 6-11. *Connected through VNC*

Through VNC, it is also possible to connect from a Windows box to a Linux server. To do this, you'll need a VNC client for Windows, such as RealVNC Viewer. This software can be downloaded from the RealVNC site.[3]

When you execute it, you'll see a window fairly similar to the one you saw when using tigervnc viewer (Figure 6-12).

---

[3]RealVNC, https://www.realvnc.com/, 2002–20016.

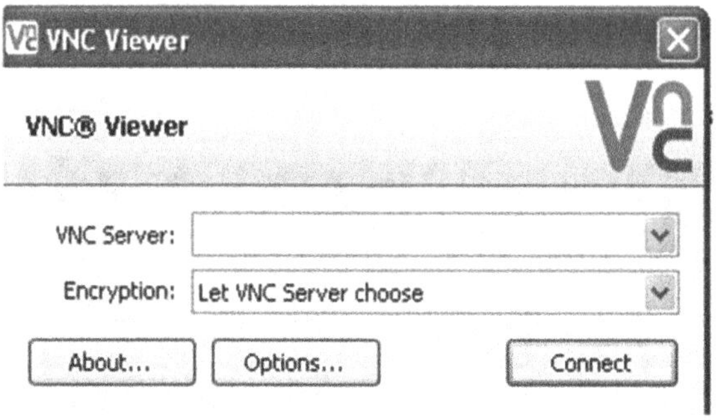

Figure 6-12. *Connecting with RealVNC Viewer*

Once you enter the IP address of the server with the display associated and the password, you'll gain access to the CentOS desktop from your Windows PC (Figure 6-13).

Figure 6-13. *Accessing the CentOS desktop from a Windows client with RealVNC Viewer*

CHAPTER 7

Web Server

If there is a service that comes to everyone's mind when talking about the Internet, it is web service. Everybody can search anything on Google, because a web server—actually lots of them—provides users with the information that they see in their browsers.

So, what happens every time someone browses the Web? When a user executes his/her favorite browser and types "www.google.com," for example, the browser queries the Domain Name System (DNS) about the Internet Protocol (IP) address of the computer: "www.google.com." Once the browser gets the answer from the DNS, it establishes a Transmission Control Protocol (TCP) connection using port 80 and requests the default web page. The server will send the page to the browser in HTML format, and this is what the user will see.

7.1. Installing the Apache Web Server

We can install the Apache server, that is, the web server, with the yum command. When using yum, it is considered good practice to clean the cache periodically and update the packages already installed.

```
1   [root@delphos ~]# yum clean all
2   [root@delphos ~]# yum update -y
```

Now we perform the actual installation.

```
1   [root@delphos ~]# yum install httpd
```

After the installation, we activate the service and configure it to start automatically. In CentOS 6:

```
1   [root@delphos ~]# service httpd start
2   Starting httpd:                                    [  OK  ]
3   [root@delphos ~]# chkconfig httpd on
4   [root@delphos ~]# chkconfig --list httpd
5   httpd 0:off 1:off 2:on 3:on 4:on 5:on 6:off
```

© Antonio Vazquez 2016
A. Vazquez, *Learn CentOS Linux Network Services*, DOI 10.1007/978-1-4842-2379-6_7

In CentOS 7:

```
1  [root@delphos ~]# systemctl start httpd
2  [root@delphos ~]# systemctl enable httpd
3  ln -s '/usr/lib/systemd/system/httpd.service' '/etc/systemd/system/
   multi-user.ta\
4  rget.wants/httpd.service'
```

As the firewall probably will be filtering out the traffic, we'll have to add a rule to permit http traffic (port 80).

In CentOS 6:

```
1  [root@delphos ~]# iptables -I INPUT 1 -m state --state NEW -m tcp -p tcp
   --dport\
2  80 -j ACCEPT
```

In CentOS 7:

```
1  [root@delphos ~]# firewall-cmd --add-service=http
2  success
```

If we prefer, we can also use this command:

```
1  [root@delphos ~]# firewall-cmd --add-port=80/tcp
2  success
```

The changes in the firewall will take effect immediately, but they won't be permanent. Once the configuration of the web server is complete, we should make these changes permanent. Chapter 10 offers more information on how to correctly set up the firewall.

Now everything should be working, so let's check it. To do this, we simply open a browser and type in the IP address or the name of the web server. As a result, we should see a test page (Figure 7-1). This test page differs, depending on the Apache version, but it is easily recognizable.

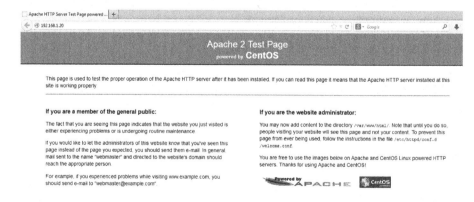

Figure 7-1. *Apache test page*

7.2. Name Resolution

In the previous example, we accessed the web server through the IP address, but this is unusual, and most people use names when accessing the Web. So, let's suppose that the web server is running in the delphos.olimpus.local computer, and we want to access to it with the URL www.olimpus.local. We could add an A or AAAA record with the name www, but it is more convenient to create an alias, that is, a CNAME record that points to the A record of the machine itself.

So, we add this new record to the zone olimpus.local:

```
1   www CNAME delphos
```

We restart the server, and we make sure the new record is successfully resolved.

```
1    [root@prometheus ~]# dig www.olimpus.local
2
3    ; <<>> DiG 9.7.3-P3-RedHat-9.7.3-8.P3.el6 <<>> www.olimpus.local
4    ;; global options: +cmd
5    ;; Got answer:
6    ;; ->>HEADER<<- opcode: QUERY, status: NOERROR, id: 42012
7    ;; flags: qr aa rd ra; QUERY: 1, ANSWER: 2, AUTHORITY: 2, ADDITIONAL: 3
8
9    ;; QUESTION SECTION:
10   ;www.olimpus.local.              IN    A
11
12   ;; ANSWER SECTION:
13   www.olimpus.local.       172800  IN    CNAME    delphos.olimpus.local.
14   delphos.olimpus.local.   172800  IN    A        192.168.1.20
15
16   ;; AUTHORITY SECTION:
17   olimpus.local.           172800  IN    NS    prometheus.olimpus.local.
18   olimpus.local.           172800  IN    NS      delphos.olimpus.local.
19
20   ;; ADDITIONAL SECTION:
21   delphos.olimpus.local.        172800  IN    AAAA  fe80::20c:29ff:fe78:4cb1
22   prometheus.olimpus.local. 172800  IN    A       192.168.1.21
23   prometheus.olimpus.local. 172800  IN    AAAA  fe80::20c:29ff:feeb:4443
24
25   ;; Query time: 2 msec
26   ;; SERVER: 192.168.1.20#53(192.168.1.20)
27   ;; WHEN: Tue Sep 16 06:37:24 2014
28   ;; MSG SIZE  rcvd: 184
```

So, now we can access the web server by using the name www.olimpus.local (Figure 7-2).

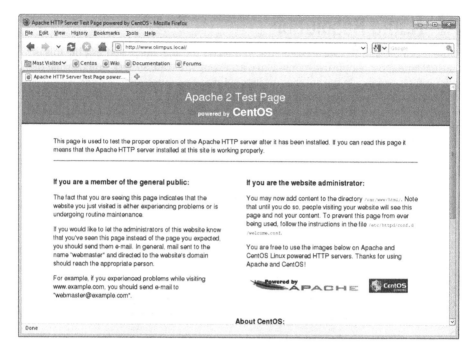

Figure 7-2. Accessing `www.olimpus.local`

7.3. Configuring the Web Site

Now, when we type "`www.olimpus.local`," we want our web page to appear, instead of the Apache test page we have seen thus far. In order to achieve this, we first take a look at the main Apache configuration file `/etc/httpd/conf/httpd.conf`. There are many options defined in this file that determine the port number the server listens on, the default web page, etc. We'll see the most important ones.

```
1    Listen 80
```

This means the server will listen to http requests on the TCP port 80.

```
1    DirectoryIndex index.html index.html.var
```

In this line, Apache specifies that the default page for the site will be `index.html` or `index.html.var`. That is, if we type "`www.olimpus.local`," Apache will automatically search for a file named `index.html` or `index.html.var`.

```
1    DocumentRoot "var/www/html"
```

This is the folder in which the web site files are located by default. When we create our custom web page, we'll have to place our files inside this folder, so let's begin.

We have to create an HTML file, name it index.html and place it in the /var/www/html folder. An in-depth explanation of the HTML language is beyond the scope of this book, so we'll create a very basic html file.

```
1   <html>
2   <head>
3   <title>Welcome to the Olimpus</title>
4   </head>
5   <body>
6   <h1>Olimpus</h1>
7   <p>Welcome to the mount Olimpus. Have a nice stay.</p>
8   </body>
9   </html>
```

Basically, an HTML file is a text file with a special structure. HTML uses tags that have to be opened and closed accordingly. The whole content must be comprised between the tags <html> and </html>.

Then there is a <head> section, in which we specify the title of the page, and a <body> section that contains the text users will see in their browsers, with a heading <h1> and a paragraph <p>.

Now if we type "www.olimpus.local" in our favorite browser, we'll see the web page we just created (Figure 7-3).

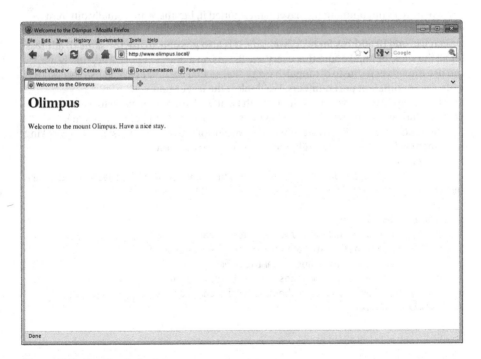

Figure 7-3. Our first web site

7.4. Virtual Hosts

Some large companies have their own dedicated server to host their web sites, but most small and medium-sized enterprises (SMEs) cannot afford that and hire a third company to host their web site. These latter companies host the web pages of many companies and, obviously, many of these sites will share the same physical server, to reduce costs.

For example, if we want to host the `www.olimpus.local` site and the `www.valhalla.local` site on the same physical server, the following is what we have to do.

We already have a DNS server configured with the `olimpus.local` zone, and a www CNAME record on it. We have to do the same for the `valhalla.local` domain (see Chapter 5). Or we can use a shortcut and simply add a line such as the following to the `/etc/hosts` file of the computer we use to connect to the web server:

```
1   192.168.1.20 www.valhalla.local
```

In this example, 192.168.1.20 is the IP address of the web server. If the IP is different, it should be changed accordingly.

Now we have to modify the `/etc/httpd/conf/httpd.conf` file.

If we're working on CentOS 6, in the `httpd.conf` file, there should be a commented line such as this one:

```
1   #NameVirtualHost *:80
```

We have to uncomment it. I haven't mentioned it, but there are actually different ways to host several sites in the same physical server. If the server has many IP addresses, we can use one IP address for every web site. It is also possible to use the same IP address for all the sites, but make sure that every site listens on a different port. And, finally, we can use the server name to distinguish every site, so that we don't have to use several IP addresses or different port numbers. We'll select the last option.

In the new Apache version shipped with CentOS 7, there is no need to use the `NameVirtualHost` directive, as this behavior is now included implicitly in Apache.

Now we configure the virtual hosts. Depending on the CentOS version we're working with, there will be some minor differences to take into account.

In CentOS 6:

In the `/etc/httpd/conf/httpd.conf` file, a bit below the `NameVirtualHost` line, we'll see a virtual host example.

```
1   #<VirtualHost *:80>
2   #    ServerAdmin webmaster@dummy-host.example.com
3   #    DocumentRoot /www/docs/dummy-host.example.com
4   #    ServerName dummy-host.example.com
5   #    ErrorLog logs/dummy-host.example.com-error_log
6   #    CustomLog logs/dummy-host.example.com-access_log common
7   #</VirtualHost>
```

We can use these lines as a template for the two sites. The final result could be something like this:

```
1   NameVirtualHost *:80
2
3   <VirtualHost *:80>
4       DocumentRoot /www/docs/olimpus.local
5       ServerName www.olimpus.local
6       ErrorLog logs/olimpus.local-error_log
7       CustomLog logs/olimpus.local-access_log common
8   </VirtualHost>
9
10
11  <VirtualHost *:80>
12      DocumentRoot /www/docs/valhalla.local
13      ServerName www.valhalla.local
14      ErrorLog logs/valhalla.local-error_log
15      CustomLog logs/valhalla.local-access_log common
16  </VirtualHost>
```

We can check the syntax of the httpd.conf file with the apachectl command.

```
1   [root@delphos ~]# apachectl -t
2   Syntax OK
```

In CentOS 7:

In CentOS 7, there is no commented VirtualHost section in the httpd.conf file, but we can take a look at /usr/share/doc/httpd-2.4.6/httpd-vhosts.conf to know how to define a virtual host.

Besides, in CentOS 7, the default configuration of Apache is far more restrictive, and we have to explicitly allow access to the folder where the pages are located.

In Apache 2.2, the version included in CentOS 6, we could allow or deny access by using the parameters Order by, Allow, and deny. However, in Apache 2.4, included with CentOS 7, we have to use the Require directive instead.

Finally, the VirtualHost section should look more or less like this:

```
1   <VirtualHost *:80>
2       DocumentRoot /www/docs/olimpus.local
3       <Directory /www/docs/olimpus.local>
4           Require all granted
5       </Directory>
6       DirectoryIndex index.html
7       ServerName www.olimpus.local
8       ErrorLog logs/olimpus.local-error_log
9       CustomLog logs/olimpus.local-access_log common
10  </VirtualHost>
11  <VirtualHost *:80>
12      DocumentRoot /www/docs/valhalla.local
```

```
13        <Directory /www/docs/valhalla.local>
14              Require all granted
15        </Directory>
16        DirectoryIndex index.html
17        ServerName www.valhalla.local
18        ErrorLog logs/valhalla.local-error_log
19        CustomLog logs/valhalla.local-access_log common
20    </VirtualHost>
```

Now we have to create the two directories we defined for the olimpus.local and valhalla.local sites.

```
1    [root@delphos html]# mkdir -p /www/docs/olimpus.local /www/docs/
     valhalla.local
```

We copy the index.html file we created previously for www.olimpus.local to its new location, and we create a similar index.html file for the www.valhalla.local site.

Before restarting the httpd service, we have to pay attention to SELinux.

If we take a look at the SELinux context of the folder /var/www/html, we see that the context is httpd_sys_content_t.

```
1    [root@delphos www]# ls -Zd /var/www/html/
2    drwxr-xr-x. root root system_u:object_r:httpd_sys_content_t:s0 /var/www/
     html/
```

But, in the newly created folders, the context is default_t.

```
1    [root@delphos www]# ls -Zd /www/docs/olimpus.local/ /www/docs/valhalla.
     local/
2    drwxr-xr-x. root root unconfined_u:object_r:default_t:s0 /www/docs/
     olimpus.local\
3    /
4    drwxr-xr-x. root root unconfined_u:object_r:default_t:s0 /www/docs/
     valhalla.loca\
5    l/
```

So, we have to change it.

```
1    [root@delphos www]# chcon -R -t httpd_sys_content_t /www/docs/
2    [root@delphos www]# ls -Zd /www/docs/olimpus.local/ /www/docs/valhalla.
     local/
3    drwxr-xr-x. root root unconfined_u:object_r:httpd_sys_content_t:s0 /www/
     docs/oli\
4    mpus.local/
5    drwxr-xr-x. root root unconfined_u:object_r:httpd_sys_content_t:s0 /www/
     docs/val\
6    halla.local/
```

Now, if we restart the httpd service, we can access both sites (Figure 7-4).

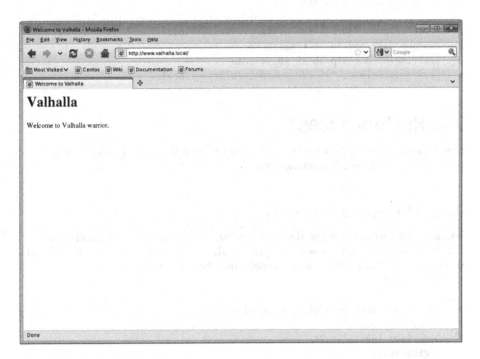

Figure 7-4. *Our second web site*

In the log files, we can see the following entries:

```
1   [root@delphos ~]# tail /etc/httpd/logs/olimpus.local-access_log
2   192.168.1.20 - - [06/Aug/2014:08:44:59 -0400] "GET / HTTP/1.1" 200 155
3
4   [root@delphos ~]# tail -f /etc/httpd/logs/valhalla.local-access_log
5   192.168.1.21 - - [06/Aug/2014:08:49:17 -0400] "GET / HTTP/1.1" 200 133
```

However, the folders and their contents still belong to the root user. If we want to grant access to the avazquez user we just created when installing CentOS, we'll have to change the owner with the chown command.

```
1   [root@delphos ~]# chown -R avazquez /www/docs/olimpus.local/
2   [root@delphos ~]# ls -lZd /www/docs/olimpus.local/
3   drwxr-xr-x. avazquez root unconfined_u:object_r:httpd_sys_content_t:s0 /
    www/docs\
4   /olimpus.local/
```

177

Now, if the user avazquez accesses the server through ssh, he will be able to create and modify the files of his web site.

```
1  [root@delphos named]# ssh avazquez@192.168.10.23
2  avazquez@192.168.10.23's password:
3  Last login: Mon Sep 26 18:50:54 2016
4  [avazquez@delphos ~]$ cd /www/docs/olimpus.local/
```

7.5. Restrict Access

Not all web sites are supposed to be accessible to anyone. We might be interested in restricting access to certain machines or users.

7.5.1. Host-Based Security

We can restrict access, based on IPs. Let's suppose we don't want the computer with IP 192.168.1.21 to access the site www.olimpus.local. The site is configured as a virtual host, so we have to include in the virtual host definition the following lines.

In CentOS 6:

```
1  <Directory /www/docs/olimpus.local>
2  Order deny,allow
3  Deny from 192.168.1.21
4  </Directory>
```

This way we define the access permissions to the web site in the /www/docs/olimpus.local folder.

```
1  Order deny,allow
```

This means the deny directives are evaluated before the allow directives, and access is allowed by default.

```
1  Deny from 192.168.1.21
```

The host with IP address 192.168.1.21 will be denied access to the site.

After the changes, the complete definition of our virtual host www.olimpus.local will be something like this:

```
1  <VirtualHost *:80>
2      DocumentRoot /www/docs/olimpus.local
3      ServerName www.olimpus.local
4      ErrorLog logs/olimpus.local-error_log
```

```
5        CustomLog logs/olimpus.local-access_log common
6            <Directory /www/docs/olimpus.local>
7                    Order deny,allow
8                    Deny from 192.168.1.21
9            </Directory>
10    </VirtualHost>
```

In CentOS 7:

As we saw earlier, the syntax has changed since previous versions of Apache. In this case, we'll have to modify the Apache configuration file with the following lines:

```
1    <Directory /www/docs/olimpus.local>
2                    Require all granted
3                    Require not ip 192.168.1.21
4    </Directory>
```

We start by granting access to everybody, with this directive:

```
1    Require all granted
```

And then, we deny access to the client with IP address 192.168.1.21.

```
1    Require not ip 192.168.1.21
```

This will be the complete VirtualHost definition in CentOS 7:

```
1    <VirtualHost *:80>
2                DocumentRoot /www/docs/olimpus.local
3                <Directory /www/docs/olimpus.local>
4                    Require all granted
5                    Require not ip 192.168.1.30
6                </Directory>
7                DirectoryIndex index.html
8                ServerName www.olimpus.local
9                ErrorLog logs/olimpus.local-error_log
10                CustomLog logs/olimpus.local-access_log common
11    </VirtualHost>
```

If we restart Apache and try to access the www.olimpus.local site from the host 192.168.1.21, we'll be redirected to the test page (Figure 7-5).

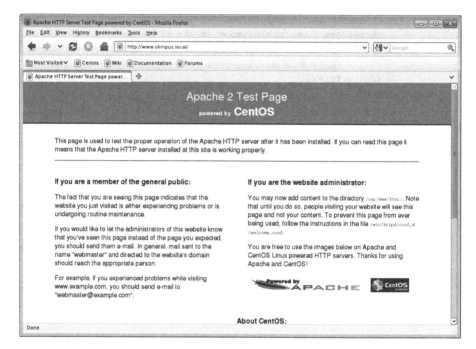

Figure 7-5. *Access denied*

Nevertheless, if we try to access `www.valhalla.local` from the same computer, we can do it without problems, because we haven't restricted the access to that site.

If we take a look at the access log of `www.olimpus.local`, we can see a line like this one:

```
1   192.168.1.21 - - [06/Aug/2014:08:47:27 -0400] "GET / HTTP/1.1" 304 -
```

We can clearly see the http code 403, which means "forbidden."

If we wanted to do the opposite, that is, to forbid access to any computer except the computer with IP address 192.168.1.21, the configuration would be similar.

In CentOS 6:

```
1   <Directory /www/docs/olimpus.local>
2               Order allow,deny
3               Allow from 192.168.1.21
4   </Directory>
```

In CentOS 7:

```
1   <Directory /www/docs/olimpus.local>
2               Require ip 192.168.1.21
3   </Directory>
```

We'll explore these parameters a bit more in depth.

```
1   Order allow,deny
```

`Allow` directives are evaluated before deny directives. Access is denied by default.

```
1   Allow from 192.168.1.21
```

The host 192.168.1.21 will be allowed access.
As a result, only the host 192.168.1.21 will be able to access the web site.

7.5.2. User-Based Security

Host-based security might not be appropriate for our needs. If, for instance, we want to restrict access to a web site by certain users on the Internet, we can't use host-based security, because we don't know from which IP addresses the clients will be connecting.

For example, let's assume we want the user thor to be the only one able to access the site www.valhalla.local.

The first thing we have to do is to create a file containing the users and associated passwords. This is the file that Apache will use later to allow or deny access. We create the file with the htpasswd command.

```
1   [root@delphos ~]# htpasswd -c /www/users_valhalla thor
2   New password:
3   Re-type new password:
4   Adding password for user thor
```

We create (Y) the /www/users_valhalla file, and we add the thor user.
As we did with the www.olimpus.local site, we now have to add a few lines to the www.valhalla.local site.

```
1   <Directory /www/docs/valhalla.local>
2           AuthType Basic
3           AuthName "Restricted Access"
4           AuthUserFile "/www/users_valhalla"
5           Require user thor
6   </Directory>
```

We'll use basic authentication (Authtype Basic). When the user tries to access this site, a window with the message "restricted access" will pop up, asking for a username and password. We'll only allow access to the user thor, and we'll check the password entered against the one stored in the /www/users_valhalla file.

This is the new definition of the valhalla site after all the changes we made.

```
1   <VirtualHost *:80>
2           DocumentRoot /www/docs/valhalla.local
3           ServerName www.valhalla.local
```

```
4      ErrorLog logs/valhalla.local-error_log
5      CustomLog logs/valhalla.local-access_log common
6      <Directory /www/docs/valhalla.local>
7          AuthType Basic
8          AuthName "Restricted Access"
9          AuthUserFile "/www/users_valhalla"
10         Require user thor
11     </Directory>
12  </VirtualHost>
```

We have to check that Apache will be able to read the file with the passwords.

```
1  [root@delphos ~]# ls -lZ /www/users_valhalla
2  -rw-r--r--. root root unconfined_u:object_r:default_t:s0 users_valhalla
```

All users have read access, but SELinux will prevent Apache from accessing this file, so we have to change this.

```
1  [root@delphos ~]# chcon -t httpd_sys_content_t /www/users_valhalla
2  [root@delphos ~]# ls -lZ /www/users_valhalla
3  -rw-r--r--. root root unconfined_u:object_r:httpd_sys_content_t:s0 /www/
   users_va\
4  lhalla
```

Now we restart the server and try to access www.valhalla.local. We'll be shown an authentication required window (Figure 7-6).

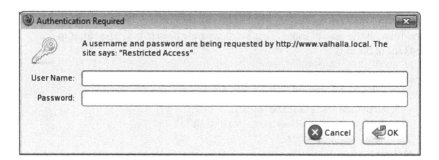

Figure 7-6. *Restricted access*

Once we enter the user and password for thor, we gain access to the site (Figure 7-7).

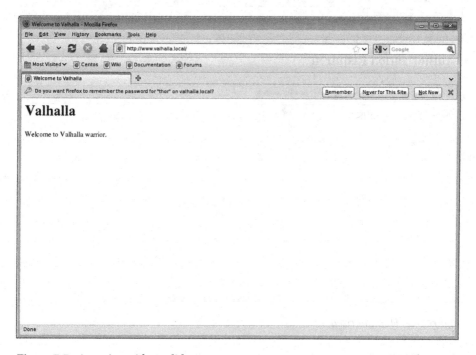

Figure 7-7. *Accessing with a valid user*

Conversely, if we don't know the username/password combination, the following is what we'll see (Figure 7-8):

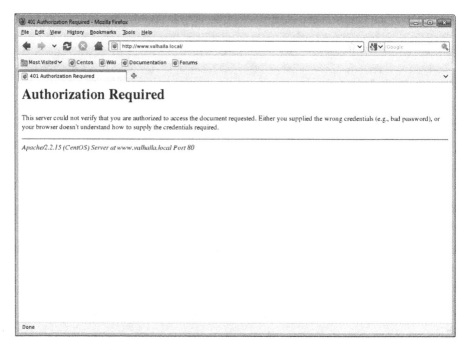

Figure 7-8. *Unauthorized user*

7.6. PHP Support

As the World Wide Web evolved, users demanded more interactivity from web pages. To fulfill that demand, many new technologies emerged, such as CGI, PHP, ASP, JavaScript, etc. One of the more widely used technologies to develop interactive sites is PHP, an open multiplatform server-side technology. The way to install it on CentOS is as simple as ever.

```
1    [root@delphos ~]# yum install php
```

To test the PHP installation, we have to create a PHP page. Obviously, this is not a book about PHP, so I won't go into it in much detail.

We create a test.php file in the home directory of the www.olimpus.local site and type the following lines:

```
1    <?php
2        phpinfo();
3    ?>
```

The PHP code must be always enclosed between the <?php and the ?> tags. Then we call the phpinfo() function, which generates a page with information about the PHP installation.

As we have installed PHP support to the server, we have to restart the httpd service, so that the applied changes take effect.

Now we open a browser and type "www.olimpus.local/test.php" in the address bar. We must connect from a client computer whose IP is allowed access; otherwise, we'll have to remove the Deny from directives we saw in the previous section. If everything is fine, we should see a page similar to that shown in Figure 7-9.

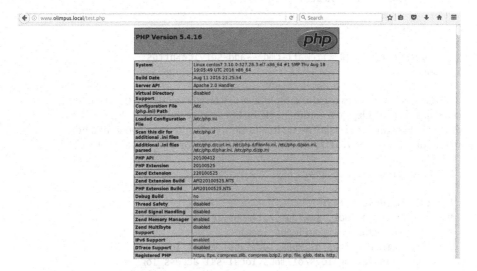

Figure 7-9. *Checking the PHP support*

So, the PHP support is working correctly.

7.7. HTTPS

We have already configured our HTTP server. Over the years, HTTP (Hypertext Transfer Protocol) proved to be a reliable protocol, but, as happened with the FTP and Telnet protocols, it wasn't designed with security in mind. So, HTTP traffic could be easily captured, as it is sent in plain text. To overcome this, HTTP Secure (HTTPS) was developed.

This way, by using a public key infrastructure, we can encrypt the communication between server and client.

To start configuring a secure web site, we'll have to install the mod_ssl package.

```
1   [root@delphos olimpus.local]# yum install mod_ssl
```

Once the package is installed, we should look at the /etc/httpd/conf.d/ssl.conf file. In the file, we can see all the parameters necessary to define a secure web site. There are also brief explanations of what every parameter does.

It is important to note also that the https protocol listens on TCP port 443, so we'll have to open it in the firewall.

In CentOS 6:

```
1  [root@delphos olimpus.local]# iptables -I INPUT -m state --state NEW -m
   tcp -p t\
2  cp --dport 443 -j ACCEPT
```

In CentOS 7:

```
1  [root@CentOS7 ~]# firewall-cmd --add-service=https
2  success
```

As we don't want to use the sample secure web site defined in the /etc/httpd/conf.d/ssl.conf file, we'll comment all the lines between the tags <VirtualHost default:443> and </VirtualHost>. In addition, we'll add these two virtual host definitions, one for www.olimpus.local and the other for www.valhalla.local:

```
1   NameVirtualHost *:443
2
3   <VirtualHost *:443>
4       DocumentRoot /www/docs/olimpus.local
5       ServerName www.olimpus.local
6       ErrorLog logs/olimpus.local-ssl_error_log
7       TransferLog logs/olimpus.local-ssl_access_log
8       LogLevel warn
9       SSLEngine on
10      SSLProtocol all -SSLv2
11      SSLCipherSuite ALL:!ADH:!EXPORT:!SSLv2:RC4+RSA:+HIGH:+MEDIUM:+LOW
12      SSLCertificateFile /etc/pki/tls/certs/www.olimpus.local.crt
13      SSLCertificateKeyFile /etc/pki/tls/private/www.olimpus.local.key
14  </VirtualHost>
15
16  <VirtualHost *:443>
17      DocumentRoot /www/docs/valhalla.local
18      ServerName www.valhalla.local
19      ErrorLog logs/valhalla.local-error_log
20      TransferLog logs/olimpus.local-ssl_access_log common
21      LogLevel warn
22      SSLEngine on
23      SSLProtocol all -SSLv2
24      SSLCipherSuite ALL:!ADH:!EXPORT:!SSLv2:RC4+RSA:+HIGH:+MEDIUM:+LOW
25      SSLCertificateFile /etc/pki/tls/certs/www.valhalla.local.crt
26      SSLCertificateKeyFile /etc/pki/tls/private/www.valhalla.local.key
27  </VirtualHost>
```

With NameVirtualHost *:443, we make it possible to share many secure web sites on the same server (see the "Virtual Hosts" section, earlier in this chapter). The DocumentRoot, ServerName, and log parameters have been used already and are self-explanatory.

The following lines beginning with SSL... are necessary to determine such parameters as the algorithm used to cipher the connection and to tell Apache where the certificate and the key files are located.

Before restarting the httpd service, we have to create the key and certificate files. Here, we can take two different approaches: we can create the certificate and the key files manually with the openssl command, or we can use the certbot tool. Both options are valid. The second is definitely easier, but knowing how to use openssl is a very interesting skill for any admin too. So I'll cover both.

7.7.1. Certificate Creation with openSSL

As I said previously, we can create the certificate and key files with the openssl command.

```
1   [root@delphos ~]# openssl genrsa -des3 -out www.olimpus.local.key
2   Generating RSA private key, 512 bit long modulus
3   ..++++++++++++
4   ....................++++++++++++
5   e is 65537 (0x10001)
6   Enter pass phrase for www.olimpus.local.key:
7   Verifying - Enter pass phrase for www.olimpus.local.key:
```

We generate an RSA key (genrsa) with triple DES cipher (-des3) and name the file containing the key www.olimpus.local.key. When creating the key, we must also assign it a pass phrase.

Now we create what is called a certificate request. This is an intermediate step in the process of creating a certificate.

```
1   [root@delphos ~]# openssl req -new -key www.olimpus.local.key -out
    www.olimpus.l\
2   ocal.csr
3   Enter pass phrase for www.olimpus.local.key:
4   You are about to be asked to enter information that will be
    incorporated
5   into your certificate request.
6   What you are about to enter is what is called a Distinguished Name or
    a DN.
7   There are quite a few fields but you can leave some blank
8   For some fields there will be a default value,
9   If you enter '.', the field will be left blank.
10  -----
11  Country Name (2 letter code) [XX]:GR
12  State or Province Name (full name) []:
```

```
13  Locality Name (eg, city) [Default City]:Athens
14  Organization Name (eg, company) [Default Company Ltd]:Mount Olimpus
15  Organizational Unit Name (eg, section) []:
16  Common Name (eg, your name or your server's hostname) []:www.olimpus.
    local
17  Email Address []:
18
19  Please enter the following 'extra' attributes
20  to be sent with your certificate request
21  A challenge password []:
22  An optional company name []:
```

We request (req) a new (-new) certificate by using the key www.olimpus.local.
key, and we indicate that this request be stored in the www.olimpus.local.csr file. In
the process, we must provide some information, such as the country code, the company
name, etc.

We'll be asked for the pass phrase we associated to the key file. We can avoid this in
future by executing the following commands:

```
1  [root@delphos ~]# cp www.olimpus.local.key www.olimpus.local.key.orig
2  [root@delphos ~]# openssl rsa -in www.olimpus.local.key.orig -out
   www.olimpus.lo\
3  cal.key
4  Enter pass phrase for www.olimpus.local.key.orig:
5  writing RSA key
```

Finally, we create the certificate itself.

```
1  [root@delphos ~]# openssl x509 -req -days 365 -in www.olimpus.local.csr
   -signkey\
2  www.olimpus.local.key -out www.olimpus.local.crt
3  Signature ok
4  subject=/C=GR/L=Athens/O=Mount Olimpus/CN=www.olimpus.local
5  Getting Private key
```

We request (-req) a certificate (x509) valid for 365 days, pass the csr and key files as
parameters, and store the certificate in the www.olimpus.local.crt file.
Now we repeat the whole process for the www.valhalla.local site.

```
1  [root@delphos ~]# openssl genrsa -des3 -out www.valhalla.local.key
2  Generating RSA private key, 512 bit long modulus
3  .......++++++++++++
4  ........................++++++++++++
5  e is 65537 (0x10001)
6  Enter pass phrase for www.valhalla.local.key:
```

```
7   Verifying - Enter pass phrase for www.valhalla.local.key:
8
9   [root@delphos ~]# openssl req -new -key www.valhalla.local.key -out
    www.valhalla\
10  .local.csr
11  Enter pass phrase for www.valhalla.local.key:
12  You are about to be asked to enter information that will be
    incorporated
13  into your certificate request.
14  What you are about to enter is what is called a Distinguished Name or
    a DN.
15  There are quite a few fields but you can leave some blank
16  For some fields there will be a default value,
17  If you enter '.', the field will be left blank.
18  -----
19  Country Name (2 letter code) [XX]:ES
20  State or Province Name (full name) []:Madrid
21  Locality Name (eg, city) [Default City]:Madrid
22  Organization Name (eg, company) [Default Company Ltd]:Valhalla
23  Organizational Unit Name (eg, section) []:
24  Common Name (eg, your name or your server's hostname) []:www.valhalla.
    local
25  Email Address []:
26
27  Please enter the following 'extra' attributes
28  to be sent with your certificate request
29  A challenge password []:
30  An optional company name []:
```

Once we have finished, we have to copy the certificate and key files to the destinations we specified in the /etc/httpd/conf.d/ssl.conf file.

```
1   [root@delphos ~]# cp www.olimpus.local.crt /etc/pki/tls/certs/
2   [root@delphos ~]# cp www.olimpus.local.key /etc/pki/tls/private/
3   [root@delphos ~]# cp www.valhalla.local.crt /etc/pki/tls/certs/
4   [root@delphos ~]# cp www.valhalla.local.key /etc/pki/tls/private/
```

Now we restart the service, launch an Internet browser, and type "https://www.olimpus.local" in the address bar. The first time we connect, we'll probably receive a warning, as our browser doesn't trust the certificate we just made. This is normal. By default, the browsers trust certificates issued by Verisign and other well-known companies, but when they find a certificate issued by some organization they don't know, they show the user a warning (Figure 7-10).

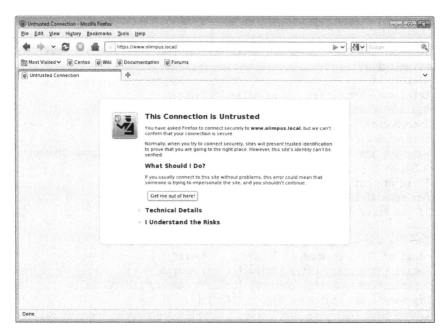

Figure 7-10. *Accessing a secure web site*

As we trust our own certificate, we add an exception (Figures 7-11 and 7-12).

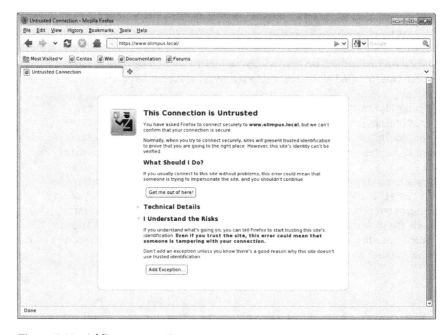

Figure 7-11. *Adding an exception*

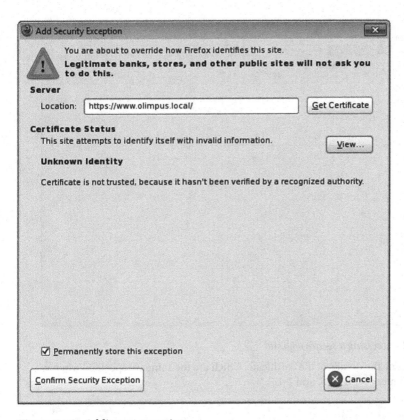

Figure 7-12. Adding an exception

And, finally, we get to the secure web site (Figure 7-13).

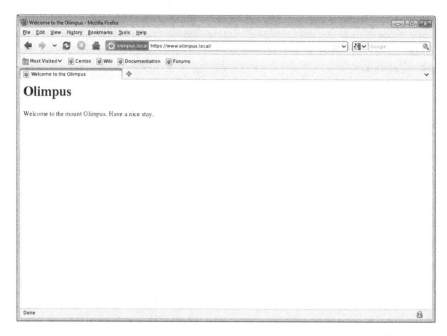

Figure 7-13. *Accessing a secure web site*

We can see the details of the certificate, which are the same we specified when we created it (Figures 7-14, 7-15, and 7-16).

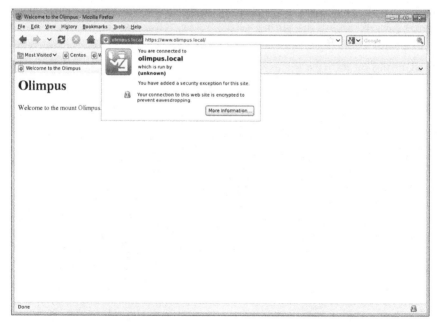

Figure 7-14. *Secure site properties*

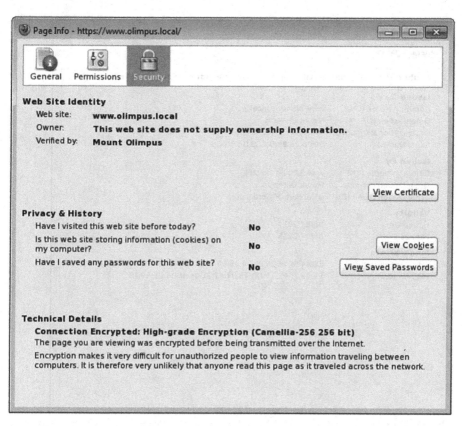

Figure 7-15. Secure site properties

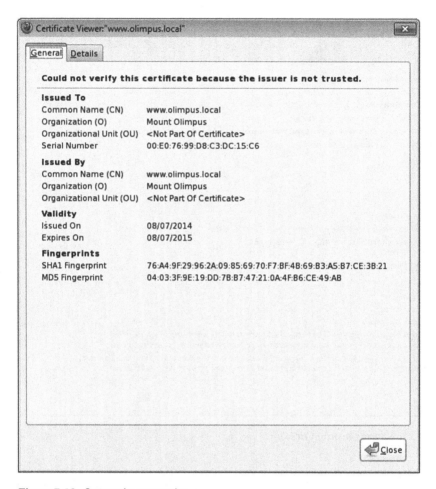

Figure 7-16. Secure site properties

The same thing occurs when we try to access the URL https://www.valhalla.local for the first time. After accepting the certificate, we can access the site through https.

Right now, we can access the sites www.olimpus.local and www.valhalla.local through both HTTP and HTPPS protocols. But maybe we want to force all communication through a secure channel. If we want to do this with the www.olimpus.local site, we have to modify its virtual host definition in the /etc/httpd/conf/httpd.conf file.

```
1   <VirtualHost *:80>
2       DocumentRoot /www/docs/olimpus.local
3       ServerName www.olimpus.local
4       Redirect / https://www.olimpus.local
5       ErrorLog logs/olimpus.local-error_log
6       CustomLog logs/olimpus.local-access_log common
7   </VirtualHost>
```

After restarting the httpd service, every time we try to access http://www.olimpus.local, we'll be redirected to https://www.olimpus.local.

7.7.2. Certificate Creation with certbot

The use of certbot greatly simplifies the process of creating the certificates required. The packages are included in the EPEL repository. So, if you haven't installed this repository yet, we'll install it now.

In CentOS 6:

First, we install the EPEL repositories.

```
1   [root@delphos ~]# yum install epel-release
```

Unfortunately, it looks like there isn't any packaged version of openbot for CentOS 6, so we'll have to install it manually.

```
1   [root@delphos ~]# wget https://dl.eff.org/certbot-auto
2   -bash: wget: command not found
3   [root@delphos ~]# yum -y install wget
4   .
5   .
6   .
7   [root@delphos ~]# wget https://dl.eff.org/certbot-auto
8   --2016-09-30 00:14:02--  https://dl.eff.org/certbot-auto
9   Resolving dl.eff.org... 173.239.79.196
10  Connecting to dl.eff.org|173.239.79.196|:443... connected.
11  HTTP request sent, awaiting response... 200 OK
12  Length: 44115 (43K) [text/plain]
13  Saving to: "certbot-auto"
14
15  100%[====================================>] 44.115     249K/s   in 0,2s
16
17  2016-09-30 00:14:03 (249 KB/s) - "certbot-auto" saved [44115/44115]
18  [root@delphos ~]# chmod a+x certbot-auto
```

Finally, we execute certbot-auto to install the program and its dependencies. It will also execute the program, once installed.

In CentOS 7:

We install the EPEL repositories, in case they are not yet installed.

```
1   [root@centos7 named]# yum install epel-release
```

Next, we can install openbot.

```
1   [root@centos7 named]# yum install python-certbot-apache
```

After installation, we only have to execute the following command:

```
1    [root@centos7 ~]# certbot --apache
```

After a few seconds, `certbot` asks the user which domain sites should be enabled for HTTPS (Figure 7-17).

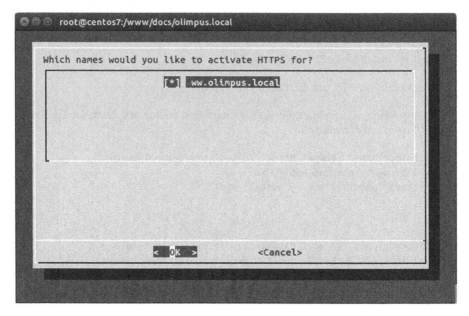

Figure 7-17.

Next, we must provide a valid e-mail (Figure 7-18).

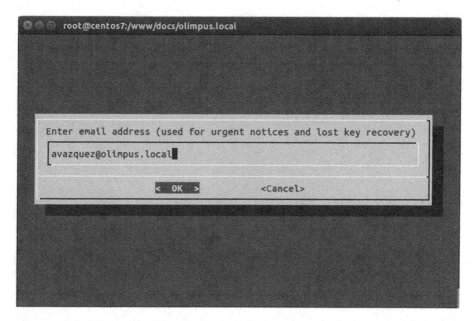

Figure 7-18. *Providing a valid e-mail*

Before generating the certificates, we must read and accept the license agreement at `https://letsencrypt.org/documents/-LE-SA-v1.1.1-August-1-2016.pdf` (Figure 7-19).

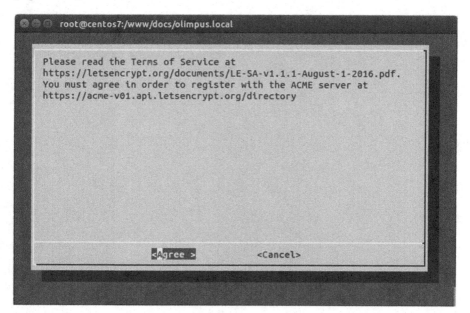

Figure 7-19. *Accepting the terms of service*

Unfortunately, in the end, we receive an error message, because our internal domain uses the suffix "local," which is not a valid suffix on the Internet, as are, for example, .com, .net, and .org. So, in this case, we can't use `certbot`. However, if you own an Internet domain, `certbot` is an easy way to configure a secure site.

CHAPTER 8

■ ■ ■

FTP Server

One of the first network protocols ever developed was the File Transfer Protocol (FTP). It is used to share files, which is indeed one of the most obvious advantages of a shared network. As one of the oldest protocols, FTP is relatively simple.

There are two different ways in which the FTP can work, based on how it handles its connections. FTP uses two different connections: the control connection and the data connection. The control connection is the first to be established and uses the port 21 by default. The data connection is established every time a listing or transfer is requested, but this can occur in two different ways:

1. The server connects to the client using the source port 20. This is called active FTP, as it is the server that opens the connection. Of course, the client will have to allow the incoming connection.

2. The server tells the client the port number it can use to establish the data connection. In this case, it is the client who actually opens the data connection. This is called passive FTP.

8.1. Installing an FTP Server on CentOS

The FTP server included in CentOS is vsftpd (very secure ftpd). It can be installed the usual way.

```
1    [root@localhost2 ~]# yum install vsftpd
```

The configuration file for the vftpd server is /etc/vsftpd/vsftpd.conf. Some of the most important options are:

```
1    anonymous_enable=YES
```

to allow anonymous connections, and

```
1    write_enable=YES
```

to be able to upload files from the client to the server.

As we already know, once installed, it's necessary to launch the associated service and make sure it starts automatically every time the computer restarts.

In CentOS 6:

```
1  [root@localhost2 ~]# service vsftpd start
2  Starting vsftpd for vsftpd: [ OK ]
3  [root@localhost2 ~]# chkconfig vsftpd on
```

In CentOS 7:

```
1  [root@CentOS7 ~]# systemctl start vsftpd
2  [root@CentOS7 ~]# systemctl enable vsftpd
3  ln -s '/usr/lib/systemd/system/vsftpd.service' '/etc/systemd/system/
   multi-user.t\
4  arget.wants/vsftpd.service'
```

As usual, we'll have to permit access to the FTP ports (20 and 21) in the firewall. In CentOS 6:

```
1  [root@delphos ~]# iptables -I INPUT 2 -p tcp --dport 20 -j ACCEPT
2  [root@delphos ~]# iptables -I INPUT 2 -p tcp --dport 21 -j ACCEPT
```

In CentOS 7:

```
1  [root@CentOS7 ~]# firewall-cmd --add-service=ftp
2  success2
```

8.2. Connecting from a Linux Client

After configuring the FTP server, we can connect from another computer as an anonymous user with any password, as it won't be checked. We'll have to use an FTP client. In most Linux applications, we can use lftp or ftp, for example. We'll install both.

```
1   [root@prometheus ~]# yum install ftp
2
3
4   [root@prometheus ~]# ftp 192.168.1.20
5   Connected to 192.168.1.20 (192.168.1.20).
6   220 (vsFTPd 2.2.2)
7   Name (192.168.1.20:root): anonymous
8   331 Please specify the password.
9   Password:
10  230 Login successful.
11  Remote system type is UNIX.
12  Using binary mode to transfer files.
13  ftp> bye
```

```
14   221 Goodbye.
15
16   [root@prometheus ~]# yum install lftp
17
18   [root@prometheus ~]# lftp 192.168.1.20
19   lftp 192.168.1.20:~>
```

The lftp program establishes an anonymous connection by default. We can disconnect at any time with bye.

The default working directory is /var/ftp, which is empty by default. We create a file text inside this folder, so we can download this file later.

```
1   [root@delphos ~]# cd /var/ftp/pub/
2   [root@delphos pub]# echo Hola > saludo.txt
```

8.2.1. Access As an Anonymous User

As we saw before, we can connect anonymously to the FTP server.

```
1    [root@prometheus ~]# ftp 192.168.1.20
2    Connected to 192.168.1.20 (192.168.1.20).
3    220 (vsFTPd 2.2.2)
4    Name (192.168.1.20:root): anonymous
5    331 Please specify the password.
6    Password:
7    230 Login successful.
8    Remote system type is UNIX.
9    Using binary mode to transfer files.
10   ftp>
```

To identify the present working directory, we can use the pwd command.

```
1   ftp> pwd
2   257 "/"
```

Now we can search for the saludo.txt file and download it.

```
1   ftp> ls
2   227 Entering Passive Mode (192,168,1,20,144,63).
3   ftp: connect: No route to host
```

If we're working with CentOS 6, we'll see that the listing doesn't execute. This is because we opened the firewall for connections to port 21, but the data connection is not being allowed. We'll have to make some minor adjustments for this to work in CentOS 6. In CentOS 7, on the other hand, these changes won't be necessary.

When introducing the FTP, I mentioned that it uses both a control connection and a data connection. Owing to the peculiar nature of the FTP, it could be quite complicated to deal with the data connections, but there is a kernel module that handles this for us automatically.

This module is ip_conntrack_ftp. We can load it with modprobe and then restart the FTP connection from the client.

```
1   [root@delphos pub]# modprobe ip_conntrack_ftp
2
3   ftp> bye
4   221 Goodbye.
5   [root@prometheus ~]# ftp 192.168.1.20
6   Connected to 192.168.1.20 (192.168.1.20).
7   220 (vsFTPd 2.2.2)
8   Name (192.168.1.20:root): anonymous
9   331 Please specify the password.
10  Password:
11  230 Login successful.
12  Remote system type is UNIX.
13  Using binary mode to transfer files.
14  ftp> ls
15  227 Entering Passive Mode (192,168,1,20,183,110).
16  150 Here comes the directory listing.
17  drwxr-xr-x    2 0        0            4096 Aug 09 19:10 pub
18  226 Directory send OK.
19  ftp>
```

If we don't want to load ip_conntrack_ftp manually every time we reboot the server, we can modify the file /etc/sysconfig/iptables and add the module in the list of iptables modules, so that the line remains like this:

```
1   IPTABLES_MODULES="ip_conntrack_ftp"
```

CentOS 7 loads automatically the ip_conntrack_ftp module, so there is no need to change any configuration file.

Now we'll try to find and download the saludo.txt file.

```
1   ftp> ls
2   227 Entering Passive Mode (192,168,1,20,63,110).
3   150 Here comes the directory listing.
4   drwxr-xr-x    2 0        0            4096 Aug 09 19:10 pub
5   226 Directory send OK.
6   ftp> cd pub
7   250 Directory successfully changed.
8   ftp> ls
9   227 Entering Passive Mode (192,168,1,20,157,163).
10  150 Here comes the directory listing.
11  -rw-r--r--    1 0        0               5 Aug 09 19:10 saludo.txt
12  226 Directory send OK.
13  ftp>
```

As saludo.txt is a text file, we have to activate the ASCII mode.

```
1   ftp> ascii
2   200 Switching to ASCII mode.
```

We download the file and exit.

```
1   ftp> get saludo.txt
2   local: saludo.txt remote: saludo.txt
3   227 Entering Passive Mode (192,168,1,20,212,55).
4   150 Opening BINARY mode data connection for saludo.txt (5 bytes).
5   WARNING! 1 bare linefeeds received in ASCII mode
6   File may not have transferred correctly.
7   226 Transfer complete.
8   5 bytes received in 0.000275 secs (18.18 Kbytes/sec)
9   ftp> bye
10  221 Goodbye.
```

Now we have the file available in the client machine.

```
1   [root@prometheus ~]# cat saludo.txt
2   Hola
```

In the preceding example, we downloaded a text file, so we had to activate the ASCII mode. But we can also download binary files, activating the binary mode. To see an example, we'll copy a binary file in the FTP directory and download it from the client.

```
1   [root@delphos pub]# cp /bin/bash /var/ftp/pub/
```

Now we connect from the client the same way we did before.

```
1   [root@prometheus ~]# ftp 192.168.1.20
2   Connected to 192.168.1.20 (192.168.1.20).
3   220 (vsFTPd 2.2.2)
4   Name (192.168.1.20:root): anonymous
5   331 Please specify the password.
6   Password:
7   230 Login successful.
8   Remote system type is UNIX.
9   Using binary mode to transfer files.
10  ftp> ls
11  227 Entering Passive Mode (192,168,1,20,203,62).
12  150 Here comes the directory listing.
13  drwxr-xr-x    2 0        0            4096 Aug 10 00:17 pub
14  226 Directory send OK.
15  ftp> cd pub
16  250 Directory successfully changed.
17  ftp> ls
```

```
18   227 Entering Passive Mode (192,168,1,20,111,228).
19   150 Here comes the directory listing.
20   -rwxr-xr-x   1 0      0          868404 Aug 10 00:17 bash
21   -rw-r--r--   1 0      0               5 Aug 09 19:10 saludo.txt
22   226 Directory send OK.
23   ftp>
```

But now we activate the binary mode instead of the ASCII mode.

```
1    ftp> binary
2    200 Switching to Binary mode.
3    ftp> get bash
4    local: bash remote: bash
5    227 Entering Passive Mode (192,168,1,20,93,208).
6    150 Opening BINARY mode data connection for bash (868404 bytes).
7    226 Transfer complete.
8    868404 bytes received in 0.0661 secs (13141.71 Kbytes/sec)
9    ftp> bye
10   221 Goodbye.
```

Until now, we have downloaded files from the server to the client, but we can also upload files from the client to the FTP server. For this to work, we need to set this parameter in the config file /etc/vsftpd/vsftpd.conf.

```
1    anon_upload_enable=YES
```

If this parameter doesn't exist or is set to NO, we change it and reload the vsftpd service.

In CentOS 6:

```
1    [root@delphos ~]# service vsftpd restart
2    Shutting down vsftpd:                      [ OK ]
3    Starting vsftpd for vsftpd:                [ OK ]
```

In CentOS 7:

```
1    [root@CentOS7 ~]# systemctl restart vsftpd
```

Of course, we'll have to give write permissions with chmod in the folder in which we want the users to upload the files.

```
1    [root@CentOS7 ~]# chmod 777 /var/ftp/pub/
```

In addition, we have to check the SELinux Booleans associated with the FTP service. The names of these Booleans vary depending on whether we are working with CentOS 6 or CentOs 7:

In CentOS 6:

```
1   [root@delphos ~]# getsebool -a |grep -i ftp
2   allow_ftpd_anon_write --> off
3   allow_ftpd_full_access --> off
4   allow_ftpd_use_cifs --> off
5   allow_ftpd_use_nfs --> off
6   ftp_home_dir --> off
7   ftpd_connect_db --> off
8   httpd_enable_ftp_server --> off
```

In CentOs 7:

```
1    [root@CentOS7 ~]# getsebool -a | grep -i ftp
2    ftp_home_dir --> off
3    ftpd_anon_write --> off
4    ftpd_connect_all_unreserved --> off
5    ftpd_connect_db --> off
6    ftpd_full_access --> off
7    ftpd_use_cifs --> off
8    ftpd_use_fusefs --> off
9    ftpd_use_nfs --> off
10   ftpd_use_passive_mode --> off
11   httpd_can_connect_ftp --> off
12   httpd_enable_ftp_server --> off
13   sftpd_anon_write --> off
14   sftpd_enable_homedirs --> off
15   sftpd_full_access --> off
16   sftpd_write_ssh_home --> off
17   tftp_anon_write --> off
18   tftp_home_dir --> off
```

We'll have to change the value of allow_ftpd_anon_write (ftpd_anon_write in CentOS 7) from off to on. We can see a more detailed description of this Boolean value with the semanage command.

```
1   [root@delphos ~]# semanage boolean -l | grep allow_ftpd_anon_write
2   allow_ftpd_anon_write -> off Allow ftp servers to upload files, used\
3   for public file transfer services. Directories must be labeled
    public_content_r\
4   w_t.
```

So, we change the value of the Boolean.
In CentOS 6:

```
1   [root@delphos ~]# setsebool allow_ftpd_anon_write on
2   [root@delphos ~]# getsebool allow_ftpd_anon_write
3   allow_ftpd_anon_write --> on
```

In CentOS 7:

```
1  [root@CentOS7 ~]# setsebool ftpd_anon_write on
2  [root@CentOS7 ~]# getsebool ftpd_anon_write
3  ftpd_anon_write --> on
```

We'll have to see the context associated with the FTP directory too.

```
1  [root@delphos ~]# ls -Z /var/ftp/
2  drwxrwxrwx. root root system_u:object_r:public_content_t:s0 pub
```

And we change the context, if necessary, so that writing is allowed too.

```
1  [root@delphos ~]# chcon -t public_content_rw_t /var/ftp/pub/
2  [root@delphos ~]# ls -Z /var/ftp/
3  drwxrwxrwx. root root system_u:object_r:public_content_rw_t:s0 pub
```

Now we're ready to upload a file from the client.

```
1   [root@prometheus ~]# ftp 192.168.1.20
2   Connected to 192.168.1.20 (192.168.1.20).
3   220 (vsFTPd 2.2.2)
4   Name (192.168.1.20:root): anonymous
5   331 Please specify the password.
6   Password:
7   230 Login successful.
8   Remote system type is UNIX.
9   Using binary mode to transfer files.
10  ftp> pwd
11  257 "/"
12  ftp> ls
13  227 Entering Passive Mode (192,168,1,20,237,214).
14  150 Here comes the directory listing.
15  drwxrwxrwx    2 0        0            4096 Aug 10 07:45 pub
16  226 Directory send OK.
17  ftp> cd pub
18  250 Directory successfully changed.
19  ftp> ascii
20  200 Switching to ASCII mode.
21  ftp> put test.txt
22  local: test.txt remote: test.txt
23  227 Entering Passive Mode (192,168,1,20,189,66).
24  150 Ok to send data.
25  226 Transfer complete.
26  16 bytes sent in 0.00019 secs (84.21 Kbytes/sec)
```

Now we can see the uploaded file in the server.

```
1   ftp> ls
2   227 Entering Passive Mode (192,168,1,20,82,229).
3   150 Here comes the directory listing.
4   -rwxr-xr-x    1 0        0           868404 Aug 10 00:17 bash
5   -rw-r--r--    1 0        0                5 Aug 09 19:10 saludo.txt
6   -rw-------    1 14       50              16 Aug 10 07:46 test.txt
7   226 Directory send OK.
8   ftp>
```

We could also access the FTP server from a web browser such as Firefox (Figure 8-1).

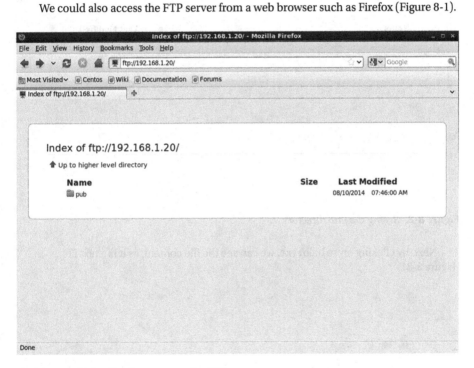

Figure 8-1. *Using Firefox to access the FTP server*

By clicking pub, we'll see its content (Figure 8-2).

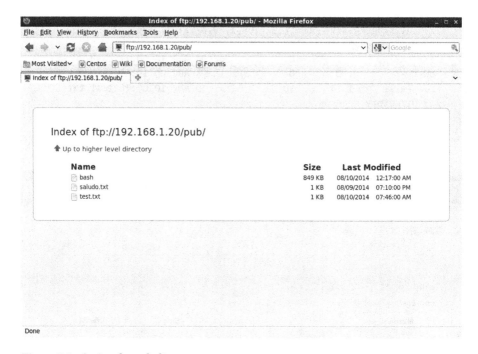

Figure 8-2. *Seeing the pub directory*

Next, by clicking on saludo.txt, we can see the file content, as it is a text file (Figure 8-3).

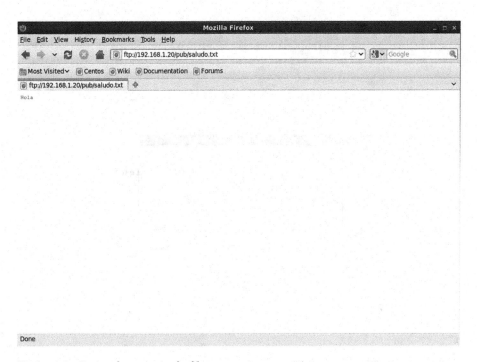

Figure 8-3. *Seeing the content of a file*

On the other hand, if we click a binary file such as bash, we'll be asked whether we want to download the file (Figure 8-4).

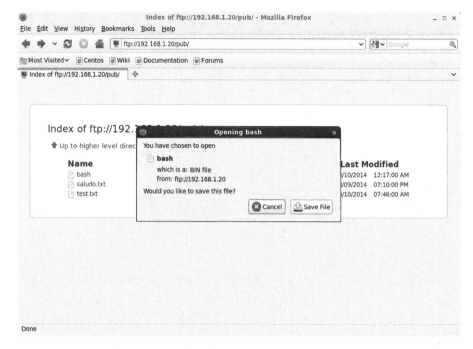

Figure 8-4. *Downloading a binary file*

It is possible that when clicking a file such as test.txt, we receive an error message (Figure 8-5).

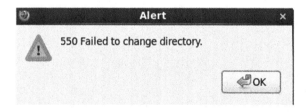

Figure 8-5. *Error downloading the file*

This means that the permissions associated with the file are not correct. If we list the permissions from the server, we get the following:

```
1  [root@delphos ~]# ls -l /var/ftp/pub/
2  total 860
3  -rwxr-xr-x. 1 root root 868404 Aug      9 20:17 bash
4  -rw-r--r--. 1 root root      5 Aug      9 15:10 saludo.txt
5  -rw-------. 1 ftp  ftp      16 Aug 10 03:46 test.txt
```

As we can see, only the owner—in this case, ftp—has permission to access the test.
txt file. This is the default behavior of the FTP server when an anonymous user uploads
a file. But we can change this by editing the /etc/vsftpd/vsftpd.conf file and including
this parameter:

```
1    anon_umask=022
```

After restarting the vsftpd service, we can upload a new file.

```
1    [root@prometheus ~]# ftp 192.168.1.20
2    Connected to 192.168.1.20 (192.168.1.20).
3    220 (vsFTPd 2.2.2)
4    Name (192.168.1.20:root): anonymous
5    331 Please specify the password.
6    Password:
7    230 Login successful.
8    Remote system type is UNIX.
9    Using binary mode to transfer files.
10   ftp> cd pub
11   250 Directory successfully changed.
12   ftp> ascii
13   200 Switching to ASCII mode.
14   ftp> put test2.txt
15   local: test2.txt remote: test2.txt
16   227 Entering Passive Mode (192,168,1,20,89,209).
17   150 Ok to send data.
18   226 Transfer complete.
19   26 bytes sent in 0.000339 secs (76.70 Kbytes/sec)
20   ftp>
```

Now the permissions will be different, and other users will have read access to the
new uploaded file.

```
1    [root@delphos ~]# ls -l /var/ftp/pub/
2    total 864
3    -rwxr-xr-x. 1 root root 868404 Aug  9 20:17 bash
4    -rw-r--r--. 1 root root      5 Aug  9 15:10 saludo.txt
5    -rw-r--r--. 1 ftp  ftp      26 Aug 10 15:52 test2.txt
6    -rw-------. 1 ftp  ftp      16 Aug 10 03:46 test.txt
```

Consequently, we'll be able to see or download the file with Firefox (Figures 8-6
and 8-7).

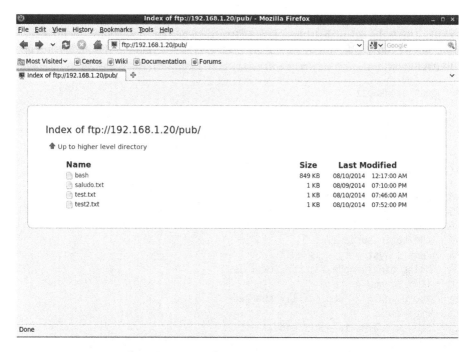

Figure 8-6. *Accessing the FTP server with Firefox again*

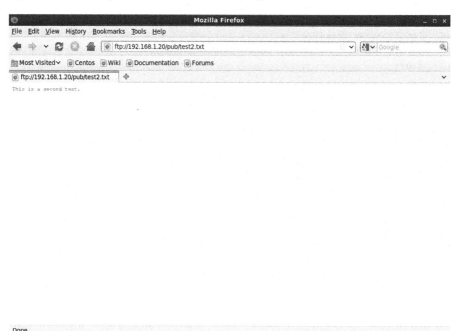

Figure 8-7. *Downloading the file test 2*

8.2.2. Connecting As a Local User

Apart from connecting as an anonymous user, we can also connect as a local user. The procedure is almost exactly the same, so I'll offer only a brief example.

First of all, we must make sure that this parameter is active in the /etc/vsftpd/vsftpd.conf file.

```
1  # Uncomment this to allow local users to log in.
2  local_enable=YES
```

In addition, we have to change a Boolean SELinux parameter.

```
1  [root@delphos ~]# setsebool ftp_home_dir on
2  [root@delphos ~]# getsebool ftp_home_dir
3  ftp_home_dir --> on
```

Let's suppose we have a local user called Socrates. If we don't, we create it now and assign it a new password.

```
1  [root@delphos ~]# useradd -m socrates
2  [root@delphos ~]# passwd socrates
3  Changing password for user socrates.
4  New password:
5  BAD PASSWORD: it is based on a dictionary word
6  Retype new password:
7  passwd: all authentication tokens updated successfully.
```

Now we can connect to the server from the client.

```
1   [root@prometheus ~]# ftp 192.168.1.20
2   Connected to 192.168.1.20 (192.168.1.20).
3   220 (vsFTPd 2.2.2)
4   Name (192.168.1.20:root): socrates
5   331 Please specify the password.
6   Password:
7   230 Login successful.
8   Remote system type is UNIX.
9   Using binary mode to transfer files.
10  ftp> pwd
11  257 "/home/socrates"
12  ftp>
```

We can download and upload files exactly the same way we did when connecting as an anonymous user.

8.3. Connecting from a Windows Client

We can also connect from a Windows client by using the command line FTP client
included with the OS (Figure 8-8).

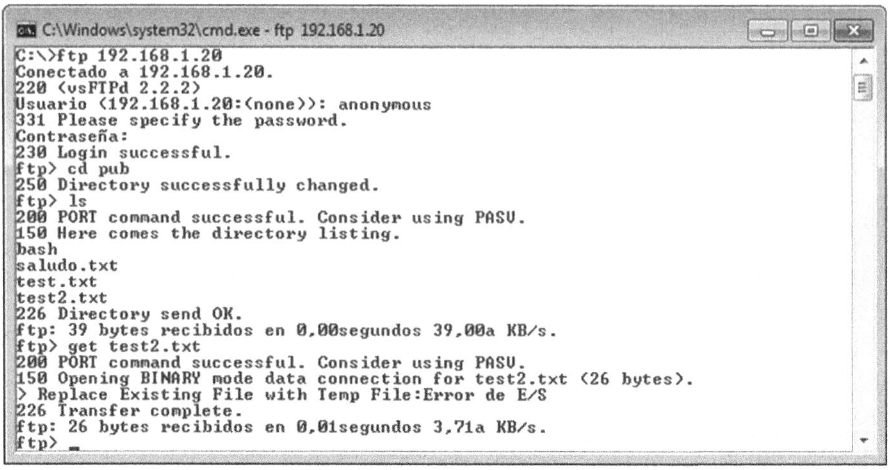

```
C:\Windows\system32\cmd.exe - ftp 192.168.1.20
C:\>ftp 192.168.1.20
Conectado a 192.168.1.20.
220 (vsFTPd 2.2.2)
Usuario (192.168.1.20:(none)): anonymous
331 Please specify the password.
Contraseña:
230 Login successful.
ftp> cd pub
250 Directory successfully changed.
ftp> ls
200 PORT command successful. Consider using PASV.
150 Here comes the directory listing.
bash
saludo.txt
test.txt
test2.txt
226 Directory send OK.
ftp: 39 bytes recibidos en 0,00segundos 39,00a KB/s.
ftp> get test2.txt
200 PORT command successful. Consider using PASV.
150 Opening BINARY mode data connection for test2.txt (26 bytes).
> Replace Existing File with Temp File:Error de E/S
226 Transfer complete.
ftp: 26 bytes recibidos en 0,01segundos 3,71a KB/s.
ftp> _
```

Figure 8-8. *Using the Windows FTP client*

But it is far more common to use a graphical client such as Filezilla (also available in
Linux). After launching the program, we'll see the screen shown in Figure 8-9.

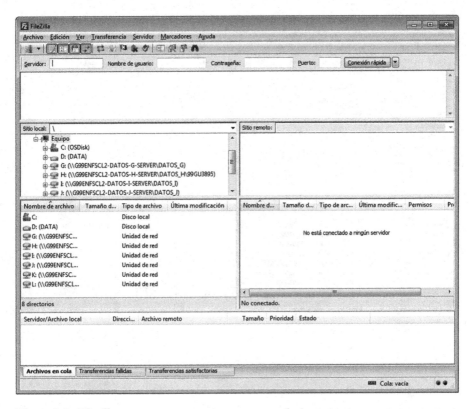

Figure 8-9. *Filezilla*

We have only to type the server, port, username, and password and click "Connection" (Figure 8-10).

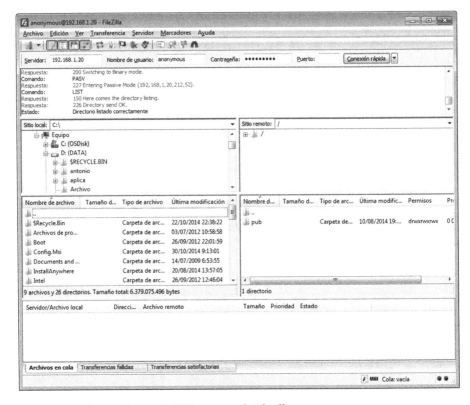

Figure 8-10. *Connecting to the FTP server with Filezilla*

To download or upload files, we have only to drag files between the local and the remote site.

8.4. Analyzing the FTP with Telnet

We'll try to learn a bit more about the FTP by using Telnet. We start by opening a `telnet` session to port 21 of the FTP server. This way, we establish the control connection.

```
1   [root@prometheus ~]# telnet 192.168.1.20 21
2   Trying 192.168.1.20...
3   Connected to 192.168.1.20.
4   Escape character is '^]'.
5   220 (vsFTPd 2.2.2)
```

Now we specify the user and the password.

```
1   USER anonymous
2   331 Please specify the password.
3   PASS anonymous
4   230 Login successful.
```

Once logged in, we execute commands. Some commands such as downloading or uploading a file require a second connection, the data connection, so we'll start by taking a look at the simplest commands.

```
1   STAT
2   211-FTP server status:
3        Connected to 192.168.1.21
4        Logged in as ftp
5        TYPE: ASCII
6        No session bandwidth limit
7        Session timeout in seconds is 300
8        Control connection is plain text
9        Data connections will be plain text
10       At session startup, client count was 1
11       vsFTPd 2.2.2 - secure, fast, stable
12  211 End of status
```

As we see, STAT shows some information about the FTP server. If we pass as a parameter the name of a directory, STAT will show the content of that directory.

```
1   STAT .
2   213-Status follows:
3   drwxr-xr-x    3 0        0          4096 Aug 09 14:58 .
4   drwxr-xr-x    3 0        0          4096 Aug 09 14:58 ..
5   drwxrwxrwx    2 0        0          4096 Aug 10 19:52 pub
6   213 End of status
7   STAT pub
8   213-Status follows:
9   drwxrwxrwx    2 0        0          4096 Aug 10 19:52 .
10  drwxr-xr-x    3 0        0          4096 Aug 09 14:58 ..
11  -rwxr-xr-x    1 0        0        868404 Aug 10 00:17 bash
12  -rw-r--r--    1 0        0             5 Aug 09 19:10 saludo.txt
13  -rw-------    1 14       50           16 Aug 10 07:46 test.txt
14  -rw-r--r--    1 14       50           26 Aug 10 19:52 test2.txt
15  213 End of status
```

To change directories, we can use the CWD command.

```
1   CWD pub
2   250 Directory successfully changed.
3   STAT .
```

```
4    213-Status follows:
5    drwxrwxrwx 2 0        0        4096 Aug 10 19:52 .
6    drwxr-xr-x 3 0        0        4096 Aug 09 14:58 ..
7    -rwxr-xr-x 1 0        0      868404 Aug 10 00:17 bash
8    -rw-r--r-- 1 0        0           5 Aug 09 19:10 saludo.txt
9    -rw------- 1 14       50         16 Aug 10 07:46 test.txt
10   -rw-r--r-- 1 14       50         26 Aug 10 19:52 test2.txt
11   213 End of status
```

To return to the parent directory, we type "CDUP."

```
1    CDUP
2    250 Directory successfully changed.
3    STAT .
4    213-Status follows:
5    drwxr-xr-x  3 0        0        4096 Aug 09 14:58 .
6    drwxr-xr-x  3 0        0        4096 Aug 09 14:58 ..
7    drwxrwxrwx  2 0        0        4096 Aug 10 19:52 pub
8    213 End of status
```

If we want to know the directory we are currently working on, we can type "PWD."

```
1    PWD
2    257 "/"
```

We can delete files if we have the appropriate permissions. We exit the session with quit and log in as a normal user, to try to delete a file.

```
1    quit
2    221 Goodbye.
3    Connection closed by foreign host.
4    [root@prometheus ~]# telnet 192.168.1.20 21
5    Trying 192.168.1.20...
6    Connected to 192.168.1.20.
7    Escape character is '^]'.
8    220 (vsFTPd 2.2.2)
9    USER antonio
10   331 Please specify the password.
11   PASS antonio
12   230 Login successful.
13   STAT .
14   213-Status follows:
15   drwx------  2 500      500      4096 Aug 09 14:12 .
16   drwxr-xr-x  4 0        0        4096 Aug 10 20:41 ..
17   -rw-------  1 500      500        37 Aug 09 14:12 .bash_history
18   -rw-r--r--  1 500      500        18 Dec 02 2011 .bash_logout
19   -rw-r--r--  1 500      500       176 Dec 02 2011 .bash_profile
20   -rw-r--r--  1 500      500       124 Dec 02 2011 .bashrc
```

```
21   -rw-rw-r--    1  500              500            5 Aug 09 14:12 hola
22   213 End of status
23   DELE hola
24   250 Delete operation successful.
25   STAT .
26   213-Status follows:
27   drwx------    2  500              500         4096 Aug 11 23:41 .
28   drwxr-xr-x    4  0                0           4096 Aug 10 20:41 ..
29   -rw-------    1  500              500           37 Aug 09 14:12 .bash_history
30   -rw-r--r--    1  500              500           18 Dec 02 2011 .bash_logout
31   -rw-r--r--    1  500              500          176 Dec 02 2011 .bash_profile
32   -rw-r--r--    1  500              500          124 Dec 02 2011 .bashrc
33   213 End of status
34   quit
35   221 Goodbye.
```

As we can see, the file named hola was successfully deleted.

So far, we have seen how to list files with the STAT command. But this is not the way FTP clients do it. They basically open a new channel—the data channel—and the listing is transferred through that channel. Let's see an example. We start by connecting to the FTP server and forcing the passive mode.

```
1    [root@prometheus ~]# telnet 192.168.1.20 21
2    Trying 192.168.1.20...
3    Connected to 192.168.1.20.
4    Escape character is '^]'.
5    220 (vsFTPd 2.2.2)
6    USER anonymous
7    331 Please specify the password.
8    PASS anonymous
9    230 Login successful.
10   CWD pub
11   250 Directory successfully changed.
12   PASV
13   227 Entering Passive Mode (192,168,1,20,204,80).
```

After forcing the passive mode, the system confirms the operation and shows six numbers. The first four represent the IP address of the server, 192.168.1.20 in this case. And the two last numbers represent the port number. To obtain the port number, we must multiply the first number for 256 and add the result to the second number. In this example, the port number would be (204*256)+80=52304.

This means that the server will open port number 52304 for data transfers. Now we can ask for a file listing with the LIST command.

```
1    LIST
2    150 Here comes the directory listing.
3    226 Directory send OK.
```

Now, to get the listing, we have to open another telnet session to port number 52304. From now on, we'll call this telnet session the data session.
Of course, first, we'll have to allow traffic to this port in the server.
In CentOS 6:

```
1   [root@delphos ~]# iptables -I INPUT 1 -p tcp --dport 52304 -j ACCEPT
```

In CentOS 7:

```
1   [root@CentOS7 ~]# firewall-cmd --add-port=52304/tcp
2   success
```

Now we can establish the data session.

```
1    [root@prometheus ~]# telnet 192.168.1.20 52304
2    Trying 192.168.1.20...
3    Connected to 192.168.1.20.
4    Escape character is '^]'.
5    -rwxr-xr-x   1 0          0            868404 Aug 10 00:17 bash
6    -rw-r--r--   1 14         50                0 Aug 11 17:56 prueba.pcl
7    -rw-r--r--   1 14         50             1853 Aug 11 14:23 prueba3.pcl
8    -rw-r--r--   1 0          0                 5 Aug 09 19:10 saludo.txt
9    -rw-------   1 14         50               16 Aug 10 07:46 test.txt
10   -rw-r--r--   1 14         50               26 Aug 10 19:52 test2.txt
11   Connection closed by foreign host.
```

The way to download a file is pretty similar. We'll try now to download an ascii file with the RETR command.

```
1    [root@prometheus ~]# telnet 192.168.1.20 21
2    Trying 192.168.1.20...
3    Connected to 192.168.1.20.
4    Escape character is '^]'.
5    220 (vsFTPd 2.2.2)
6    USER anonymous
7    331 Please specify the password.
8    PASS anonymous
9    230 Login successful.
10   CWD pub
11   250 Directory successfully changed.
12   TYPE A
13   200 Switching to ASCII mode.
14   PASV
15   227 Entering Passive Mode (192,168,1,20,44,102).
```

In this case, the port number open in the server for data transfers will be 11366. So, we open it in the firewall.

```
1    [root@delphos ~]# iptables -I INPUT 1 -p tcp --dport 11366 -j ACCEPT
```

Now we try to download the file with the RETR command.

```
1    RETR saludo.txt
2    150 Opening BINARY mode data connection for saludo.txt (5 bytes).
```

In the second terminal window, we'll have to open a telnet session to port 11366 and redirect the output to a file.

```
1    [root@prometheus ~]# telnet 192.168.1.21 11366 > saludo.txt
2    Connection closed by foreign host.
```

Once the transfer is complete, we'll see this message in the first telnet session, the control session.

```
1    226 Transfer complete.
```

8.5. Secure FTP

As we all know, FTP is an old protocol and wasn't designed with security in mind. We have already seen that we can use the SSH protocol to transfer files in a secure way (see Chapter 6). But we can also generate a certificate and configure vsftp to use TLS.

8.5.1. Generating the Certificate

We have already seen how to generate a certificate (see Chapter 7), so I won't go into much detail now. First, we create the key.

```
1    [root@delphos ~]# openssl genrsa -des3 -out FTPsecure.key
2    Generating RSA private key, 512 bit long modulus
3    ...................++++++++++++++
4    ...................++++++++++++++
5    e is 65537 (0x10001)
6    Enter pass phrase for FTPsecure.key:
7    Verifying - Enter pass phrase for FTPsecure.key:
```

Then, we generate a certificate request.

```
1    [root@delphos ~]# openssl req -new -key FTPsecure.key -out FTPsecure.csr
2    Enter pass phrase for FTPsecure.key:
3    You are about to be asked to enter information that will be
     incorporated
4    into your certificate request.
```

```
 5   What you are about to enter is what is called a Distinguished Name or
     a DN.
 6   There are quite a few fields but you can leave some blank
 7   For some fields there will be a default value,
 8   If you enter '.', the field will be left blank.
 9   -----
10   Country Name (2 letter code) [XX]:GR
11   State or Province Name (full name) []:Athens
12   Locality Name (eg, city) [Default City]:
13   Organization Name (eg, company) [Default Company Ltd]:olimpus
14   Organizational Unit Name (eg, section) []:
15   Common Name (eg, your name or your server's hostname) []:
16   Email Address []:
17
18   Please enter the following 'extra' attributes
19   to be sent with your certificate request
20   A challenge password []:
21   An optional company name []:
22   [root@delphos ~]#
```

Now we remove the password associated with the key file.

```
1   [root@delphos ~]# cp FTPsecure.key FTPsecure.key.orig
2   [root@delphos ~]# openssl rsa -in FTPsecure.key.orig -out FTPsecure.key
3   Enter pass phrase for FTPsecure.key.orig:
4   writing RSA key
```

And, finally, we generate the certificate.

```
1   [root@delphos ~]# openssl x509 -req -days 365 -in FTPsecure.csr -signkey
    FTPsecu\
2   re.key -out FTPsecure.crt
3   Signature ok
4   subject=/C=GR/ST=Athens/L=Default City/O=olimpus
5   Getting Private key
```

Now we copy both the key and the certificate file to /etc/pki/tls/certs.

```
1   [root@delphos ~]# cp FTPsecure.key /etc/pki/tls/certs/
2   [root@delphos ~]# cp FTPsecure.crt /etc/pki/tls/certs
```

8.5.2. Configuring vsftpd As an FTP Secure Server

As we already have the certificate, we can change the configuration file (/etc/vsftpd/
vsftpd.conf) accordingly to support FTP Secure. We should add the following lines:

```
1   ssl_enable=YES
2   allow_anon_ssl=YES
```

```
3   ssl_tlsv1=YES
4   ssl_sslv2=NO
5   ssl_sslv3=NO
6   rsa_cert_file=/etc/pki/tls/certs/FTPsecure.crt
7   rsa_private_key_file=/etc/pki/tls/certs/FTPsecure.key
8   ssl_ciphers=HIGH
```

Usually, FTP clients use the passive mode by default. In order for this mode to work with secure connections, we must add the following parameters to the /etc/vsftpd/ vsftpd.conf file.

```
1   pasv_enable=YES
2   pasv_max_port=10100
3   pasv_min_port=10090
```

We explicitly allow passive mode and define a range of ports that will be used for the data connection.
We also have to allow incoming traffic to that range of ports.
In CentOS 6:

```
1   [root@delphos vsftpd]# iptables -I INPUT 2 -p tcp --destination-port
    10090:10100\
2   -j ACCEPT
```

In CentOS 7:

```
1   [root@CentOS7 ftp]# firewall-cmd --add-port=10090-10100/tcp
2   success
```

Now we restart the service and try to establish a secure connection. We should take into account that not all FTP clients support FTP Secure, so we have to use a client that actually can establish a secure connection, for example, Filezilla.

8.5.3. Connecting with Filezilla

As we have to configure a secure connection, we can't simply establish a fast connection, as we did under the section "Connecting from a Windows Client." Instead, we have to access Site Manager (File ➤ Site Manager; see Figures 8-11 and 8-12).

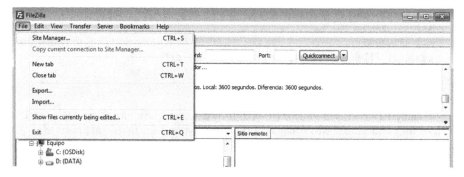

Figure 8-11. *Accessing Site Manager*

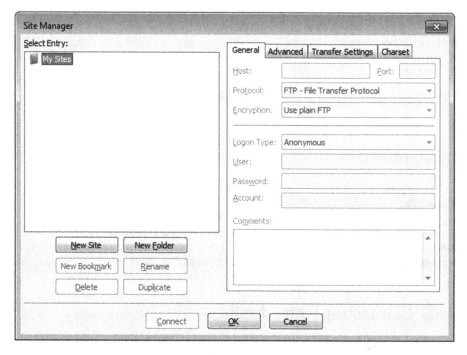

Figure 8-12. *Site Manager*

We click New Site and fulfill the form (Figure 8-13).

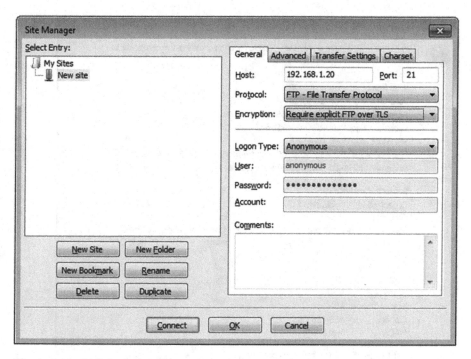

Figure 8-13. *Defining a new site*

When we click Connect, we'll see the following message (Figure 8-14).

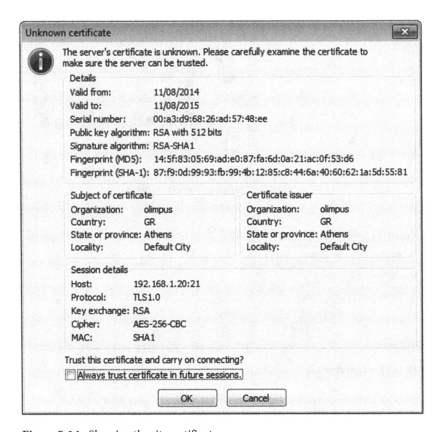

Figure 8-14. *Showing the site certificate*

After accepting the certificate, we can upload and download files the same way we did before (Figure 8-15).

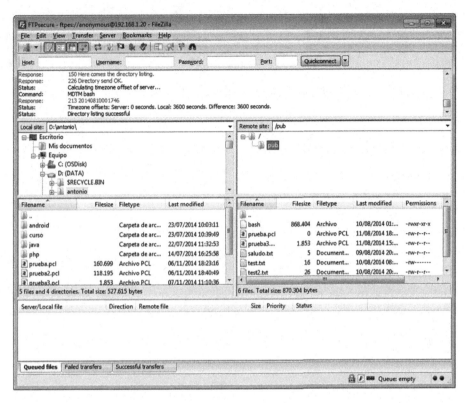

Figure 8-15. *Connected to a secure FTP site*

CHAPTER 9

Mail Server

E-mails have changed completely the way we communicate with one another. Today, someone in New York can send an e-mail to a friend in Moscow in an easy and inexpensive way. If, for example, user achilles@olimpus.local wants to send a message to thor@valhalla.local, he sends this message to his mail server. The mail server will query the DNS server about the address of the mail server for the valhalla.local domain, and it will send the message to that server. Finally, the mail server at valhalla.local sorts the e-mail and moves the message into thor's mailbox.

9.1. Communication Between Local Users

Linux, as well as the other UNIX systems, is a multiuser operating system. Usually, every default installation includes a mail server that makes possible the communication among the different users.

This feature usually works "out of the box," without any further configuration in the server. Only a mail client is required. If there is none, it can be installed. In CentOS, a common client is mail, included in the mailx package.

```
1   [root@delphos ~]# yum install mailx
```

For example, let's suppose we have two users, antonio and jose. If we don't have these two users, we can create them (see Chapter 2). User antonio can send an e-mail to user jose by doing the following:

```
1   [antonio@delphos ~]$ mail -s "Meeting" jose
2   Hi Jose!
3   The boss wants to see us
4   .
5   EOT
```

antonio executes mail and passes as arguments the subject of the message ("Meeting") and the recipient (jose). Then he types the message itself and finishes with a dot (.) and a return.

A. Vazquez, *Learn CentOS Linux Network Services*, DOI 10.1007/978-1-4842-2379-6_9

From this moment on, when the user jose logs in to the system, he can use the same command mail to view his messages.

```
1  [jose@delphos ~]$ mail
2  Heirloom Mail version 12.4 7/29/08.    Type ? for help.
3  "/var/spool/mail/jose": 1 message 1    new
4  >N  1 antonio@delphos.olim    Mon Aug   11 21:55        19/634
   "Meeting"
5  &
```

To read antonio's message, he has only to type "1."

```
1  & 1
2  Message 1:
3  From antonio@delphos.olimpus.local      Mon Aug 11 21:55:55 2014
4  Return-Path: <antonio@delphos.olimpus.local>
5  X-Original-To: jose
6  Delivered-To: jose@delphos.olimpus.local
7  Date: Mon, 11 Aug 2014 21:55:55 -0400
8  To: jose@delphos.olimpus.local
9  Subject: Meeting
10 User-Agent: Heirloom mailx 12.4 7/29/08
11 Content-Type: text/plain; charset=us-ascii
12 From: antonio@delphos.olimpus.local
13 Status: R
14
15 Hi Jose!
16 The boss wants to see us
17
18 &
```

To answer the e-mail, he types "r" + "number_of_message."

```
1  & r 1
2  To: antonio@delphos.olimpus.local jose@delphos.olimpus.local
3  Subject: Re: Meeting
4
5  antonio@delphos.olimpus.local wrote:
6
7  > Hi Jose!
8  > The boss wants to see us
9  OK. I see you at the office then.
10 .
11 EOT
12 &
```

If the user wants to save the message, he can do it with the s or save command. This will create an mbox file in the user's personal folder, in this case, /home/jose/mbox. We can choose which messages we want to save, or we can save them all. Finally, to exit the program, we type "q" or "quit."

Now, antonio will be able to view jose's answer.

```
1   [antonio@delphos ~]$ mail
2   Heirloom Mail version 12.4 7/29/08. Type ? for help.
3   "/var/spool/mail/antonio": 1 message 1 new
4   >N 1 jose@delphos.olimpus Tue Aug 12 00:19 24/885 "Re: Meeting"
5   & 1
6   Message 1:
7   From jose@delphos.olimpus.local Tue Aug 12 00:19:39 2014
8   Return-Path: <jose@delphos.olimpus.local>
9   X-Original-To: antonio@delphos.olimpus.local
10  Delivered-To: antonio@delphos.olimpus.local
11  Date: Tue, 12 Aug 2014 00:19:39 -0400
12  To: jose@delphos.olimpus.local, antonio@delphos.olimpus.local
13  Subject: Re: Meeting
14  User-Agent: Heirloom mailx 12.4 7/29/08
15  Content-Type: text/plain; charset=us-ascii
16  From: jose@delphos.olimpus.local
17  Status: R
18
19  antonio@delphos.olimpus.local wrote:
20
21  > Hi Jose!
22  > The boss wants to see us
23  OK. I see you at he office then
24
25  &
```

9.2. Communication Between Remote Systems

We've just seen how easy it is to send e-mails between local users. But most of the time, we have to communicate with users in remote systems. In such cases, our mail server must be able to determine the identity of the remote mail server and successfully deliver the message.

In order to send mail between remote servers, we have to make some changes to the default configuration.

As I stated before, the mail service is usually installed by default, and it listens for connections on port 25, but only for local connections, as we can see in the following:

```
1   [root@delphos ~]# lsof -i :25
2   COMMAND  PID USER   FD   TYPE DEVICE SIZE/OFF NODE  NAME
3   master  1240 root   12u  IPv4  11027      0t0 TCP   localhost:smtp (LISTEN)
4   master  1240 root   13u  IPv6  11029      0t0 TCP   localhost:smtp (LISTEN)
```

If for some reason the service isn't running, we can start it the usual way.
In CentOS 6:

```
1   [root@delphos ~]# service postfix start
```

In CentOS 7:

```
1   [root@CentOS7 ~]# systemctl start postfix
```

If the service is not installed on the system, it can also be installed.

```
1   [root@delphos ~]# yum install postfix
```

There are two main configuration files in Postfix: /etc/postfix/master.cf and /etc/postfix/main.cf. If we open the /etc/postfix/main.cf file, we'll see a section called RECEIVING MAIL.

```
1    .
2    .
3    .
4    # RECEIVING MAIL
5
6    # The inet_interfaces parameter specifies the network interface
7    # addresses that this mail system receives mail on. By default,
8    # the software claims all active interfaces on the machine. The
9    # parameter also controls delivery of mail to user@[ip.address].
10   #
11   # See also the proxy_interfaces parameter, for network addresses that
12   # are forwarded to us via a proxy or network address translator.
13   #
14   # Note: you need to stop/start Postfix when this parameter changes.
15   #
16   #inet_interfaces = all
17   #inet_interfaces = $myhostname
18   #inet_interfaces = $myhostname, localhost
19   inet_interfaces = localhost
20
21   # Enable IPv4, and IPv6 if supported
22   inet_protocols = all
23   .
24   .
25   .
```

We have to change the line inet_interfaces = localhost to inet_interfaces = all and restart the service.

In CentOS 6:

```
1   [root@delphos ~]# service postfix restart
2   Shutting down postfix:                                    [ OK ]
3   Starting postfix:                                         [ OK ]
```

In CentOS 7:

```
1  [root@CentOS7 ~]# systemctl restart postfix
```

Now the service will listen for remote as well as local connections.

```
1  [root@delphos ~]# lsof -i :25
2  COMMAND  PID USER   FD   TYPE  DEVICE SIZE/OFF NODE NAME
3  master  2902 root   12u  IPv4   19551     0t0  TCP *:smtp (LISTEN)
4  master  2902 root   13u  IPv6   19553     0t0  TCP *:smtp (LISTEN)
```

But, of course, we must also permit this traffic in the firewall of the server.
In CentOS 6:

```
1  [root@delphos ~]# iptables -I INPUT 2 -p tcp --dport 25 -j ACCEPT
```

In CentOS 7:

```
1  [root@CentOS7 ~]# firewall-cmd --add-service=smtp
2  success
```

To check this out, we'll connect from a remote system to send a mail to antonio. We'll do this by manually establishing a connection to port 25 with telnet.

```
1  [root@prometheus ~]# telnet 192.168.1.20 25
2  Trying 192.168.1.20...
3  Connected to 192.168.1.20.
4  Escape character is '^]'.
5  220 delphos.olimpus.local ESMTP Postfix
6  EHLO client
7  250-delphos.olimpus.local
8  250-PIPELINING
9  250-SIZE 10240000
10 250-VRFY
11 250-ETRN
12 250-ENHANCEDSTATUSCODES
13 250-8BITMIME
14 250 DSN
15 MAIL FROM:jose
16 250 2.1.0 Ok
17 RCPT TO:antonio
18 250 2.1.5 Ok
19 DATA
20 354 End data with <CR><LF>.<CR><LF>
21 Hello Antonio. It looks like we have to work together on a new project.
22 .
23 250 2.0.0 Ok: queued as 9BDFB184B
24 QUIT
```

```
25   221 2.0.0 Bye
26   Connection closed by foreign host.
27   [root@prometheus ~]#
```

Now we'll see a brief description of the commands used in the previous example.

- EHLO: Used by the client to introduce itself
- MAIL FROM: Specifies the sender
- RCPT TO: Specifies the recipient
- DATA: Tells the server the user is about to start typing the actual message. The message is ended by hitting the Enter key, typing a dot, and hitting the Enter key again.
- QUIT: Used to exit the connection

When the user antonio checks his mail again, he will see the message.

```
1    [antonio@delphos ~]$ mail
2    Heirloom Mail version 12.4 7/29/08.  Type ? for help.
3    "/var/spool/mail/antonio": 2 messages 1 new
4        1 jose@delphos.olimpus  Tue Aug 12 00:19  25/896    "Re: Meeting"
5    >N  2 jose@delphos.olimpus  Tue Aug 12 01:06  10/402
6    & 2
7    Message     2:
8    From jose@delphos.olimpus.local          Tue Aug 12 01:06:05 2014
9    Return-Path: <jose@delphos.olimpus.local>
10   X-Original-To: antonio
11   Delivered-To: antonio@delphos.olimpus.local
12   Status: R
13
14   Hello Antonio. It looks like we have to work together on a new project.
15
16   &
```

9.3. Mail Service and DNS

In the previous examples, we sent a couple of e-mails using "antonio" as the recipient name, but this is not usual at all. It is far more common to employ usernames such as antonio@olimpus.local, antonio@centos.org, or antonio@redhat.com as recipient names.

When a mail server has to send an e-mail for antonio@olimpus.local, what it needs to do first is determine the mail server of the domain olimpus.local. In order to get that information, it queries a Domain Name System (DNS) server.

In Chapter 4, I described how to set up a DNS server, so from now on, I'll assume that we have a working DNS server with information about the zone olimpus.local.

The zone file could be something similar to the following:

```
1   $ORIGIN .
2   $TTL 172800    ; 2 days
3   olimpus.local           IN SOA   olimpus.local. root.olimpus.local. (
4                                     2014090111 ; serial
5                                     60         ; refresh (1 minute)
6                                     7200       ; retry (2 hours)
7                                     604800     ; expire (1 week)
8                                     172800     ; minimum (2 days)
9                                     )
10                          NS       delphos.olimpus.local.
11                          NS       prometheus.olimpus.local.
12                          MX       10 delphos.olimpus.local.
13                          DNSKEY   256 3 5 (
14                                   AwEAAb386KgB7QrWAWBZ9+uSaHjHmpW+3TpcGkCfh9T4
15                                   Znl6BJVb/kPp6DmfeTRzjFUQSbAGRiI3yvzJ9+iEUhra
16                                   dME=
17                                   ) ; key id = 28332
18                          DNSKEY   257 3 5 (
19                                   AwEAAeGilVrj9hxnmjRY9Yd9SqrBMwtiqKwfSda3wXhn
20                                   d3koFZQzVI129xRVxEhaXpQvcH4tZG724hE/NF/zq6jI
21                                   H2q6OtUOposlWLnRTE4CteOEMP/Q4dSpSzLqjT4+cPrw
22                                   Fyfgvv7q+dHBHJOTiWJjeSffFDFcACPfqY3KIFHNxgD3
23                                   bBwdO/GXgLDACBVoH7qVCNRBosuji24lmxwYu9qOOqX5
24                                   sTF1mhmKpOm4uO2CEVhSnTeXlER4XermehqLhOLlodWl
25                                   R75EmAYc13SvMS9CoFc66eXEOpSLOl7F9eZQ/RHh/Wob
26                                   x74moN1uSwP32fTYhJZr3GXOTey+kfnpvhBIxXRa6nbB
27                                   2jfLsNOPMb4ZEYTAXOICtevRDYptuM3ytakPd3elNfrm
28                                   px9vxkFMye1/18diS/VWXD7RBc8wpbKOaQBMYV94dKhB
29                                   a3F6SV9tbXF7nTadG7kOI+USOkUSfppCjWr+TTwdfvGR
30                                   e/M7XPM1riBv/zUgSp7XzOKWdYT2mQjPR4xl21FcsSwy
31                                   tehCWoS+xGEd3y9AaW7RHAwPjeexMR30458/h1cqQcEs
32                                   QCQlt13uboqjFon3s4iHcHIqtpnBUC/TaonMA39pBTXt
33                                   VFPO+EV3YJBKFgGf1qZRW9aFAU+BHAnaRt2svPmBId7n
34                                   40778a14Jgaco4b64Y6Ij3Mx8as5
35                                   ) ; key id = 9187
36  $ORIGIN olimpus.local.
37  $TTL 21600     ; 6 hours
38  antonio-virtual-machine A        192.168.1.45
39                          TXT      "0020ebba00f97540d54b8850290bf1ecb7"
40  $TTL 172800    ; 2 days
41  aphrodite               A        192.168.1.22
42  delphos                 A        192.168.1.20
43                          AAAA     fe80::20c:29ff:fe78:4cb1
44  dns                     CNAME    delphos
45  $TTL 21600     ; 6 hours
46  G99D02467402cor         A        192.168.1.40
```

```
47                                TXT    "31cd0178098b2d89febcf6fb6c86a02352"
48   $TTL 172800    ; 2 days
49   mail                         CNAME  prometheus
50   neptune                      A      192.168.1.240
51                                AAAA   fe80::20c:29ff:fe78:abcd
52   prometheus                   A      192.168.1.21
53                                AAAA   fe80::20c:29ff:feeb:4443
54   www                          CNAME  delphos
```

For the mail service to work properly, there should be a mail exchange (MX) record defined in the olimpus.local domain that points to the mail server. In this example, the MX record is

```
1   MX      10 delphos.olimpus.local.
```

The number 10 that appears in the record is called the "preference." In this case, we only have an MX record, but we could have many more. By assigning different preferences, we can load-balance the service. The lower the preference value, the more it is prefered by the DNS server. So, for instance, if we had both a really fast server and an old and not so fast server acting as mail servers, we could assign a preference of 10 to the first and one of 20 to the second, so that most of the e-mails would be processed by the fast computer.

Obviously, the client from which we are sending the e-mail should have the correct DNS configuration (see Chapter 4). We can check this with the dig command.

```
1    [root@prometheus ~]# dig -t mx olimpus.local
2
3    ; <<>> DiG 9.7.3-P3-RedHat-9.7.3-8.P3.el6 <<>> -t mx olimpus.local
4    ;; global options: +cmd
5    ;; Got answer:
6    ;; ->>HEADER<<- opcode: QUERY, status: NOERROR, id: 41569
7    ;; flags: qr aa rd ra; QUERY: 1, ANSWER: 1, AUTHORITY: 2, ADDITIONAL: 4
8
9    ;; QUESTION SECTION:
10   ;olimpus.local.                   IN    MX
11
12   ;; ANSWER SECTION:
13   olimpus.local.        172800     IN    MX        10 delphos.
                                                      olimpus.local.
14
15   ;; AUTHORITY SECTION:
16   olimpus.local.        172800     IN    NS        delphos.olimpus.
                                                      local.
17   olimpus.local.        172800     IN    NS        prometheus.
                                                      olimpus.local.
18
19   ;; ADDITIONAL SECTION:
20   delphos.olimpus.local.  172800   IN    A         192.168.1.20
```

```
21   delphos.olimpus.local.   172800    IN    AAAA
     fe80::20c:29ff:fe78:4cb1
22   prometheus.olimpus.local. 172800   IN    A       192.168.1.21
23   prometheus.olimpus.local. 172800   IN    AAAA
     fe80::20c:29ff:feeb:4443
24
25   ;; Query time: 7 msec
26   ;; SERVER: 192.168.1.20#53(192.168.1.20)
27   ;; WHEN: Sat Sep 20 01:15:44 2014
28   ;; MSG SIZE  rcvd: 182
```

Now we should edit the /etc/postfix/main.cf file in the mail server, to specify that it will receive mail from the olimpus.local domain. We do this by editing the mydestination parameter, which has the following value by default:

```
1   mydestination = $myhostname, localhost.$mydomain, localhost
```

We could simply add the olimpus.local domain to the end of the line, but it would be better to add the variable $domain and change its value in the beginning of the same file. The parameter $mydomain is used in many other parameters, and it has this value assigned by default:

```
1   #mydomain = domain.tld
```

So, we have to change both parameters: mydomain and mydestination to this:

```
1   mydomain = olimpus.local
2
3   mydestination = $myhostname, localhost.$mydomain, localhost, $mydomain
```

But before moving on to the next step, we should change one more parameter to specify the server's fully qualified domain name (FQDN).

```
1   myhostname = delphos.olimpus.local
```

We save the changes and restart the service.
In CentOS 6:

```
1   [root@delphos soft]# service postfix restart
2   Shutting down postfix:                        [ OK ]
3   Starting postfix:                             [ OK ]
```

In CentOS 7:

```
1   [root@CentOS7 ~]# systemctl restart postfix
```

Now we perform the same test as that in the "Communication Between Local Users" section, but using FQDNs.

237

```
1   [antonio@delphos ~]$ mail -s "New meeting" jose@olimpus.local
2   Hi Jose!
3
4   It looks like we'll have to assist to a new meeting this Friday.
5   .
6   EOT
```

Now jose will be able to see the message the same way as before.

```
1   [jose@delphos ~]$ mail
2   Heirloom Mail version 12.4 7/29/08.  Type ? for help.
3   "/var/spool/mail/jose": 4 messages 2 new 3 unread
4       1 antonio@delphos.olim  Mon Aug 11 21:55    20/645     "Meeting"
5   U   2 jose@delphos.olimpus   Mon Aug 11 22:05     25/890      "Re:
    Meeting"
6   >N  3 jose@delphos.olimpus    Tue Aug 12 00:19     24/879      "Re:
    Meeting"
7   N   4 antonio@delphos.cent    Tue Aug 12 13:54     20/672      "New
    meeting"
8   & 4
9   Message   4:
10  From antonio@delphos.centos.local    Tue Aug 12 13:54:04 2014
11  Return-Path: <antonio@delphos.centos.local>
12  X-Original-To: jose@olimpus.local
13  Delivered-To: jose@olimpus.local
14  Date: Tue, 12 Aug 2014 13:54:02 -0400
15  To: jose@olimpus.local
16  Subject: New meeting
17  User-Agent: Heirloom mailx 12.4 7/29/08
18  Content-Type: text/plain; charset=us-ascii
19  From: antonio@delphos.centos.local
20  Status: R
21
22  Hi Jose!
23
24  It looks like we'll have to assist to a new meeting this Friday.
25
26  &
```

As we can see, the mail was correctly addressed to jose@olimpus.local, but the sender address was marked as antonio@delphos.centos.local instead of antonio@olimpus.local. To change this behavior, we'll have to edit the parameter myorigin, so that all e-mails sent from this server are tagged with the correct domain.

```
1   myorigin = $mydomain
```

9.4. Routing Mails

So far, we have exchanged e-mails between users in the same server and, of course, the same domain. But this is not at all usual. Actually, most of the time, we'll be sending e-mails to different domains.

In our case, we'll suppose that the user thor@valhalla.local wants to send an email to the user socrates@olimpus.local. We already have a mail server for the domain olimpus.local, but we need another server to manage mail for the valhalla.local domain. We have already seen how to install the operating system (Chapter 1) as well as the postfix package (in the section "Communication Between Remote Systems"). We also need a new DNS zone for the valhalla.local domain (see Chapter 4).

A sample zone file could be the following:

```
1   $TTL 172800
2   valhalla.local.    IN SOA valhalla.local. root.valhalla.local. (
3                      20141203        ; serial
4                      60              ; refresh (1 minute)
5                      7200            ; retry (2 hours)
6                      604800          ; expire (1 week)
7                      17280           ; minimum (2 days)
8                      )
9
10                     NS       odin.valhalla.local.
11                     MX       10 odin.valhalla.local.
12
13  odin               A        192.168.10.21
```

We can check that the new zone is resolving correctly with the dig command.

```
1   [root@prometheus named]# dig @192.168.1.21 axfr valhalla.local
2
3   ; <<>> DiG 9.7.3-P3-RedHat-9.7.3-8.P3.el6 <<>> @192.168.1.21 axfr
    valhalla.local
4   ; (1 server found)
5   ;; global options: +cmd
6   valhalla.local.          172800   IN   SOA   valhalla.local. root.
                                                  valhalla.lo\
7   cal. 20141203 60 7200 604800 17280
8   valhalla.local.          172800   IN   NS    odin.valhalla.local.
9   valhalla.local.          172800   IN   MX    10 odin.valhalla.local.
10  odin.valhalla.local.     172800   IN   A     192.168.10.21
11  valhalla.local.          172800   IN   SOA   valhalla.local. root.
                                                  valhalla.lo\
12  cal. 20141203 60 7200 604800 17280
13  ;; Query time: 1 msec
14  ;; SERVER: 192.168.1.21#53(192.168.1.21)
15  ;; WHEN: Sat Sep 20 14:58:49 2014
16  ;; XFR size: 5 records (messages 1, bytes 160)
```

In the new mail server for valhalla.local, we'll have to do the same changes as before. We open the /etc/postfix/main.cf file and edit the following values:

```
1   inet_interfaces = all
2   mydomain = valhalla.local
3   mydestination = $myhostname, localhost.$mydomain, localhost, $mydomain
4   myhostname = odin.valhalla.local
```

After making these changes and restarting the postfix service, we'll perform a simple test. This test consists of sending a message from user thor@valhalla.local to user loki@valhalla.local.

As the user thor, we type the message and send it with mail.

```
1   [thor@prometheus ~]$ mail -s "Important" loki@valhalla.local
2   Loki, we have to talk.
3   .
4   EOT
```

If everything has worked as expected, loki should be able to see the message from thor.

```
1    [loki@prometheus ~]$ mail
2    Heirloom Mail version 12.4 7/29/08.        Type ? for help.
3    "/var/spool/mail/loki": 1 message 1 new
4    >N  1 thor@odin.valhalla.l    Sat Sep 20 15:21     18/615
     "Important"
5    & 1
6    Message   1:
7    From thor@odin.valhalla.local  Sat Sep 20 15:21:43 2014
8    Return-Path: <thor@odin.valhalla.local>
9    X-Original-To: loki@valhalla.local
10   Delivered-To: loki@valhalla.local
11   Date: Sat, 20 Sep 2014 15:21:41 +0200
12   To: loki@valhalla.local
13   Subject: Important
14   User-Agent: Heirloom mailx 12.4 7/29/08
15   Content-Type: text/plain; charset=us-ascii
16   From: thor@odin.valhalla.local
17   Status: R
18
19   Loki, we have to talk.
20
21   &
```

Now it's time to send mail between the olimpus.local and the valhalla.local domains. First, we must be sure that both mail servers can resolve both domains correctly.

```
1   [root@delphos ~]# cat /etc/resolv.conf
2
3   nameserver 192.168.1.21
4
5   [root@delphos ~]# dig -t mx olimpus.local
6
7   ; <<>> DiG 9.7.3-P3-RedHat-9.7.3-8.P3.el6 <<>> @192.168.1.21 -t mx
    olimpus.local
8   ; (1 server found)
9   ;; global options: +cmd
10  ;; Got answer:
11  ;; ->>HEADER<<- opcode: QUERY, status: NOERROR, id: 64244
12  ;; flags: qr aa rd ra; QUERY: 1, ANSWER: 1, AUTHORITY: 2, ADDITIONAL: 4
13
14  ;; QUESTION SECTION:
15  ;olimpus.local.                  IN      MX
16
17  ;; ANSWER SECTION:
18  olimpus.local.          172800   IN      MX        10 delphos.
                                                        olimpus.local.
19
20  ;; AUTHORITY SECTION:
21  olimpus.local.          172800   IN      NS        prometheus.
                                                        olimpus.local.
22  olimpus.local.          172800   IN      NS        delphos.olimpus.
                                                        local.
23
24  ;; ADDITIONAL SECTION:
25  delphos.olimpus.local.  172800   IN      A         192.168.1.20
26  delphos.olimpus.local.  172800   IN      AAAA
    fe80::20c:29ff:fe78:4cb1
27  prometheus.olimpus.local. 172800 IN      A         192.168.1.21
28  prometheus.olimpus.local. 172800 IN      AAAA
    fe80::20c:29ff:feeb:4443
29
30  ;; Query time: 2 msec
31  ;; SERVER: 192.168.1.21#53(192.168.1.21)
32  ;; WHEN: Wed Aug 13 07:33:18 2014
33  ;; MSG SIZE   rcvd: 182
34
35  [root@delphos ~]# dig -t mx valhalla.local
36
37  ; <<>> DiG 9.7.3-P3-RedHat-9.7.3-8.P3.el6 <<>> -t mx valhalla.local
38  ;; global options: +cmd
39  ;; Got answer:
40  ;; ->>HEADER<<- opcode: QUERY, status: NOERROR, id: 27902
41  ;; flags: qr aa rd ra; QUERY: 1, ANSWER: 1, AUTHORITY: 1, ADDITIONAL: 1
42
```

```
43   ;; QUESTION SECTMail ServerRouting mailsION:
44   ;valhalla.local.                 IN      MX
45
46   ;; ANSWER SECTION:
47   valhalla.local.        172800    IN      MX         10 odin.valhalla.
                                                         local.
48
49   ;; AUTHORITY SECTION:
50   valhalla.local.        172800    IN      NS         odin.valhalla.
                                                         local.
51
52   ;; ADDITIONAL SECTION:
53   odin.valhalla.local.   172800    IN      A          192.168.10.21
54
55   ;; Query time: 2 msec
56   ;; SERVER: 192.168.1.21#53(192.168.1.21)
57   ;; WHEN: Wed Aug 13 07:33:55 2014
58   ;; MSG SIZE  rcvd: 83
59
60   [root@prometheus ~]# cat /etc/resolv.conf
61   nameserver 192.168.1.21
62
63   [root@prometheus ~]# dig -t mx olimpus.local
64
65   ; <<>> DiG 9.7.3-P3-RedHat-9.7.3-8.P3.el6 <<>> -t mx olimpus.local
66   ;; global options: +cmd
67   ;; Got answer:
68   ;; ->>HEADER<<- opcode: QUERY, status: NOERROR, id: 7692
69   ;; flags: qr aa rd ra; QUERY: 1, ANSWER: 1, AUTHORITY: 2, ADDITIONAL: 4
70
71   ;; QUESTION SECTION:
72   ;olimpus.local.                   IN      MX
73
74   ;; ANSWER SECTION:
75   olimpus.local.         172800    IN      MX         10 delphos.
     olimpus.local.
76
77   ;; AUTHORITY SECTION:
78   olimpus.local.         172800    IN      NS         prometheus.olimpus.
     local.
79   olimpus.local.         172800    IN      NS         delphos.olimpus.
     local.
80
81   ;; ADDITIONAL SECTION:
82   delphos.olimpus.local. 172800    IN      A          192.168.1.20
83   delphos.olimpus.local. 172800    IN      AAAA
     fe80::20c:29ff:fe78:4cb1
84   prometheus.olimpus.local. 172800 IN      A          192.168.1.21
```

```
85   prometheus.olimpus.local. 172800 IN      AAAA
     fe80::20c:29ff:feeb:4443
86
87   ;; Query time: 1 msec
88   ;; SERVER: 192.168.1.20#53(192.168.1.20)
89   ;; WHEN: Sat Sep 20 15:51:15 2014
90   ;; MSG SIZE  rcvd: 182
91
92   [root@prometheus ~]# dig -t mx valhalla.local
93
94   ; <<>> DiG 9.7.3-P3-RedHat-9.7.3-8.P3.el6 <<>> -t mx valhalla.local
95   ;; global options: +cmd
96   ;; Got answer:
97   ;; ->>HEADER<<- opcode: QUERY, status: NOERROR, id: 17313
98   ;; flags: qr aa rd ra; QUERY: 1, ANSWER: 1, AUTHORITY: 1, ADDITIONAL: 1
99
100  ;; QUESTION SECTION:
101  ;valhalla.local. IN MX
102
103  ;; ANSWER SECTION:
104  valhalla.local. 172800 IN MX 10 odin.valhalla.local.
105
106  ;; AUTHORITY SECTION:
107  valhalla.local. 172800 IN NS odin.valhalla.local.
108
109  ;; ADDITIONAL SECTION:
110  odin.valhalla.local. 172800 IN A 192.168.10.21
111
112  ;; Query time: 1 msec
113  ;; SERVER: 192.168.1.21#53(192.168.1.21)
114  ;; WHEN: Sat Sep 20 15:52:17 2014
115  ;; MSG SIZE  rcvd: 83
116
117  [root@prometheus ~]#
```

Of course, in both servers, the Simple Mail Transfer Protocol (SMTP) port should be open. In CentOS 6:

```
1   [root@delphos ~]# iptables -I INPUT 2 -p tcp --dport 25 -j ACCEPT
2
3   [root@prometheus ~]# iptables -I INPUT 2 -p tcp --dport 25 -j ACCEPT
```

In CentOS 7:

```
1   [root@CentOS7 ~]# firewall-cmd --add-service=smtp
2   success
```

243

Now we are ready to send the e-mail.

```
1  [socrates@delphos ~]$ mail -s "Help" thor@valhalla.local
2  Hello Thor.
3  We need your help.
4  .
5  EOT
```

And thor will get the message.

```
1   [thor@prometheus ~]$ mail
2   Heirloom Mail version 12.4 7/29/08.     Type ? for help.
3   "/var/spool/mail/thor": 4 messages 4 new
4   >N  1 socrates@olimpus.loc      Sat Sep 20 16:27          22/804
    "Help"
5   & 1
6   Message    1:
7   From socrates@olimpus.local  Sat Sep 20 16:27:18 2014
8   Return-Path: <socrates@olimpus.local>
9   X-Original-To: thor@valhalla.local
10  Delivered-To: thor@valhalla.local
11  Date: Wed, 13 Aug 2014 08:00:37 -0400
12  To: thor@valhalla.local
13  Subject: Help
14  User-Agent: Heirloom mailx 12.4 7/29/08
15  Content-Type: text/plain; charset=us-ascii
16  From: socrates@olimpus.local
17  Status: R
18
19  Hello Thor.
20  We need your help.
21
22  &
```

And he will be able to answer, if he wants to.

```
1   & r 1
2   To: socrates@olimpus.local thor@valhalla.local
3   Subject: Re: Help
4
5   socrates@olimpus.local wrote:
6
7   > Hello Thor.
8   > We need your help.
9   No problem. I'll be glad to help.
10  .
11  EOT
12  &
```

socrates will be happy to see thor's answer.

```
1    [socrates@delphos ~]$ mail
2    Heirloom Mail version 12.4 7/29/08.      Type ? for help.
3    "/var/spool/mail/socrates": 3 messages 3 new
4    >N   1 thor@odin.valhalla.l     Wed Aug 13 09:11      27/1042       "Re:
     Help"
5    & 1
6    Message  1:
7    From thor@odin.valhalla.local  Wed Aug 13 09:11:21 2014
8    Return-Path: <thor@odin.valhalla.local>
9    X-Original-To: socrates@olimpus.local
10   Delivered-To: socrates@olimpus.local
11   Date: Sat, 20 Sep 2014 17:17:38 +0200
12   To: thor@valhalla.local, socrates@olimpus.local
13   Subject: Re: Help
14   User-Agent: Heirloom mailx 12.4 7/29/08
15   Content-Type: text/plain; charset=us-ascii
16   From: thor@odin.valhalla.local
17   Status: R
18
19   socrates@olimpus.local wrote:
20
21   > Hello Thor.
22   > We need your help.
23   No problem. I'll be glad to help.
24
25   &
```

9.5. Using a Mail Client

So far, we've been sending and receiving mail from a console in the server. But most people don't do this. Instead, they have a mail client in their computers, such as Microsoft Outlook or Mozilla Firebird, that handles e-mail.

For this, the mail client establishes a connection with the mail server by using a protocol such as POP3 or IMAP. So, obviously, we have to install a POP3/IMAP server in our mail server.

An open source IMAP/POP3 server included in most Linux/UNIX systems is dovecot. We'll install it the usual way, as follows:

```
1    [root@delphos named]# yum install dovecot
```

Right after the installation, we'll start the service and activate it every time the system boots.

In CentOS 6:

```
1  [root@delphos ~]# service dovecot start
2  Starting Dovecot Imap:                                    [ OK ]
3  [root@delphos ~]# chkconfig dovecot on
4  [root@delphos ~]# chkconfig --list dovecot
5  dovecot          0:off   1:off   2:on   3:on   4:on   5:on   6:off
6  [root@delphos ~]#
```

In CentOS 7:

```
1  [root@CentOS7 ~]# systemctl start dovecot
2  [root@CentOS7 ~]# systemctl enable dovecot
3  ln -s '/usr/lib/systemd/system/dovecot.service' '/etc/systemd/system/
   multi-user.\
4  target.wants/dovecot.service'
```

To configure the server, we'll edit the main configuration file, /etc/dovecot/
dovecot.conf. By default, the server listens for connections by using any of these three
protocols: IMAP, POP3, and LMTP. So, we don't have to change this value. In addition to
this file, we can see that there are many more configuration files in the /etc/dovecot/
conf.d/ folder. One of these additional files is 10-auth.conf, which we'll have to
modify to allow plain-text authentication. The exact parameter we need to change is the
following:

```
1  disable_plaintext_auth = no
```

If we're using CentOS 7, we also have to edit the /etc/dovecot/conf.d/10-ssl.conf
file. In this file, we'll see the following line:

```
1  ssl = required
```

In order to allow plain-text authentication from another computer, we'll have to
change it to the following:

```
1  ssl = yes
```

We must also indicate the location of the spool directory and the user's mailboxes.
This information is included in the /etc/dovecot/conf.d/10-mail.conf file. We'll add
the following line:

```
1  mail_location = mbox:~/mbox:INBOX=/var/mail/%u
```

We also have to change another parameter in the /etc/dovecot/conf.d/10-mail.
conf file.

```
1  mail_access_groups = mail
```

9.5.1. POP3

While we access the mailbox through POP3, we have to block the access to other processes. We can configure this in the 20-pop3.conf file by changing the following parameter:

```
1   # Keep the mailbox locked for the entire POP3 session.
2   pop3_lock_session = yes
```

And we open the port in the firewall.
In CentOS 6:

```
1   [root@delphos ~]# iptables -I INPUT 2 -p tcp --dport 110 -j ACCEPT
```

In CentOS 7:

In CentOS 7, there isn't a predefined XML file in /usr/lib/firewalld/services (see Chapter 10), so we'll have to open TCP port 110.

```
1   [root@CentOS7 ~]# firewall-cmd --add-port=110/tcp
2   success
```

After all these changes, we restart the service and test the connection by telnetting port 110 in the server.

```
1   [root@prometheus ~]# telnet 192.168.1.20 110
2   Trying 192.168.1.20...
3   Connected to 192.168.1.20.
4   Escape character is '^]'.
5   +OK Dovecot ready.
```

Once connected, we log in.

```
1   USER socrates
2   +OK
3   PASS socrates
4   +OK Logged in.
```

From now on, we can list the e-mails with the LIST command.

```
1   LIST
2   +OK 3 messages:
3   1 1010
4   2 1010
5   3 763
6   .
```

And we can open any of the e-mails with RETR.

```
1   RETR 1
2   +OK 1010 octets
3   Return-Path: <thor@odin.valhalla.local>
4   X-Original-To: socrates@olimpus.local
5   Delivered-To: socrates@olimpus.local
6   Received: from odin.valhalla.local (prometheus.olimpus.local
    [192.168.1.21])
7           by delphos.centos.local (Postfix) with ESMTP id 3B2521301
8           for <socrates@olimpus.local>; Wed, 13 Aug 2014 09:11:21 -0400
    (EDT)
9   Received: by odin.valhalla.local (Postfix, from userid 503)
10          id 5888742F56; Sat, 20 Sep 2014 17:17:38 +0200 (CEST)
11  Date: Sat, 20 Sep 2014 17:17:38 +0200
12  To: thor@valhalla.local, socrates@olimpus.local
13  Subject: Re: Help
14  References: <20140813120037.D2DA61876@delphos.centos.local>
15  In-Reply-To: <20140813120037.D2DA61876@delphos.centos.local>
16  User-Agent: Heirloom mailx 12.4 7/29/08
17  MIME-Version: 1.0
18  Content-Type: text/plain; charset=us-ascii
19  Content-Transfer-Encoding: 7bit
20  Message-Id: <20140920151738.5888742F56@odin.valhalla.local>
21  From: thor@odin.valhalla.local
22
23  socrates@olimpus.local wrote:
24
25  > Hello Thor.
26  > We need your help.
27  No problem. I'll be glad to help.
28  .
```

When we're done, we can close the connection with QUIT.

```
1   QUIT
2   +OK Logging out.
3   Connection closed by foreign host.
```

As the POP3 server is working perfectly, users can now read their e-mail by using a mail client such as Mozilla Thunderbird. Let's see how to do it.

In the workstation (Linux, Windows, or Mac), we make sure that we can resolve the address of the mail server. We can check this in Windows with the nslookup command (Figure 9-1).

```
C:\Windows\system32\cmd.exe - nslookup                        [ _ ][ □ ][ x ]

C:\Users\Antonio>nslookup
Servidor predeterminado:  prometheus.olimpus.local
Address:  192.168.1.21

> set type=MX
> olimpus.local
Servidor:  prometheus.olimpus.local
Address:  192.168.1.21

olimpus.local    MX preference = 10, mail exchanger = delphos.olimpus.local
olimpus.local    nameserver = delphos.olimpus.local
olimpus.local    nameserver = prometheus.olimpus.local
delphos.olimpus.local    internet address = 192.168.1.20
delphos.olimpus.local    AAAA IPv6 address = fe80::20c:29ff:fe78:4cb1
prometheus.olimpus.local    internet address = 192.168.1.21
prometheus.olimpus.local    AAAA IPv6 address = fe80::20c:29ff:feeb:4443
> valhalla.local
Servidor:  prometheus.olimpus.local
Address:  192.168.1.21

valhalla.local    MX preference = 10, mail exchanger = odin.valhalla.local
valhalla.local    nameserver = odin.valhalla.local
odin.valhalla.local    internet address = 192.168.1.21
>
```

Figure 9-1. nslookup

If name resolution fails, we'll have to check the network configuration (see Chapter 3).

The mail client we'll use is Mozilla Thunderbird. We can download it from www.mozilla.org/thunderbird.

The way to install it is pretty easy, and choosing the default values should be enough to get the software installed.

After the installation, if we launch Thunderbird, we'll see the screen shown in Figure 9-2.

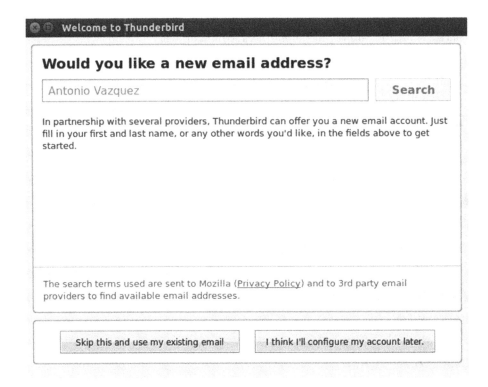

Figure 9-2. Launching Thunderbird

Thunderbird gives us the possibility of receiving a new e-mail account, but for the moment, this is not what we want, so we choose the option Skip this and use my existing email account. In the new window, we enter the necessary data into the appropriate boxes (Figure 9-3).

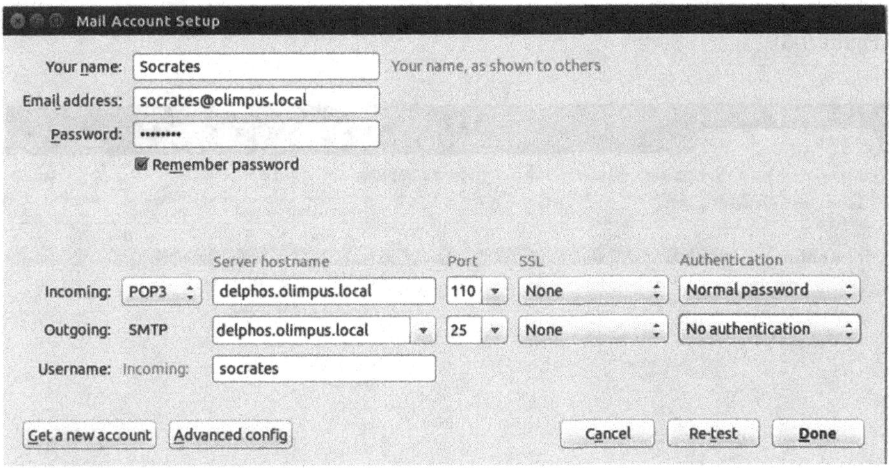

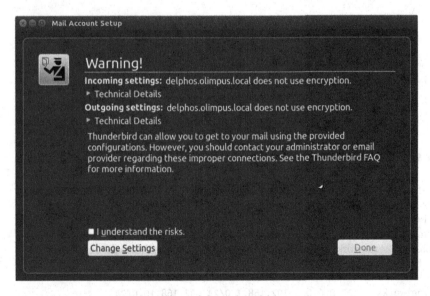

Figure 9-3. Configuring a POP3 account

As we're not using TLS, we receive a warning about it (Figure 9-4). For the moment, we acknowledge and accept the risks.

Figure 9-4. *Warning! The traffic won't be ciphered*

Now the user socrates can download his messages by clicking Get Messages (Figure 9-5).

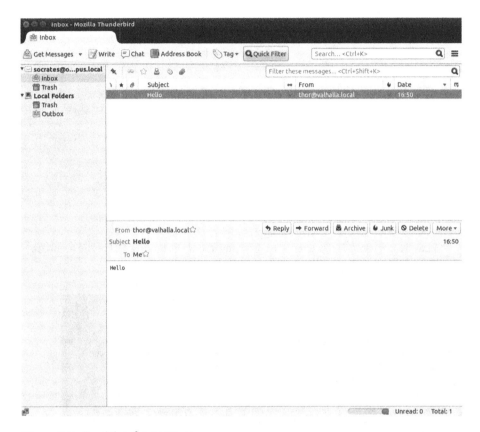

Figure 9-5. *Receiving the messages*

If the client computer is in the same network as the mail server, everything should work as expected; otherwise, we should edit the parameter mynetworks in the /etc/ postfix/main.cf file to include the network the client computer belongs to. For example, if the mail server has the IP address 192.168.1.20 and the client computer is in the 192.168.10.0/24 network, we should have a parameter such as this in the /etc/postfix/ main.cf file:

```
1    mynetworks = 127.0.0.0/8 192.168.1.0/24 192.168.10.0/24
```

9.5.2. IMAP

We have seen how to get incoming mail through POP3. But, by default, when we receive mail from the server, the messages are actually copied to the client and deleted from the server. So, if we try to connect to the server from another computer, the mailbox will be empty until a new e-mail arrives.

This is not what happens when we use IMAP. Conversely, in this case, messages are kept in the server, and they are synchronized with the client.

We already saw previously in this section that dovecot can act both as a POP3 server and as an IMAP server. So, we don't have to change anything in the main configuration, although we will have to allow traffic to port 143 in the firewall.

In CentOS 6:

```
1    [root@delphos ~]# iptables -I INPUT 2 -p tcp --dport 143 -j ACCEPT
```

In CentOS 7:

```
1    [root@CentOS7 ~]# firewall-cmd --add-port=143/tcp
2    success
```

Anyway, before configuring the client, we can test the server by establishing a connection with telnet.

First, we open a telnet session to port 143.

```
1    [root@delphos ~]# telnet localhost 143
2    Trying ::1...
3    Connected to localhost.
4    Escape character is '^]'.
5    * OK [CAPABILITY IMAP4rev1 LITERAL+ SASL-IR LOGIN-REFERRALS ID ENABLE
     IDLE START\
6    TLS AUTH=PLAIN] Dovecot ready.
```

Next, we identify ourselves by typing ". LOGIN username password."

```
1    . LOGIN plato plato
2    . OK [CAPABILITY IMAP4rev1 LITERAL+ SASL-IR LOGIN-REFERRALS ID ENABLE
     IDLE SORT \
3    SORT=DISPLAY THREAD=REFERENCES THREAD=REFS MULTIAPPEND UNSELECT CHILDREN
     NAMESPA\
4    CE UIDPLUS LIST-EXTENDED I18NLEVEL=1 CONDSTORE QRESYNC ESEARCH ESORT
     SEARCHRES W\
5    ITHIN CONTEXT=SEARCH LIST-STATUS]        Logged in
```

We list the folders with LIST.

```
1   . LIST "" "*"
2   * LIST (\NoInferiors \UnMarked) "/" "Trash"
3   * LIST (\NoInferiors \Marked) "/" "INBOX"
4   . OK List completed.
```

Then we examine the INBOX folder to see whether there are any messages.

```
1   . EXAMINE INBOX
2   * FLAGS (\Answered \Flagged \Deleted \Seen \Draft)
3   * OK [PERMANENTFLAGS ()] Read-only mailbox.
4   * 1 EXISTS
5   * 0 RECENT
6   * OK [UIDVALIDITY 1407985588] UIDs valid
7   * OK [UIDNEXT 2] Predicted next UID
8   * OK [HIGHESTMODSEQ 1] Highest
9   . OK [READ-ONLY] Select completed.
```

As there is a message, we can see its content with FETCH.

```
1   . FETCH 1 BODY[]
2   * 1 FETCH (BODY[] {671}
3   Return-Path: <socrates@olimpus.local>
4   X-Original-To: plato@olimpus.local
5   Delivered-To: plato@olimpus.local
6   Received: from [192.168.10.100] (unknown [192.168.10.100])
7           by delphos.centos.local (Postfix) with ESMTP id 508A318B3
8           for <plato@olimpus.local>; Wed, 13 Aug 2014 23:15:16 -0400
            (EDT)
9   Message-ID: <5487191A.9070502@olimpus.local>
10  Date: Tue, 09 Dec 2014 16:45:30 +0100
11  From: Socrates <socrates@olimpus.local>
12  User-Agent: Mozilla/5.0 (Windows NT 6.1; rv:31.0) Gecko/20100101
    Thunderbird/31.\
13  3.0
14  MIME-Version: 1.0
15  To: plato@olimpus.local
16  Subject: Test
17  Content-Type: text/plain; charset=utf-8; format=flowed
18  Content-Transfer-Encoding: 7bit
19
20  Hello Plato
21  )
22  . OK Fetch completed.
```

Finally, we exit with LOGOUT.

```
1    . LOGOUT
2    * BYE Logging out
3    . OK Logout completed.
4    Connection closed by foreign host.
```

Now Plato can configure Thunderbird to access its mailbox from his home computer through IMAP. This is what he (we) will have to do.

After launching Thunderbird, we must click the Skip this and use my existing email box (Figure 9-6) and complete the form with the user's data (Figure 9-7).

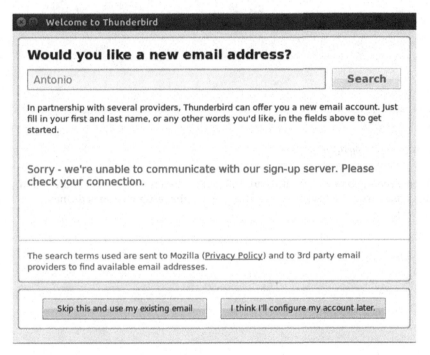

Figure 9-6. Configuring an IMAP account

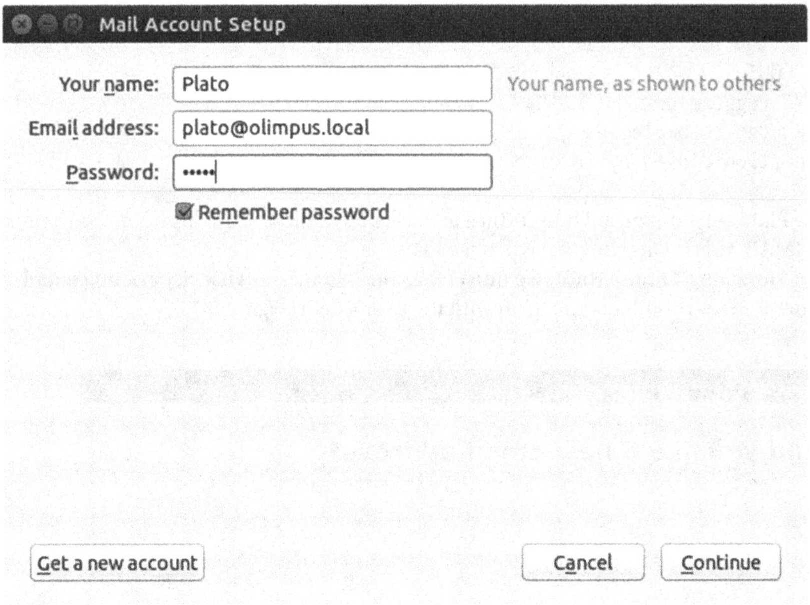

Figure 9-7. Fulfilling the form

There seems to be an issue with autoconfiguration in some versions of Thunderbird, so if that is the case, we'll have to use the IP address of the server instead of the name (Figure 9-8).

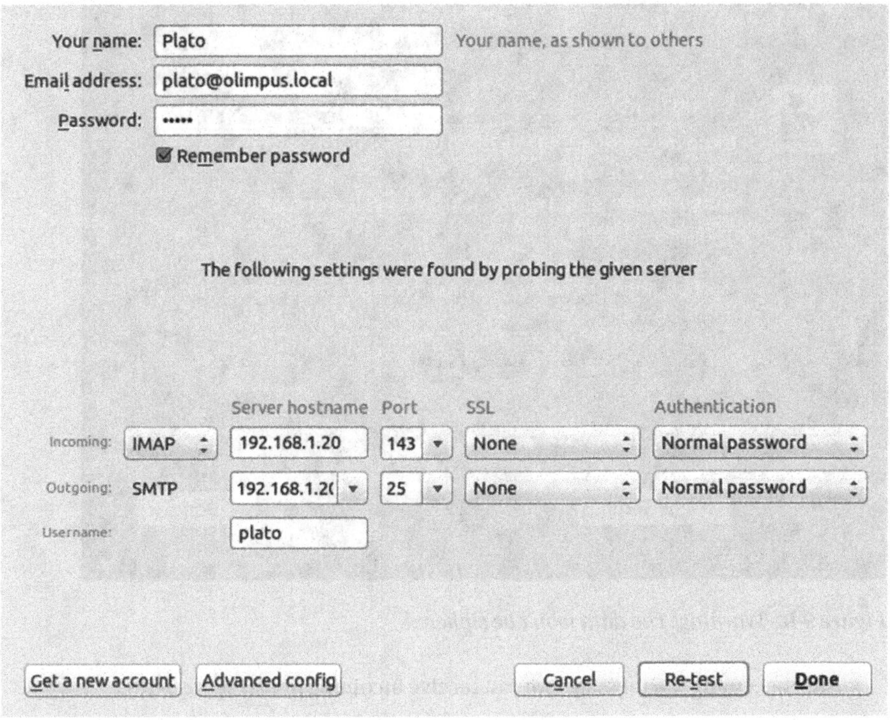

		Server hostname	Port	SSL	Authentication
Incoming:	IMAP ⇕	192.168.1.20	143 ▾	None ⇕	Normal password ⇕
Outgoing:	SMTP	192.168.1.2(▾	25 ▾	None ⇕	Normal password ⇕
Username:		plato			

Your name: Plato — Your name, as shown to others
Email address: plato@olimpus.local
Password: •••••
☑ Remember password

The following settings were found by probing the given server

[Get a new account] [Advanced config]   [Cancel] [Re-test] [Done]

Figure 9-8. Configuring the mail account

The program warns the user that the connection has not been ciphered (Figure 9-9).

Figure 9-9. Warning! The data won't be ciphered

After accepting the message, we can receive incoming mail (Figure 9-10).

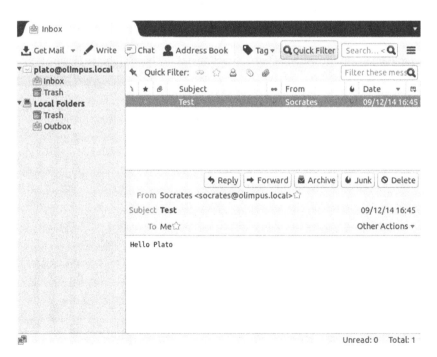

Figure 9-10. Receiving mail through IMAP

9.6. SMTP Authentication

So far, we have been able to connect to the SMTP server and send e-mails without any authentication. By default, the STMP server allows or denies the ability to send e-mail, based on the network address. This is not advisable at all, as someone might use the mail server for a harmful purpose, such as sending spam.

To avoid this, we can use authentication. Postfix does not provide authentication natively, but it can be configured together with other software packages, such as cyrus or dovecot, to provide authentication. For our purposes here, we'll use dovecot.

In order to find out if our version of Postfix supports a SASL (Simple Authentication and Security Layer), we can execute the following command:

```
1   [root@delphos ~]# postconf -a
2   cyrus
3   dovecot
```

The result means that we can configure SASL with cyrus or dovecot.

We have to open the /etc/dovecot/conf.d/10-master.conf file and edit the section service_auth like this:

```
1   service auth {
2     # auth_socket_path points to this userdb socket by default. It's
      typically
3     # used by dovecot-lda, doveadm, possibly imap process, etc. Its
      default
4     # permissions make it readable only by root, but you may need to
      relax these
5     # permissions. Users that have access to this socket are able to get
      a list
6     # of all usernames and get results of everyone's userdb lookups.
7     #unix_listener auth-userdb {
8     #   mode = 0666
9     #   user = postfix
10    #   group = postfix
11    #}
12
13    # Postfix smtp-auth
14    unix_listener /var/spool/postfix/private/auth {
15      mode = 0666
16      user = postfix
17      group = postfix
18    }
19
20
21    # Auth process is run as this user.
22    #user = $default_internal_user
23  }
```

In addition, to make authentication work with Outlook Express and Windows mail, we must also edit the /etc/dovecot/conf.d/10-auth.conf file and change the auth_ mechanisms parameter.

```
1  auth_mechanisms = plain login
```

After making the changes, we just have to restart the dovecot service.
Now we have to make some changes in Postfix too. We open the /etc/postfix/main.cf file and add the following lines:

```
1  smtpd_sasl_type = dovecot
2  smtpd_sasl_path = private/auth
3  smtpd_sasl_auth_enable = yes
```

There is also another parameter that we should add, to make sure authentication works with any mail client. Otherwise, certain programs, such as Outlook Express, might not work.

```
1  broken_sasl_auth_clients = yes
```

After restarting the Postfix server, we can establish a Telnet connection to check whether the authentication is working.

```
1   [root@prometheus ~]# telnet delphos.olimpus.local 25
2   Trying 192.168.1.20...
3   Connected to delphos.olimpus.local.
4   Escape character is '^]'.
5   220 delphos.centos.local ESMTP Postfix
6   EHLO prometheus.olimpus.local
7   250-delphos.centos.local
8   250-PIPELINING
9   250-SIZE 10240000
10  250-VRFY
11  250-ETRN
12  250-AUTH PLAIN LOGIN
13  250-ENHANCEDSTATUSCODES
14  250-8BITMIME
15  250 DSN
```

As we can see in the line 250-AUTH PLAIN LOGIN, the server now supports authentication.
We can try to actually authenticate ourselves through the server connection. To perform a plain authentication, we have to code the username and the password in base64. For example, if we want to authenticate the user "plato" with password "plato," we have to code both terms first.

Probably the easiest way to do this is by using Python. Using the username and password in the preceding example, we can get the base64 string this way:

```
1  [root@delphos ~]# python -c 'import base64 ; print base64.
   b64encode("\000plato\0\
2  00plato")'
3  AHBsYXRvAHBsYXRv
```

In the telnet session we opened previously, we have to type the following:

```
1  AUTH PLAIN AHBsYXRvAHBsYXRv
```

If everything works well, we'll see the following answer from the server:

```
1  235 2.7.0 Authentication successful
```

We can keep sending e-mail as usual.

```
1   MAIL FROM:plato@olimpus.local
2   250 2.1.0 Ok
3   RCPT TO:socrates@olimpus.local
4   250 2.1.5 Ok
5   DATA
6   354 End data with <CR><LF>.<CR><LF>
7   From:plato@olimpus.local
8   Subject:Authentication test
9   We had to authenticate to send this email
10  .
11  250 2.0.0 Ok: queued as 7B03C18B9
12  QUIT
13  221 2.0.0 Bye
14  Connection closed by foreign host.
```

As of now, the server supports authentication, but it also accepts e-mail from unauthenticated clients whose network addresses are included in the mynetworks parameter of the main configuration file /etc/postfix/main.cf. To avoid this, we change this parameter back.

```
1  mynetworks = 127.0.0.0/8
```

We also have to add the following new parameters, to restrict the ability to send mail only to authenticated users:

```
1  smtpd_client_restrictions = permit_sasl_authenticated, reject_unknown_
   client_hos\
2  tname, reject
3  smtpd_sender_restrictions = permit_sasl_authenticated, reject
```

261

This way, we allow authenticated users to send e-mail (permit_sasl_ authenticated), and we reject mail from clients whose hostname is not known (reject_ unknown_client_hostname).

■ **Note** This configuration might be too restrictive, however, because now, it will reject messages from other mail servers, such as the valhalla.local mail server. So, perhaps after verifying that SMTP authentication is working as expected, you should eliminate the reject parameter, in order not to have it interfere with the rest of the exercises in the book.

Now anybody wanting to send mail from our server will have to be authenticated. We can check this with Thunderbird. First, we have to click the View settings for this account link (Figure 9-11).

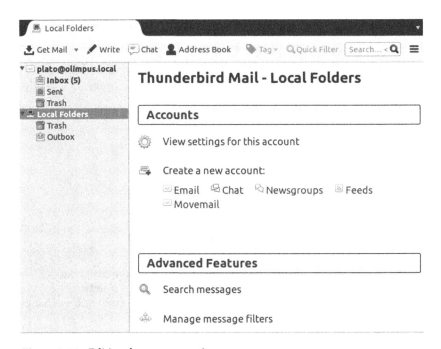

Figure 9-11. Editing the account settings

Next, we edit the account settings (Figure 9-12) and modify the authentication method to "No authentication" (Figure 9-13).

plato@olimpus.local
Server Settings
Copies & Folders
Composition & Addressing
Junk Settings
Synchronization & Storage
Return Receipts
Security
Local Folders
Junk Settings
Disk Space
Outgoing Server (SMTP)
Account Actions
Outgoing Server (SMTP) Settings
When managing your identities you can use a server from this list by selecting it as the Outgoing Server (SMTP), or you can use the default server from this list by selecting "Use Default Server".
plato - 192.168.1.20 (Default)
Add...
Edit...
Remove
Set Default
Description: <not specified>
Server Name: 192.168.1.20
Port: 25
User Name: plato
Authentication method: No authentication
Connection Security: None
Cancel
OK

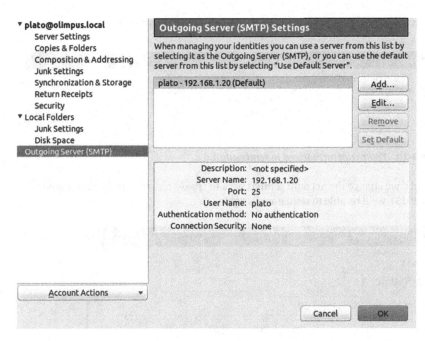

Figure 9-12. Outgoing mail settings

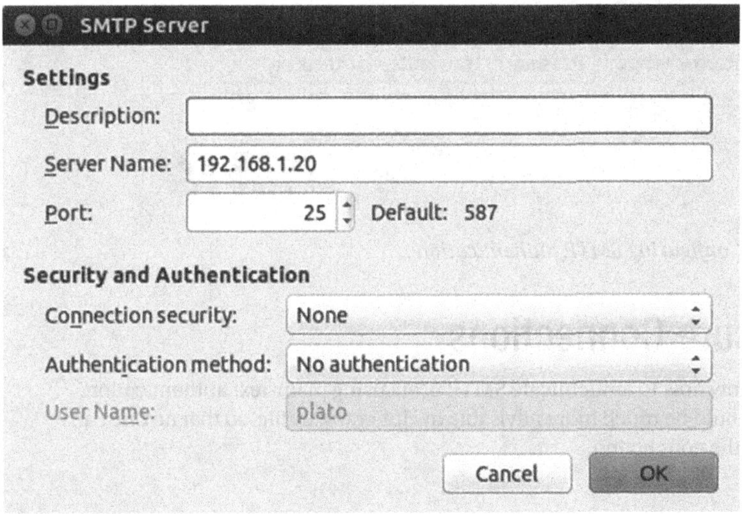

SMTP Server
Settings
Description:
Server Name: 192.168.1.20
Port: 25 Default: 587
Security and Authentication
Connection security: None
Authentication method: No authentication
User Name: plato
Cancel
OK

Figure 9-13. Selecting no authentication

If now we try to send an e-mail, we'll receive an error (Figure 9-14).

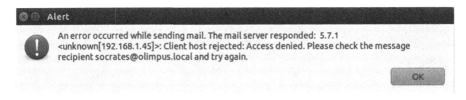

Figure 9-14. You're not authorized to send e-mail

And if we change the account settings back to "Password, transmitted insecurely" (Figure 9-15), we'll be able to send e-mails again.

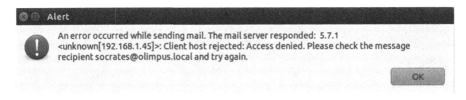

Figure 9-15. Configuring SMTP authentication

9.7. Secure Connections

We already know how to authenticate SMTP users using plain-text authentication. Of course, it would be much more advisable to cipher the traffic, so that no one can eavesdrop on the connection.

9.7.1. Securing the SMTP Connection

First of all, we have to generate the certificates. We have seen this process in Chapters 7 and 8, so here I'll only show the necessary commands, without further explanation.

```
1    [root@delphos ~]# openssl genrsa -des3 -out MAILsecure.key
2    .
3    .
4    .
5    [root@delphos ~]# openssl req -new -key MAILsecure.key -out MAILsecure.
     csr
6    .
7    .
8    .
9    [root@delphos ~]# cp MAILsecure.key MAILsecure.key.orig
10   [root@delphos ~]# openssl rsa -in MAILsecure.key.orig -out MAILsecure.
     key
11   .
12   .
13   .
14   [root@delphos ~]# openssl x509 -req -days 365 -in MAILsecure.csr
     -signkey MAILse\
15   cure.key -out MAILsecure.crt
```

We copy the certificate and the key file to the default location.

```
1    [root@delphos ~]# cp MAILsecure.crt /etc/postfix/
2    [root@delphos ~]# cp MAILsecure.key /etc/postfix/
```

Now we have to add the following parameters to the /etc/postfix/main.cf file.

```
1    smtpd_use_tls = yes
2    smtpd_tls_cert_file = /etc/postfix/MAILsecure.crt
3    smtpd_tls_key_file = /etc/postfix/MAILsecure.key
```

Now we restart the service.
In CentOS 6:

```
1    [root@delphos ~]# service postfix restart
2    Shutting down postfix:                           [ OK ]
3    Starting postfix:                                [ OK ]
```

In CentOS 7:

```
1    [root@CentOS7 ~]# systemctl restart postfix
```

Next, in Thunderbird (or whatever mail client you're using), we change the SMTP settings. We can see the original settings in Figure 9-16.

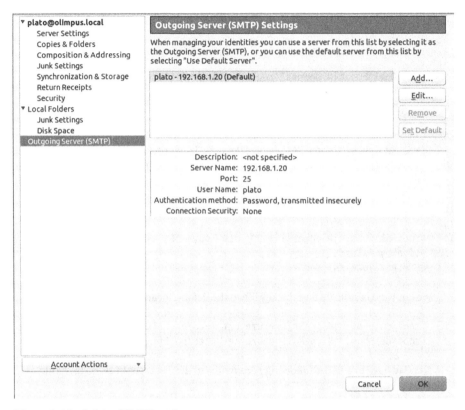

Figure 9-16. *Original SMTP settings*

We should change the setting to something similar to what is shown in Figure 9-17.

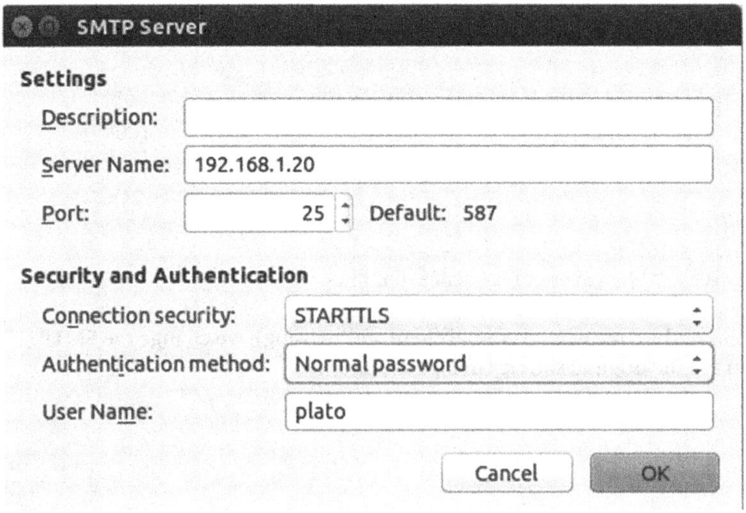

Figure 9-17. *New SMTP settings*

We accept the changes and try to send an e-mail (Figure 9-18).

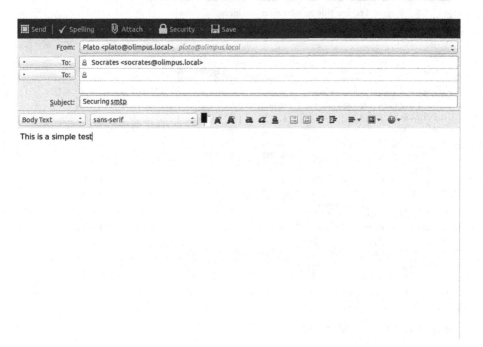

Figure 9-18. *New SMTP settings*

The first time we send an e-mail after changing the settings, we receive the following warning (Figure 9-19).

Figure 9-19. *New SMTP settings*

We confirm the security exception, and the message is sent.

9.7.2. IMAPS

In addition to using a secure connection in order to send e-mail, we could—and should—use a secure connection to receive our mail.

In this case, it is not necessary to create the certificates, as the default installation already creates in /etc/pki/dovecot/certs/dovecot.pem a sample certificate that we can use. Of course, we can create our custom certificate if we want to. In order to do this, we only have to create a certificate as we did in previous chapters of this book.

We should reopen Server Settings in the mail account and select Security Settings ➤ SSL/TLS (Figure 9-20).

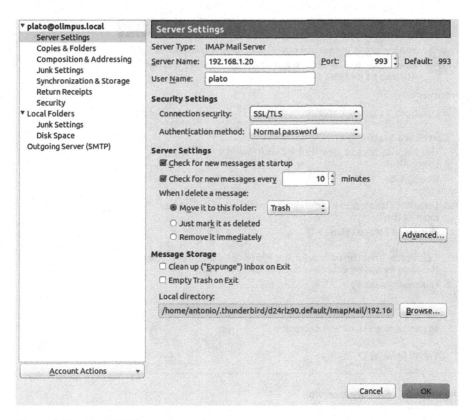

Figure 9-20. *New IMAPS settings*

In the server, we open TCP port 993, to allow incoming connections to the IMAPS port.

In CentOS 6:

```
1   [root@delphos dovecot]# iptables -I INPUT 2 -p tcp --dport 993 -j
    ACCEPT
```

In CentOS 7:

```
1   [root@CentOS7 ~]# firewall-cmd --add-service=imaps
2   success
```

Now when we try to receive mail for the first time, we receive the usual warning message (Figure 9-21).

Figure 9-21. *Security exception*

If we click "View..." we can see that this is the sample certificate installed by default with dovecot (Figure 9-22).

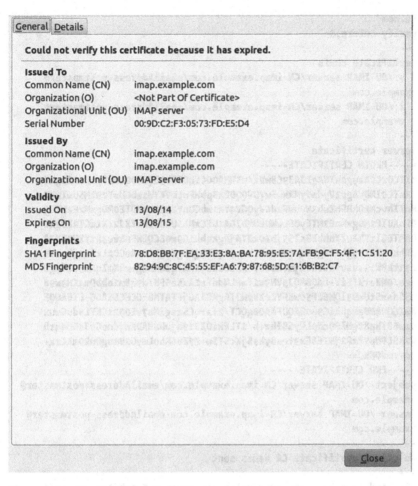

Figure 9-22. *View certificate*

Now we can receive mail through a secure port.

We could also test the connection from a command line, but, as the connection is ciphered, we can't use telnet and must employ openssl instead.

```
1   [root@dummy-server ~]# openssl s_client -connect 192.168.1.20:993
2   CONNECTED(00000003)
3   depth=0 OU = IMAP server, CN = imap.example.com, emailAddress =
    postmaster@examp\
4   le.com
5   verify error:num=18:self signed certificate
6   verify return:1
7   depth=0 OU = IMAP server, CN = imap.example.com, emailAddress =
    postmaster@examp\
```

```
 8    le.com
 9    verify return:1
10    ---
11    Certificate chain
12    0 s:/OU=IMAP server/CN=imap.example.com/emailAddress=postmaster@
      example.com
13      i:/OU=IMAP server/CN=imap.example.com/emailAddress=postmaster@
      example.com
14    ---
15    Server certificate
16    -----BEGIN CERTIFICATE-----
17    MIICQzCCAaygAwIBAgIJAJ3C8wVz/eXUMAoGCSqGSIb3DQEBBQUAMFgxFDASBgNV
18    BAsTCOlNQVAgc2VydmVyMRkwFwYDVQQDExBpbWFwLmV4YW1wbGUuY29tMSUwIwYJ
19    KoZIhvcNAQkBFhZwb3NObWFzdGVyQGV4YW1wbGUuY29tMB4XDTE0MDgxMzE2NTEy
20    OFoXDTE1MDgxMzE2NTEyOFowWDEUMBIGA1UECxMLSU1BUCBzZXJ2ZXIxGTAXBgNV
21    BAMTEGltYXAuZXhhbXBsZS5jb20xJTAjBgkqhkiG9w0BCQEWFnBvc3RtYXN0ZXJA
22    ZXhhbXBsZS5jb20wgZ8wDQYJKoZIhvcNAQEBBQADgY0AMIGJAoGBALrix1jhz1bD
23    z31tkBW13svsvfXu6uvwjmyNO6v7onaGOsRvjr/ATqI4Nn4g+mRNmIqAm3cefygO
24    wge/OMXefKfEiV+LdQBMQJ5VN3x1fwPLNddFx1AxKaGFK/W9q8m1ohbQm4XH3w98
25    NSSdsxStUWD3lQWEEP5OwKFYZe2VmwJTAgMBAAGjFTATMBEGCWCGSAGG+EIBAQQE
26    AwIGQDANBgkqhkiG9w0BAQUFAAOBgQCT/2fazqCSzsgiMs7vE0921GKYLvduGvux
27    vxw68Tkp8tgHlPQcNpLVyS8fhz+h/1TLEwiOZJ19njuBaHADEwjdooGvJs6U4qrb
28    W1XSLDNpYZzP1jNIE8Gx3tgs8yksSjKcSTSw+Z7Z86MboLmyO2BmugOukOmXCzx+
29    9d+rmVO8KQ==
30    -----END CERTIFICATE-----
31    subject=/OU=IMAP server/CN=imap.example.com/emailAddress=postmaster@
      example.com
32    issuer=/OU=IMAP server/CN=imap.example.com/emailAddress=postmaster@
      example.com
33    ---
34    No client certificate CA names sent
35    ---
36    SSL handshake has read 1301 bytes and written 311 bytes
37    ---
38    New, TLSv1/SSLv3, Cipher is DHE-RSA-AES256-SHA
39    Server public key is 1024 bit
40    Secure Renegotiation IS supported
41    Compression: zlib compression
42    Expansion: zlib compression
43    SSL-Session:
44        Protocol  :  TLSv1
45        Cipher    :  DHE-RSA-AES256-SHA
46        Session-ID :
          1DD2E48B77CB8D14487AF5322B27B60B8B41E45BC5F4B080F92CCF98B1C8FCF9
47        Session-ID-ctx:
48    Master-Key:
      DC23DBAF2E3244F4DCEFE51F6266F2462C6B46824FFF24523618AF885E19FA2D\
```

```
49   B82F347FAA8EB9808F7E7AB067183104
50       Key-Arg     : None
51       Krb5 Principal: None
52       PSK identity: None
53       PSK identity hint: None
54       TLS session ticket:
55       0000 - fd fd cb 5d 36 a7 31 ac-fe 52 03 df f6 09 41 f6
         ...]6.1..R....A.
56       0010 - 2a 65 a7 94 ee 40 86 e0-5a 8a 3c ab 72 2a 7c 78
         *e...@..Z.<.r*|x
57       0020 - b4 7a 8d a9 1b 0f bd f3-97 1a 03 0b c4 25 0b 50
         .z..........%.P
58       0030 - 6d d2 14 41 ce dc 2c 96-2c a7 a5 fd ad 20 80 60
         m..A..,.,.... .`
59       0040 - 7c 0b 51 c4 a8 09 10 93-b2 a8 49 fa d8 23 d2 41
         |.Q.......I..#.A
60       0050 - 42 13 29 ff 3a a6 12 a3-fa 68 48 6d e1 bd 7d 62
         B.).:....hHm..}b
61       0060 - b6 9c 70 07 9d 18 fc 6d-65 d4 6e 52 a9 62 94 12
         ..p....me.nR.b..
62       0070 - b6 b3 e3 7b 95 26 ca e1-df df 05 0f 4c f1 6a b2
         ...{.&......L.j.
63       0080 - 96 34 01 d5 ad 31 87 cb-7e d6 41 d4 c1 2b 8b 46
         .4...1..~.A..+.F
64       0090 - 82 eb 6a f3 31 4a ab 8a-24 cb a1 ba 7f 7e 1e 13
         ..j.1J..$....~..
65
66   Compression: 1 (zlib compression)
67   Start Time: 1411844428
68   Timeout  : 300 (sec)
69   Verify return code: 18 (self signed certificate)
70   ---
71   * OK [CAPABILITY IMAP4rev1 LITERAL+ SASL-IR LOGIN-REFERRALS ID ENABLE
     IDLE AUTH=\
72   PLAIN AUTH=LOGIN] Dovecot ready.
73   . LOGIN plato plato
74   . OK [CAPABILITY IMAP4rev1 LITERAL+ SASL-IR LOGIN-REFERRALS ID ENABLE
     IDLE SORT \
75   SORT=DISPLAY THREAD=REFERENCES THREAD=REFS MULTIAPPEND UNSELECT
     CHILDREN NAMESPA\
76   CE UIDPLUS LIST-EXTENDED I18NLEVEL=1 CONDSTORE QRESYNC ESEARCH ESORT
     SEARCHRES W\
77   ITHIN CONTEXT=SEARCH LIST-STATUS] Logged in
78   . LIST "" "*"
79   * LIST (\NoInferiors \Marked) "/" "Trash"
80   * LIST (\NoInferiors \UnMarked) "/" "Sent"
81   * LIST (\NoInferiors \UnMarked) "/" "Drafts"
```

```
 82   * LIST (\NoInferiors \UnMarked) "/" "INBOX"
 83   . OK List completed.
 84   . EXAMINE INBOX
 85   * FLAGS (\Answered \Flagged \Deleted \Seen \Draft)
 86   * OK [PERMANENTFLAGS ()] Read-only mailbox.
 87   * 1 EXISTS
 88   * 0 RECENT
 89   * OK [UIDVALIDITY 1407985588] UIDs valid
 90   * OK [UIDNEXT 15] Predicted next UID
 91   * OK [HIGHESTMODSEQ 1] Highest
 92   . OK [READ-ONLY] Select completed.
 93   . FETCH 1 BODY[]
 94   * 1 FETCH (BODY[] {671}
 95   Return-Path: <socrates@olimpus.local>
 96   X-Original-To: plato@olimpus.local
 97   Delivered-To: plato@olimpus.local
 98   Received: from [192.168.10.100] (unknown [192.168.10.100])
 99           by delphos.centos.local (Postfix) with ESMTPSA id D290718C4
100           for <plato@olimpus.local>; Thu, 14 Aug 2014 13:14:39 -0400
      (EDT)
101   Message-ID: <54985763.60404@olimpus.local>
102   Date: Mon, 22 Dec 2014 18:39:47 +0100
103   From: Socrates <socrates@olimpus.local>
104   User-Agent: Mozilla/5.0 (Windows NT 6.1; rv:31.0) Gecko/20100101
      Thunderbird/31.\
105   3.0
106   MIME-Version: 1.0
107   To: plato@olimpus.local
108   Subject: test imaps
109   Content-Type: text/plain; charset=utf-8; format=flowed
110   Content-Transfer-Encoding: 7bit
111
112   IMAPS
113   )
114   . OK Fetch completed.
115   . LOGOUT
116   * BYE Logging out
117   . OK Logout completed.
118   closed
```

9.7.3. POP3S

If you want to use POP3S instead of POP3, the procedure to follow is almost identical to that in the previous "IMAPS" section. You should also edit the server settings and choose the POPS port 995.

9.8. Spam

The invention of e-mail facilitated communications around the world, but it also promoted a new problem, unsolicited mail or spam. To minimize this, there are many solutions available that scan mail, searching for certain patterns associated with spam, such as terms related to sex or certain drugs.

One of these solutions is SpamAssassin, which is also open source. We can install it with the following command:

```
1   [root@delphos ~]# yum install spamassassin
```

Once installed, we can take a look at the /etc/mail/spamassassin/local.cf configuration file.

```
1   [root@delphos ~]# cat /etc/mail/spamassassin/local.cf
2   # These values can be overridden by editing ~/.spamassassin/user_prefs.cf
3   # (see spamassassin(1) for details)
4
5   # These should be safe assumptions and allow for simple visual sifting
6   # without risking lost emails.
7
8   required_hits 5
9   report_safe 0
10  rewrite_header Subject [SPAM]
```

SpamAssassin consists of a series of Perl scripts used to analyze mail according to different criteria, to determine whether an e-mail is spam or not. According to the result of the different scripts, SpamAssassin scores the e-mail. The higher the score, the higher the possibility of the mail being spam. The parameter required_hits 5 indicates that SpamAssassin will mark an e-mail as spam if its score is five or higher. We might have to tune this value according to our needs, as a high value might mark as spam e-mails that are not, while a low value might do just the opposite, making spam messages appear be clean.

The other two parameters that exist in the default configuration are report_safe and rewrite_header. report_safe can take the values 0, 1, or 2. If the value is set to 0, an e-mail marked as spam is sent as it is, modifying only the headers to show that it is spam. On the other hand, if the value is set to 1 or 2, a new report message is generated by SpamAssassin and sent to the recipient. The original spam message will be attached to the report message. The difference between the values 1 and 2 is that in the first case, the spam message is coded as content message/rfc822, while in the second case, it will be coded as content text/plain. The last option is the safest, as some mail clients might execute message/rfc822, and the user won't even notice. Thus, a spammer could infect the recipient's computer with a virus.

In order to test spamassassin, we can pass it a test message. In /usr/share/doc/ spamassassin-3.3.1/, we have two sample text files, one that is spam and one that is not. If we analyze the "clean" file with spamassassin, this is what we get:

```
1   [root@delphos ~]# spamassassin /usr/share/doc/spamassassin-3.3.1/
    sample-nonspam.\
2   txt
3   Aug 14 14:46:32.896 [13140] warn: config: created user preferences
    file: /root/.\
4   spamassassin/user_prefs
5   Return-Path: <tbtf-approval@world.std.com>
6   X-Spam-Checker-Version: SpamAssassin 3.3.1 (2010-03-16) on
7         delphos.olimpus.local
8   X-Spam-Level:
9   X-Spam-Status: No, score=-0.0 required=5.0 tests=T_RP_MATCHES_RCVD
10        autolearn=ham version=3.3.1
11  Delivered-To: foo@foo.com
12  .
13  .
14  .
```

The relevant part of the analysis lies in the first lines, with the X-Spam headers. We can see that the mail is considered not to be spam, because it has a score of 0.

But if we now analyze the spam sample, the result will be completely different.

```
1   [root@delphos ~]# spamassassin /usr/share/doc/spamassassin-3.3.1/
    sample-spam.txt
2   X-Spam-Checker-Version: SpamAssassin 3.3.1 (2010-03-16) on
3         delphos.olimpus.local
4   X-Spam-Flag: YES
5   X-Spam-Level: **************************************************
6   X-Spam-Status: Yes, score=1000.0 required=5.0 tests=GTUBE,NO_RECEIVED,
7         NO_RELAYS autolearn=no version=3.3.1
8   X-Spam-Report:
9         * -0.0 NO_RELAYS Informational: message was not relayed via
          SMTP
10        * 1000 GTUBE BODY: Generic Test for Unsolicited Bulk Email
11        * -0.0 NO_RECEIVED Informational: message has no Received
          headers
12  Subject: [SPAM] Test spam mail (GTUBE)
13  Message-ID: <GTUBE1.1010101@example.net>
14  Date: Wed, 23 Jul 2003 23:30:00 +0200
15  From: Sender <sender@example.net>
16  To: Recipient <recipient@example.net>
17  Precedence: junk
18  MIME-Version: 1.0
19  Content-Type: text/plain; charset=us-ascii
20  Content-Transfer-Encoding: 7bit
```

```
21   X-Spam-Prev-Subject: Test spam mail (GTUBE)
22
23   This is the GTUBE, the
24        Generic
25        Test for
26        Unsolicited
27        Bulk
28        Email
29
30   If your spam filter supports it, the GTUBE provides a test by which you
31   can verify that the filter is installed correctly and is detecting
     incoming
32   spam. You can send yourself a test mail containing the following
     string of
33   characters (in upper case and with no white spaces and line breaks):
34
35   XJS*C4JDBQADN1.NSBN3*2IDNEN*GTUBE-STANDARD-ANTI-UBE-TEST-EMAIL*C.34X
36
37   You should send this test mail from an account outside of your network.
```

In this case, the message is considered spam, because it has a score of 1000, which is, of course, way above the threshold score of 5.

Now that we know that spamassassin works as expected, we must integrate it into postfix. The easiest way to do this is probably by using procmail. procmail is a mail delivery agent (MDA). This means that procmail takes mail from the mail transfer agent (MTA)—in this case, postfix—and delivers it to the user's mailbox. After this, the user can employ any mail user agent (MUA), such as Mozilla Thunderbird or Microsoft Outlook, to retrieve mail.

We'll have to create a file, named /etc/procmailrc, with the following content:

```
1    :0 hbfw
2    | /usr/bin/spamc
```

This means that we're going to apply a filter (f) to the headers (h) and body (b) of the message, and the system will wait (w) until the filter is applied.

We also have to edit the postfix configuration file /etc/postfix/main.cf. By default, it has the following line:

```
1    #mailbox_command = /some/where/procmail
```

We'll have to change that line into this:

```
1    mailbox_command = /usr/bin/procmail
```

And we restart the postfix and spamassassin services.
In CentOS 6:

```
1  [root@delphos ~]# service postfix restart
2  Shutting down postfix:                              [ OK ]
3  Starting postfix:                                   [ OK ]
4  [root@delphos ~]# service spamassassin restart
5  Stopping spamd:                                     [ OK ]
6  Starting spamd:                                     [ OK ]
```

In CentOS 7:

```
1  [root@CentOS7 ~]# systemctl restart postfix
2  [root@CentOS7 ~]# systemctl restart spamassassin
```

Now let's imagine that there is an interloper attempting to send spam to plato@ olimpus.local. They might send a message such as the one in Figure 9-23.

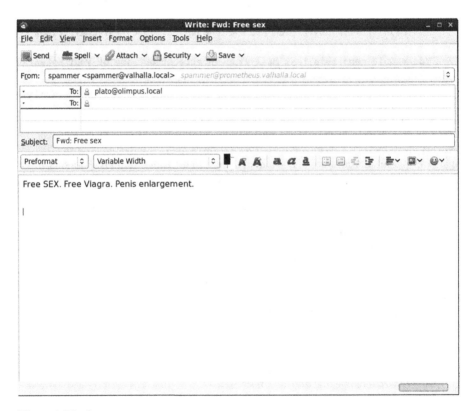

Figure 9-23. *A spam message*

When the user plato opens his mailbox, he will see the message tagged as spam (Figure 9-24).

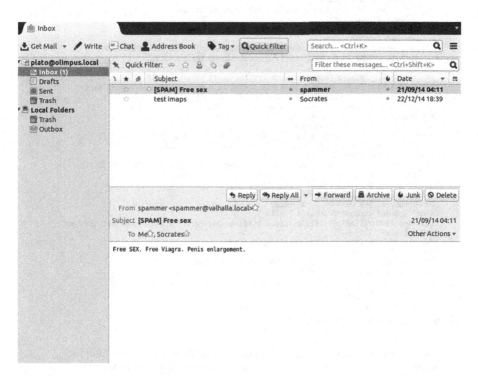

Figure 9-24. *Mailbox showing the spam message*

If he opens the mail message and then clicks Other actions ➤ View source, he will see the mail headers added by spamassassin (Figure 9-25).

```
● ● ●    Source of: imap://plato@192.168.1.20:993/fetch%3EUID%3E/INBOX%3E18 - M
    Return-Path: <spammer@valhalla.local>
    X-Spam-Checker-Version: SpamAssassin 3.3.1 (2010-03-16) on
        delphos.olimpus.local
    X-Spam-Flag: YES
    X-Spam-Level: *****
    X-Spam-Status: Yes, score=5.0 required=5.0 tests=ALL_TRUSTED,BODY_ENHANCEMENT2,
        DATE_IN_FUTURE_96_Q,DRUGS_ERECTILE autolearn=no version=3.3.1
    X-Spam-Report:
        * -1.0 ALL_TRUSTED Passed through trusted hosts only via SMTP
        *  2.3 DATE_IN_FUTURE_96_Q Date: is 4 days to 4 months after Received: date
        *  1.5 BODY_ENHANCEMENT2 BODY: Information on getting larger body parts
        *  2.2 DRUGS_ERECTILE Refers to an erectile drug
    X-Original-To: plato@olimpus.local
    Delivered-To: plato@olimpus.local
    Received: from odin.valhalla.local (prometheus.olimpus.local [192.168.1.21])
        by delphos.centos.local (Postfix) with ESMTP id 7A61618C4;
        Thu, 14 Aug 2014 16:51:53 -0400 (EDT)
    Received: from prometheus.olimpus.local (prometheus.olimpus.local [192.168.1.21])
        by odin.valhalla.local (Postfix) with ESMTP id 5BC404318D;
        Sun, 21 Sep 2014 04:11:36 +0200 (CEST)
    Message-ID: <541E33D8.9090306@valhalla.local>
    Date: Sun, 21 Sep 2014 04:11:36 +0200
    From: spammer <spammer@valhalla.local>
    User-Agent: Mozilla/5.0 (X11; U; Linux i686; en-US; rv:1.9.2.24) Gecko/20111109 Cen
    MIME-Version: 1.0
    To: plato@olimpus.local, socrates@olimpus.local
    Subject: [SPAM] Free sex
    Content-Type: text/plain; charset=ISO-8859-1; format=flowed
    Content-Transfer-Encoding: 7bit
```

Figure 9-25. spamassassin headers

As the message has been tagged as spam, we can create a message filter in Thunderbird to delete those messages or move them to a different folder.

9.9. Webmail

In a corporate network, people usually access their mailboxes through mail clients by using such protocols as POP3S, IMAPS, etc. But, on the other hand, home users usually prefer to access their mailboxes through webmail. Well-known Internet companies such as Google, Yahoo!, or Hotmail offer this service.

In order for our server to provide a webmail service, we'll use squirrelmail software, which is downloadable from the Internet.[1] For this software to work properly, we need a running web server with PHP support (see Chapter 7), as well as an IMAP server.

squirrelmail is available in the EPEL repository too, so it can be installed with yum, as usual. However, this time, we'll focus on the manual installation, as there are times when an admin has to install software this way.

---

[1]SquirrelMail, http://squirrelmail.org, 1999–2016.

After downloading the squirrelmail-webmail-1.4.22.tar.gz file, we uncompress it in a folder from which it can be accessed by the Apache web server. If you have completed Chapter 7 of this, book you'll have a web site (www.olimpus.local) whose files are stored in /www/docs/olimpus.local. You can download and unpack the software into that location.

```
1   [root@delphos html]# cd /www/docs/olimpus.local/
2   [root@delphos olimpus.local]# ls
3   index.html  squirrelmail-webmail-1.4.22.tar.gz  test.php
4   [root@delphos olimpus.local]# tar -xzvf squirrelmail-
    webmail-1.4.22.tar.gz
```

We rename the folder created to something easier to remember, such as webmail.

```
1   [root@delphos olimpus.local]# ls
2   index.html                        squirrelmail-webmail-1.4.22.tar.gz
3   squirrelmail-webmail-1.4.22       test.php
4   [root@delphos olimpus.local]# mv squirrelmail-webmail-1.4.22 webmail
5   [root@delphos olimpus.local]# ls
6   index.html  squirrelmail-webmail-1.4.22.tar.gz  test.php  webmail
```

squirrelmail requires a folder in which to create and suppress a few temporary files. By default, this folder is /var/local/squirrelmail/data/. We create it like this:

```
1   [root@delphos olimpus.local]# mkdir -p /var/local/squirrelmail/data
2   [root@delphos olimpus.local]#
```

squirrelmail also requires write access to this directory, so we have to grant the appropriate rights to the Apache user, as Apache is the user that executes squirrelmail. We can do this by assigning the ownership of the folder to the Apache user.

```
1   [root@delphos olimpus.local]# ls -ld /var/local/squirrelmail/data/
2   drwxr-xr-x. 2 root root 4096 Aug 14 21:47 /var/local/squirrelmail/data/
3   [root@delphos olimpus.local]# chown apache /var/local/squirrelmail/data/
4   [root@delphos olimpus.local]# ls -ld /var/local/squirrelmail/data/
5   drwxr-xr-x. 2 apache root 4096 Aug 14 21:47 /var/local/squirrelmail/
    data/
```

We must also create another folder to manage the mail attachments. By default, this directory is /var/lo- cal/squirrelmail/attach. We create it and grant the ownership to the Apache user.

```
1   [root@delphos olimpus.local]# mkdir /var/local/squirrelmail/attach
2   [root@delphos olimpus.local]# chown apache /var/local/squirrelmail/
    attach/
```

Now we have to access the webmail/config subfolder and launch the Perl script conf.pl.

```
1    [root@delphos olimpus.local]# cd webmail/config
2    [root@delphos config]# ./conf.pl
```

We'll see the following menu:

```
1    SquirrelMail Configuration : Read: config_default.php (1.4.0)
2    ---------------------------------------------------------------
3    Main Menu --
4    1. Organization Preferences
5    2. Server Settings
6    3. Folder Defaults
7    4. General Options
8    5. Themes
9    6. Address Books
10   7. Message of the Day (MOTD)
11   8. Plugins
12   9. Database
13   10. Languages
14
15   D.  Set pre-defined settings for specific IMAP servers
16
17   C   Turn color on
18   S   Save data
19   Q   Quit
20
21   Command >>
```

We edit Server Settings (option 2), and we see the following screen:

```
1    SquirrelMail Configuration    : Read: config_default.php (1.4.0)
2    ---------------------------------------------------------------
3    Server Settings
4
5    General
6    -------
7    1.  Domain                    : example.com
8    2.  Invert Time               : false
9    3.  Sendmail or SMTP          : SMTP
10
11   A.  Update IMAP Settings      : localhost:143 (other)
12   B.  Update SMTP Settings      : localhost:25
13
14   R   Return to Main Menu
15   C   Turn color on
16   S   Save data
17   Q   Quit
18
19   Command >>
```

We change the domain to olimpus.local.

```
1   Command >> 1
2
3   The domain name is the suffix at the end of all email addresses. If
4   for example, your email address is jdoe@example.com, then your domain
5   would be example.com.
6
7   [example.com]: olimpus.local
8   SquirrelMail Configuration   : Read: config_default.php (1.4.0)
9   ---------------------------------------------------------------
10  Server Settings
11
12  General
13  -------
14  1.  Domain                    : olimpus.local
15  2.  Invert Time               : false
16  3.  Sendmail or SMTP          : SMTP
17
18  A.  Update IMAP Settings      : localhost:143 (other)
19  B.  Update SMTP Settings      : localhost:25
20
21  R   Return to Main Menu
22  C   Turn color on
23  S   Save data
24  Q   Quit
```

As we are using SMTP authentication, we'll have to update the SMTP settings too (option B).

```
1   Command >> B
2   SquirrelMail Configuration   : Read: config.php (1.4.0)
3   ---------------------------------------------------------------
4   Server Settings
5
6   General
7   -------
8   1.  Domain                    : olimpus.local
9   2.  Invert Time               : false
10  3.  Sendmail or SMTP          : SMTP
11
12  SMTP Settings
13  -------------
14  4.   SMTP Server              : localhost
15  5.   SMTP Port                : 25
16  6.   POP before SMTP          : false
17  7.   SMTP Authentication      : none
18  8.   Secure SMTP (TLS)        : false
```

```
19   9.   Header encryption key    :
20
21   A.   Update IMAP Settings     : localhost:143 (other)
22   H.   Hide SMTP Settings
23
24   R    Return to Main Menu
25   C    Turn color on
26   S    Save data
27   Q    Quit
28
29   Command >>
```

We type 7 and specify the authentication mechanism.

```
1    Command >> 7
2
3    If you have already set the hostname and port number, I can try to
4    automatically detect the mechanisms your SMTP server supports.
5    Auto-detection is *optional* - you can safely say "n" here.
6
7    Try to detect auth mechanisms? [y/N]: y
8    Trying to detect supported methods (SMTP)...
9    Testing none:            SUPPORTED
10   Testing login:           SUPPORTED
11   Testing plain:           SUPPORTED
12   Testing CRAM-MD5:        NOT SUPPORTED
13   Testing DIGEST-MD5:      NOT SUPPORTED
14
15   What authentication mechanism do you want to use for SMTP connections?
16   none - Your SMTP server does not require authorization.
17   login - Plaintext. If you can do better, you probably should.
18   plain - Plaintext. If you can do better, you probably should.
19   cram-md5 - Slightly better than plaintext.
20   digest-md5 - Privacy protection - better than cram-md5.
21
22   *** YOUR SMTP SERVER MUST SUPPORT THE MECHANISM YOU CHOOSE HERE ***
23   If you don't understand or are unsure, you probably want "none"
24
25   none, login, plain, cram-md5, or digest-md5 [none]: plain
26   SMTP authentication uses IMAP username and password by default.
27
28   Would you like to use other login and password for all SquirrelMail
29   SMTP connections? [y/N]:
30   SquirrelMail Configuration : Read: config.php (1.4.0)
31   -----------------------------------------------------------
32   Server Settings
33
34   General
```

```
35    -------
36    1.  Domain                        : olimpus.local
37    2.  Invert Time                   : false
38    3.  Sendmail or SMTP              : SMTP
39
40    SMTP Settings
41    -------------
42    4.  SMTP Server                   : localhost
43    5.  SMTP Port                     : 25
44    6.  POP before SMTP               : false
45    7.  SMTP Authentication           : plain (with IMAP username and
                                            password)
46    8.  Secure SMTP (TLS)             : false
47    9.  Header encryption key  :
48
49    A.  Update IMAP Settings          : localhost:143 (other)
50    H.  Hide SMTP Settings
51
52    R   Return to Main Menu
53    C   Turn color on
54    S   Save data
55    Q   Quit
56
57    Command >>
```

When we have finished changing the settings, we select S to save the data and Q to quit. In addition to changing the server settings, we have to tell SELinux to allow Apache to start connections.

There is a SELinux Boolean whose default value rejects network connections made from Apache. We have to change that value.

```
1    [root@delphos config]# getsebool httpd_can_network_connect
2    httpd_can_network_connect --> off
3    [root@delphos config]# setsebool httpd_can_network_connect on
4    [root@delphos config]# getsebool httpd_can_network_connect
5    httpd_can_network_connect --> on
```

After doing this, we can check whether the configuration is correct or not by opening a web browser and typing the following address: "http://192.168.1.20/webmail/src/configtest.php."

We can see an error regarding a PHP option (Figure 9-26). This error shouldn't be a problem for the server to work properly. In any case, we can fix it easily. We only have to edit the /etc/php.ini file and change the value of the parameter short_open_tag from Off to On.

285

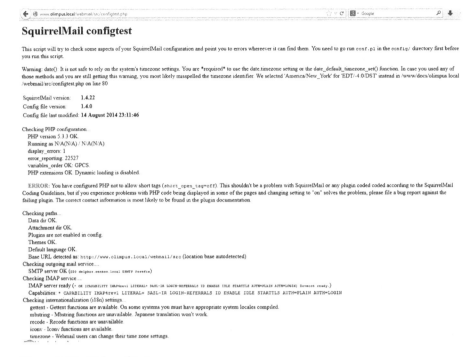

Figure 9-26. *Webmail test page*

After restarting Apache, we access the test page again (Figure 9-27) and shouldn't see any more errors.

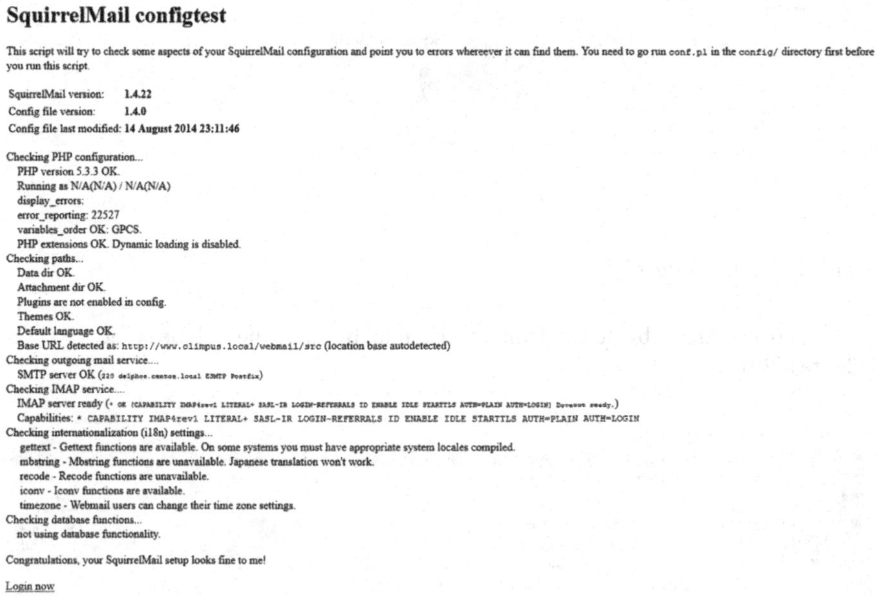

SquirrelMail configtest

This script will try to check some aspects of your SquirrelMail configuration and point you to errors whereever it can find them. You need to go run conf.pl in the config/ directory first before you run this script.

SquirrelMail version: 1.4.22
Config file version: 1.4.0
Config file last modified: 14 August 2014 23:11:46

Checking PHP configuration...
    PHP version 5.3.3 OK.
    Running as N/A(N/A) / N/A(N/A)
    display_errors:
    error_reporting: 22527
    variables_order OK: GPCS.
    PHP extensions OK. Dynamic loading is disabled.
Checking paths...
    Data dir OK.
    Attachment dir OK.
    Plugins are not enabled in config.
    Themes OK.
    Default language OK.
    Base URL detected as: http://www.olimpus.local/webmail/src (location base autodetected)
Checking outgoing mail service...
    SMTP server OK (220 delphos.centos.local ESMTP Postfix)
Checking IMAP service...
    IMAP server ready (· OK (CAPABILITY IMAP4rev1 LITERAL+ SASL-IR LOGIN-REFERRALS ID ENABLE IDLE STARTTLS AUTH=PLAIN AUTH=LOGIN] Dovecot ready.)
    Capabilities: * CAPABILITY IMAP4rev1 LITERAL+ SASL-IR LOGIN-REFERRALS ID ENABLE IDLE STARTTLS AUTH=PLAIN AUTH=LOGIN
Checking internationalization (i18n) settings...
    gettext - Gettext functions are available. On some systems you must have appropriate system locales compiled.
    mbstring - Mbstring functions are unavailable. Japanese translation won't work.
    recode - Recode functions are unavailable.
    iconv - Iconv functions are available.
    timezone - Webmail users can change their time zone settings.
Checking database functions...
    not using database functionality.

Congratulations, your SquirrelMail setup looks fine to me!

Login now

Figure 9-27. Webmail test page. The configuration is correct.

In CentOS 6:

```
1  [root@delphos config]# service httpd restart
2  Stopping httpd:                              [ OK ]
3  Starting httpd:                              [ OK ]
```

In CentOS 7:

```
1  [root@CentOS7 ~]# systemctl restart httpd
```

Now we can click the "Login now" link at the bottom of the page and enter the username and password (Figure 9-28).

Figure 9-28. *Login page*

The user is now able to send and receive mail by using the web browser (Figure 9-29).

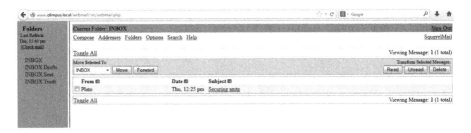

Figure 9-29. *Accessing a mailbox with a web browser*

■ ■ ■

CHAPTER 10

Firewalls

In today's dangerous cyberworld, it is mandatory to have some defense measures against either intentional or unintentional attacks. Firewalls allow us to block or allow traffic into our computer or network, based on different criteria, such as IP address, port range, etc.

In a large network, the admin usually defines several "zones," that is, groups of computers with similar security requirements. For example, if we have a web server and an FTP server that are available from the Internet, these computers require far more protection than an FTP server that is only accessible by local users. So there could be a zone called "external" for the servers accessible from the Internet and a zone called "internal" for the local servers. A corporate firewall should be installed in the perimeter of the network, to deal with the traffic to and from every zone.

But firewalls can also be used locally. Today, almost every computer, either server or workstation, includes a firewall installed by default.

This firewall functionality is managed in CentOS 6 by `iptables`, a powerful suite that allows users to create rules, redirect traffic, etc.

On the other hand, CentOS 7 uses the `firewalld` command instead, even though it is still possible to use `iptables` too. I'll provide more details in upcoming sections.

10.1. Firewall in CentOS 6

In CentOS 6, we have to use `iptables` to manage the firewall. We can check the rules currently in use with the `iptables -L` command.

```
1   [root@prometheus ~]# iptables -L
2   Chain INPUT (policy ACCEPT)
3   target      prot opt source        destination
4   ACCEPT      all  -- anywhere       anywhere        state RELATED,ESTAB\
5   LISHED
6   ACCEPT      icmp -- anywhere       anywhere
7   ACCEPT      all  -- anywhere       anywhere
8   ACCEPT      tcp  -- anywhere       anywhere        state NEW tcp dpt:s\
9   sh
10  REJECT      all  -- anywhere       anywhere        reject-with icmp-ho\
11  st-prohibited
12
```

© Antonio Vazquez 2016
A. Vazquez, *Learn CentOS Linux Network Services*, DOI 10.1007/978-1-4842-2379-6_10

```
13  Chain FORWARD (policy ACCEPT)
14  target      prot opt source    destination
15  REJECT      all -- anywhere    anywhere         reject-with icmp-ho\
16  st-prohibited
17
18  Chain OUTPUT (policy ACCEPT)
19  target    prot opt source      destination
```

We can see that, by default, CentOS allows access to all packets that belong to an already established connection.

```
1  ACCEPT   all  --    anywhere             anywhere   state RELATED,ESTAB\
2  LISHED
```

That's the reason why in some of the previous chapters, we allowed incoming traffic to a certain port this way:

```
1  [root@localhost named]# iptables -I INPUT 2 -m state --state NEW -m tcp
   -p tcp -\
2  -dport 53 -j ACCEPT
```

In this case, we are telling iptables to accept any packet requesting a new connection to port 53. I don't want to start a discussion about the inner workings of TCP, but I'll point out that the packets can have different flags associated to them. For example, if a computer wants to establish a new connection to port 53 of a server, it will send a TCP packet with the SYN flag active. If the server accepts the connection, it will send back a response with the SYN and ACK flags active. If it doesn't, it will send a packet with the RST flag.

In previous cases, we have allowed incoming traffic in a slightly different way.

```
1  [root@delphos ~]# iptables -I INPUT 2 -p tcp --dport 21 -j ACCEPT
```

In the preceding case, we are allowing all TCP packets addressed at port 21.

The first approach is more specific and, thus, slightly better.

Now we'll try to start from the beginning, with an empty configuration. We erase the current configuration in memory with iptables -F.

```
1  [root@prometheus ~]# iptables -F
```

We check that the configuration is actually empty.

```
1  [root@prometheus ~]# iptables -L
2  Chain INPUT (policy ACCEPT)
3  target    prot opt source      destination
4
5  Chain FORWARD (policy ACCEPT)
6  target    prot opt source      destination
7
8  Chain OUTPUT (policy ACCEPT)
9  target    prot opt source      destination
```

We can see three sections:

- INPUT for incoming traffic
- OUTPUT for outcoming traffic
- FORWARD for traffic forwarded to another destination

For now, I won't discuss forwarding traffic, so we'll focus on incoming and outcoming traffic.

After executing `iptables -L`, we can see that the default policy for incoming traffic is ACCEPT.

```
1   Chain INPUT (policy ACCEPT)
```

This means that, by default, all incoming traffic will be allowed. If we scan the open ports of the server with nmap, we'll see something similar to this:

```
1    [root@prometheus ~]# nmap 192.168.1.20
2
3    Starting Nmap 5.21 ( http://nmap.org ) at 2014-09-20 04:33 CEST
4    Nmap scan report for www.valhalla.local (192.168.1.20)
5    Host is up (0.0043s latency).
6    Not shown: 992 filtered ports
7    PORT     STATE  SERVICE
8    20/tcp   closed ftp-data
9    21/tcp   open   ftp
10   22/tcp   open   ssh
11   25/tcp   open   smtp
12   53/tcp   open   domain
13   80/tcp   open   http
14   443/tcp  open   https
15   990/tcp  closed ftps
16   MAC Address: 00:0C:29:78:4C:B1 (VMware)
17
18   Nmap done: 1 IP address (1 host up) scanned in 5.92 seconds
```

We're going to apply a more restrictive default policy. First, we'll allow explicitly connections to the ssh port, and then we'll change the default input policy to DROP.

```
1    [root@delphos ~]# iptables -A INPUT -p tcp --dport 22 -j ACCEPT
2    [root@delphos ~]# iptables -P INPUT DROP
```

If we scan the ports again from the same computer, this is what we'll see:

```
1    [root@prometheus ~]# nmap 192.168.1.20
2
3    Starting Nmap 5.21 ( http://nmap.org ) at 2014-09-20 05:13 CEST
4    Nmap scan report for www.valhalla.local (192.168.1.20)
5    Host is up (0.00027s latency).
```

```
6    Not shown: 999 filtered ports
7    PORT    STATE   SERVICE
8    22/tcp open    ssh
9    MAC Address: 00:0C:29:78:4C:B1 (VMware)
10
11   Nmap done: 1 IP address (1 host up) scanned in 4.88 seconds
```

As expected, only the services explicitly allowed are shown.
Now we can keep allowing access to certain services, such as http.

```
1    [root@delphos ~]# iptables -A INPUT -p tcp --dport 80 -j ACCEPT
```

We added (-A) a new rule allowing access to the http service. If we list the current
configuration of the firewall, we'll see this:

```
1    [root@delphos ~]# iptables -L
2    Chain INPUT (policy DROP)
3    target     prot opt source              destination
4    ACCEPT     tcp  --  anywhere            anywhere             tcp dpt:ssh
5    ACCEPT     tcp  --  anywhere            anywhere             tcp dpt:http
6
7    Chain FORWARD (policy ACCEPT)
8    target     prot opt source              destination
9
10   Chain OUTPUT (policy ACCEPT)
11   target     prot opt source              destination
```

So far, we granted access to port 80 to any computer trying to access, but we can
be much more specific. We can grant or deny access to network or host addresses.
For example, we might want to deny http access to the computer with IP address
192.168.10.23.
In this case, we type the following:

```
1    [root@delphos ~]# iptables -I INPUT 1 -p tcp -s 192.168.10.23 --dport
     80 -j DROP
```

Now the configuration of the firewall will be this:

```
1    Chain INPUT (policy DROP)
2    target     prot opt source              destination
3    DROP       tcp  --  192.168.10.23       anywhere             tcp dpt:http
4    ACCEPT     tcp  --  anywhere            anywhere             tcp dpt:ssh
5    ACCEPT     tcp  --  anywhere            anywhere             tcp dpt:http
6
7    Chain FORWARD (policy ACCEPT)
8    target     prot opt source              destination
9
10   Chain OUTPUT (policy ACCEPT)
11   target     prot opt source              destination
```

And if we try to access the web server from the computer with IP address 192.168.10.23, it won't be possible (Figure 10-1).

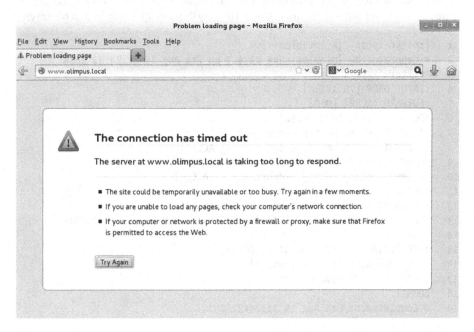

Figure 10-1. *Access rejected*

In the iptables configuration, the lines are processed sequentially, so we must pay attention to the order when adding new rules. If two rules can be applied to the network, the first always prevails.

For example, as of now, the computer 192.168.10.23 can't access the web server. Now let's imagine that the order of the rules in the INPUT chain is something like this:

```
1  Chain INPUT (policy DROP)
2  target    prot opt source              destination
3  ACCEPT    tcp  --  anywhere            anywhere        tcp dpt:http
4  DROP      tcp  --  192.168.10.23       anywhere        tcp dpt:http
5  ACCEPT    tcp  --  anywhere            anywhere        tcp dpt:ssh
```

In this case, when 192.168.10.23 tries to establish a connection, the first rule is examined. As the incoming traffic matches the criteria (source anywhere, destination port http, etc.), the connection is allowed, and, therefore, the second rule is never applied.

So far, we have added rules, but we can delete rules as well. If we want to allow 192.168.10.23 to access the web server again, we can do it with this command:

```
1  [root@delphos ~]# iptables -D INPUT 1
```

We delete (-D) the rule at the first (1) position.

10.1.1. Saving and Restoring the Configuration

We can save the firewall configuration at any moment with the `iptables-save` command.
If we execute it without any arguments, it will display the current configuration onscreen.

```
1   [root@delphos ~]# iptables-save
2   # Generated by iptables-save v1.4.7 on Fri Aug 15 21:24:32 2014
3   *filter
4   :INPUT DROP [79:12524]
5   :FORWARD ACCEPT [0:0]
6   :OUTPUT ACCEPT [750:39252]
7   -A INPUT -p tcp -m tcp --dport 22 -j ACCEPT
8   -A INPUT -p tcp -m tcp --dport 80 -j ACCEPT
9   -A INPUT -p udp -m udp --dport 53 -j ACCEPT
10  -A INPUT -p tcp -m tcp --dport 443 -j ACCEPT
11  COMMIT
12  # Completed on Fri Aug 15 21:24:32 2014
13  # Generated by iptables-save v1.4.7 on Fri Aug 15 21:24:32 2014
14  *nat
15  :PREROUTING ACCEPT [304741:26740262]
16  :POSTROUTING ACCEPT [974:60691]
17  :OUTPUT ACCEPT [974:60691]
18  COMMIT
19  # Completed on Fri Aug 15 21:24:32 2014
```

We can easily redirect the output to a file, to have a backup.

```
1   [root@delphos ~]# iptables-save > iptablesbackup
```

If we ever have to restore the firewall configuration, we can do it with `iptables-restore`.
Let's see an example.

First, we empty the configuration.

```
1   [root@delphos ~]# iptables -F
2   [root@delphos ~]# iptables -L
3   Chain INPUT (policy DROP)
4   target     prot opt source          destination
5
6   Chain FORWARD (policy ACCEPT)
7   target     prot opt source          destination
8
9   Chain OUTPUT (policy ACCEPT)
10  target     prot opt source          destination
```

And now we restore the configuration.

```
1   [root@delphos ~]# iptables-restore iptablesbackup
2   [root@delphos ~]# iptables -L
```

```
3   Chain INPUT (policy DROP)
4   target     prot opt source     destination
5   ACCEPT     tcp  -- anywhere    anywhere              tcp dpt:ssh
6
7   Chain FORWARD (policy ACCEPT)
8   target        prot opt source     destination
9
10  Chain OUTPUT (policy ACCEPT)
11  target        prot opt source     destination
```

We have seen how to back up and restore the configuration manually, but iptables is executed as a service, and if we restart iptables with the command service iptables restart, iptables will load its configuration from the /etc/sysconfig/iptables file. The content of this file could be something like this:

```
1   [root@delphos ~]# cat /etc/sysconfig/iptables
2   # Generated by iptables-save v1.4.7 on Sat Aug  9 16:38:57 2014
3   *nat
4   :PREROUTING ACCEPT [358749:34585361]
5   :POSTROUTING ACCEPT [3800:310043]
6   :OUTPUT ACCEPT [3800:310043]
7   COMMIT
8   # Completed on Sat Aug            9 16:38:57 2014
9   # Generated by iptables-save v1.4.7 on Sat Aug  9 16:38:57 2014
10  *filter
11  :INPUT ACCEPT [0:0]
12  :FORWARD ACCEPT [0:0]
13  :OUTPUT ACCEPT [2304:234903]
14  -A INPUT -p tcp -m state --state NEW -m tcp --dport 443 -j ACCEPT
15  -A INPUT -p tcp -m tcp --dport 21 -j ACCEPT
16  -A INPUT -p tcp -m tcp --dport 20 -j ACCEPT
17  -A INPUT -m state --state RELATED,ESTABLISHED -j ACCEPT
18  -A INPUT -p icmp -j ACCEPT
19  -A INPUT -i lo -j ACCEPT
20  -A INPUT -p tcp -m state --state NEW -m tcp --dport 22 -j ACCEPT
21  -A INPUT -p udp -m state --state NEW -m udp --dport 53 -j ACCEPT
22  -A INPUT -p tcp -m state --state NEW -m tcp --dport 53 -j ACCEPT
23  -A INPUT -p tcp -m state --state NEW -m tcp --dport 80 -j ACCEPT
24  -A INPUT -j REJECT --reject-with icmp-host-prohibited
25  -A FORWARD -j REJECT --reject-with icmp-host-prohibited
26  COMMIT
27  # Completed on Sat Aug   9 16:38:57 2014
```

So, if we want to change this default configuration, we should either overwrite the file with iptables- save or use the program system-config-firewall, which is perhaps more friendly (Figure 10-2).

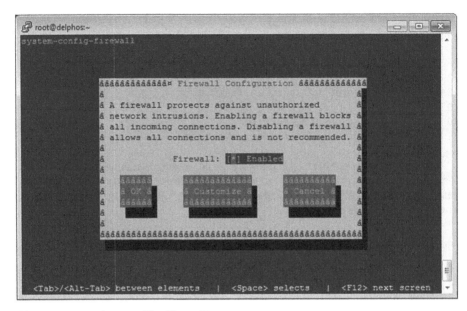

Figure 10-2. `system-config-firewall`

If we click Customize, we can select the services we want to make available. For example, if we want to make the web service accessible, we check it and click Close (Figure 10-3). On the other hand, if we want to allow access to a specific port not listed, we click Forward and enter it manually. When finally we click Close, the program informs the user that the current configuration will be overwritten (Figure 10-4).

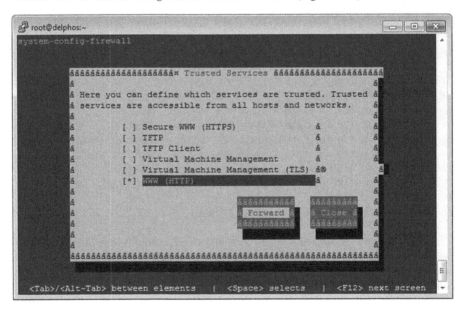

Figure 10-3. *Allowing incoming traffic with* `system-config-firewall`

296

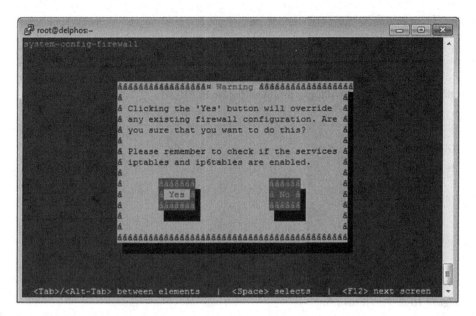

Figure 10-4. *Overwriting the configuration*

10.1.2. Port Redirection

So far, we have seen how to use iptables to filter traffic. We do this by modifying the filter table, which is the default table, by the way. Thus, the following two commands are equivalent:

```
1   [root@delphos ~]# iptables -t filter -I INPUT 1 -p tcp --dport 80 -j
    ACCEPT
2   [root@delphos ~]# iptables -I INPUT 1 -p tcp --dport 80 -j ACCEPT
```

But iptables can modify more tables apart from filter. One of these tables is nat, which allows us to change network parameters such as the destination address or port.

In order for some of these changes to work properly, the computer must be able to route network traffic. By default, this characteristic is disabled. If this is the case, we'll have to enable it by changing the value of the net.ipv4.ip_forward system parameter.

```
1   [root@delphos ~]# sysctl net.ipv4.ip_forward
2   net.ipv4.ip_forward = 0
3   [root@delphos ~]# sysctl -w net.ipv4.ip_forward=1
4   net.ipv4.ip_forward = 1
```

Now let's suppose we have a working web server listening on port 80. We might want our server to listen in a different port too. We can achieve this by modifying the nat table with iptables.

```
1   [root@delphos ~]# iptables -t nat -A PREROUTING -p tcp --dport 8888 -j
    REDIRECT \
2   --to-port 80
```

Now if we try to open a http connection over port 8888, we'll be redirected to port 80 and access the web site without a problem (Figure 10-5).

Figure 10-5. *Port forwarding*

10.1.3. Redirecting Traffic to a Different Host

We've seen in the previous section how to forward traffic between different ports in the local server. But iptables allows us to redirect the traffic to a different host. For example, if we have to update a web server, we might want to redirect web traffic to another server.

■ **Note** Procedures similar to this one are also used by hackers to perform what is called a "man in the middle" attack. So, depending on company policy, this port redirection could be considered inappropriate or even illegal. Therefore, if you have doubts regarding whether or not you're allowed to use this technique, don't use it.

Similar to what we did when forwarding traffic to a different port, we also have to change the nat table.

As it happens that some default firewall rules might interfere with the redirection, we start by erasing the current configuration.

```
1   [root@delphos ~]# iptables -t nat -F
2   [root@delphos ~]# iptables -t filter -F
```

Let's suppose we want to redirect http (port 80) traffic from our server to another computer with IP address 192.168.10.41. We'll have to instruct iptables to change the destination address of those network packets addressed to TCP port 80.

```
1   [root@delphos ~]# iptables -t nat -A PREROUTING -p tcp --dport 80 -j
    DNAT --to-d\
2   estination 192.168.10.41
```

Now these packets will be routed to their new destination, because we activated IP forwarding previously. But we'll have to change the source address too, so that the packets are returned to our server and, finally, sent back to the original client.

```
1   [root@delphos ~]# iptables -t nat -A POSTROUTING -p tcp --dport 80 -j
    SNAT --to-\
2   source 192.168.1.20
```

10.1.4. Logging Packets

Sometimes, it can be useful to log network packets. Let's imagine we're running a service, and some users complain that they get an error when trying to access the service.

The first thing we do is to take a look at the log files. But, sometimes, we won't even see an entry in the log. In these cases, however, we can use iptables to log the packets addressed to that port.

For example, if we want to log connections to the http port, we could do the following:

```
1   [root@delphos ~]# iptables -I INPUT 1 -p tcp --dport 80 -j LOG --log-
    prefix "HTT\
2   P Traffic"
```

The entries are logged by default in the /var/log/messages file, so if someone accesses port 80, we'll see in the log file many entries like these:

```
1   Oct 10 04:52:44 delphos kernel: HTTP TrafficIN=eth0 OUT=
    MAC=00:0c:29:78:4c:b1:7\
2   4:46:a0:a5:2e:1b:08:00 SRC=192.168.1.1 DST=192.168.1.20 LEN=40 TOS=0x00
    PREC=0x0\
3   0 TTL=4 ID=27373 DF PROTO=TCP SPT=54758 DPT=80 WINDOW=0 RES=0x00 RST
    URGP=0
4   Oct 10 04:52:44 delphos kernel: HTTP TrafficIN=eth0 OUT=
    MAC=00:0c:29:78:4c:b1:7\
5   4:46:a0:a5:2e:1b:08:00 SRC=192.168.1.1 DST=192.168.1.20 LEN=40 TOS=0x00
    PREC=0x0\
6   0 TTL=2 ID=27372 DF PROTO=TCP SPT=54758 DPT=80 WINDOW=63773 RES=0x00 ACK
    FIN URG\
7   P=0
```

If, on the contrary, we don't see any new entry, we conclude that the connection is filtered at any point before reaching the server.

10.2. Firewall in CentOS 7

The firewall in CentOS 7 can be managed with the command line utility firewall-cmd.
I'll try to familiarize you with it.

First, we'll see whether the service is currently running.

```
1  [root@localhost ~]# systemctl status firewalld
2  firewalld.service - firewalld - dynamic firewall daemon
3     Loaded: loaded (/usr/lib/systemd/system/firewalld.service; enabled)
4     Active: active (running) since Wed 2014-11-26 15:15:34 CET; 1h 25min
       ago
5   Main  PID: 778  (firewalld)
6     CGroup: /system.slice/firewalld.service
7             778 /usr/bin/python  -Es  /usr/sbin/firewalld  --nofork
               --nopid
8
9   Nov 26 15:15:34 localhost.localdomain systemd[1]: Started firewalld -
     dynamic...
10  Hint: Some lines were ellipsized, use -l to show in full.CentOS 7,
     firewallsservice
```

The main configuration file is /etc/firewalld/firewalld.conf, but we'll see here
how to see and change the configuration with the use of commands.

In firewalld, we have some zones defined by default, and every one of these
zones allows or rejects certain connections. They're usually given descriptive names,
such as home, internal, etc. Evidently, in the internal zone, there will be more allowed
connections than in the external zone. We can check the currently defined zones like this:

```
1  [root@localhost ~]# firewall-cmd --get-zones
2  block dmz drop external home internal public trusted work
```

We can also see the XML files associated to every zone in the /usr/lib/firewalld/
zones/ folder.

```
1  [root@localhost ~]# ls /usr/lib/firewalld/zones/
2  block.xml    drop.xml    home.xml      public.xml      work.xml
3  dmz.xml      external.xml internal.xml  trusted.xml
```

We can also see the default zone we are currently in.

```
1  [root@localhost ~]# firewall-cmd --get-default-zone
2  public
```

It could be possible to have different network interfaces associated to different zones.
We can check this, as follows:

```
1  [root@localhost ~]# firewall-cmd --get-active-zones
2  public
3  interfaces: eno16777736
```

In this case, we have only a network interface, and it is associated with the public zone. If we want to change the default zone, we can do it like this:

```
1  [root@localhost ~]# firewall-cmd --set-default-zone=internal
2  success
3  [root@localhost ~]# firewall-cmd --get-default-zone
4  internal
```

We can also check the services currently allowed in a zone.

```
1  [root@localhost ~]# firewall-cmd --zone=internal --list-services
2  dhcpv6-client ipp-client mdns samba-client ssh
```

The services are also defined in /usr/lib/firewalld/services/.

```
1   [root@localhost ~]# ls /usr/lib/firewalld/services/
2   amanda-client.xml    ipp-client.xml    mysql.xml         rpc-bind.xml
3   bacula-client.xml    ipp.xml           nfs.xml           samba-client.xml
4   bacula.xml           ipsec.xml         ntp.xml           samba.xml
5   dhcpv6-client.xml    kerberos.xml      openvpn.xml       smtp.xml
6   dhcpv6.xml           kpasswd.xml       pmcd.xml          ssh.xml
7   dhcp.xml             ldaps.xml         pmproxy.xml       telnet.xml
8   dns.xml              ldap.xml          pmwebapis.xml     tftp-client.xml
9   ftp.xml              libvirt-tls.xml   pmwebapi.xml      tftp.xml
10  high-availability.xml libvirt.xml      pop3s.xml         transmission-
    client.xml
11  https.xml            mdns.xml          postgresql.xml    vnc-server.xml
12  http.xml             mountd.xml        proxy-dhcp.xml    wbem-https.xml
13  imaps.xml            ms-wbt.xml        radius.xml
```

For example, following is the file for the HTTP service:

```
1  [root@localhost ~]# cat /usr/lib/firewalld/services/http.xml
2  <?xml version="1.0" encoding="utf-8"?>
3  <service>
4    <short>WWW (HTTP)</short>
5    <description>HTTP is the protocol used to serve Web pages. If you
       plan to make\
6  your Web server publicly available, enable this option. This option is
    not requ\
7  ired for viewing pages locally or developing Web pages.</description>
8    <port protocol="tcp" port="80"/>
9  </service>
```

In order to allow access to a certain service, the preferred option is to explicitly allow one of the services defined in /usr/lib/firewalld/services/ or create a new file, if it doesn't exist. Nevertheless, it is also possible to allow access to a port number without specifying a service. We can check what ports are allowed (apart from those associated with the allowed services).

```
1   [root@localhost ~]# firewall-cmd --zone=internal --list-ports
2   [root@localhost ~]#
```

For example, to allow access to the http service, we do the following.

```
1   [root@localhost ~]# firewall-cmd --zone=internal --add-service=http
2   success
```

Another way to allow http traffic is to open TCP port 80.

```
1   [root@CentOS7 ~]# firewall-cmd --add-port=80/tcp
2   success
```

As we can see, now the http traffic is allowed.

```
1   [root@localhost ~]# firewall-cmd --zone=internal --list-services
2   dhcpv6-client http ipp-client mdns samba-client ssh
```

We can get even more information with the –list-all option.

```
1    [root@localhost ~]# firewall-cmd --zone=internal --list-all
2    internal (default, active)
3      interfaces: eno16777736
4      sources:
5      services: dhcpv6-client http ipp-client mdns samba-client ssh
6      ports:
7      masquerade: no
8      forward-ports:
9      icmp-blocks:
10     rich rules:
```

The http traffic is now allowed, but this change is temporary, and it will be reverted once the firewalld service is restarted. If we want the change to be permanent, we'll have to use the –permanent option.

```
1   [root@localhost ~]# firewall-cmd --permanent --zone=internal --add-
    service=http
2   success
```

We can also remove a service from the firewall configuration. We can remove it temporarily.

```
1   [root@CentOS7 ~]# firewall-cmd --remove-service=http
2   success
```

Or we can remove it permanently.

```
1   [root@CentOS7 ~]# firewall-cmd --permanent --remove-service=http
2   success
```

As we saw when talking about iptables, we can permit or deny traffic to a single host or network address. When using firewall-cmd, we can do it by writing what are called rich rules. For example, if we want to permit access to the http port to all the computers except the computer with IP 192.168.1.30, this is what we'd do:

```
1  [root@CentOS7 ~]# firewall-cmd --add-service=http
2  success
3  [root@CentOS7 ~]# firewall-cmd --add-rich-rule='rule family="ipv4"
   source addres\
4  s="192.168.1.30" service name="http" reject'
5  success
```

Now the computer with address 192.168.1.30 will be unable to access the web server. We can reverse the situation easily by deleting the rich rule, as follows:

```
1  [root@CentOS7 ~]# firewall-cmd --remove-rich-rule='rule family="ipv4"
   source add\
2  ress="192.168.1.20" service name="http" reject'
3  success
```

10.2.1. Saving and Restoring Configuration

When using the new firewalld in CentOS 7, the configuration is kept in many different files, as opposed to iptables, which could keep the firewall configuration in a single file.

For this reason, if we ever have to save the firewall configuration to restore it later in the same—or a different—computer, the simplest way is probably using iptables. Even though it is recommended to use firewall-cmd to manage the firewall, we still can use iptables. The way to save or restore the rules with iptables has been already seen in the "Saving and Restoring the Configuration" section.

To switch from firewalld to iptables, we only have to stop and disable the firewalld service and start and enable the iptables service, as follows:

```
1  [root@CentOS7 firewalld]# systemctl stop firewalld
2  [root@CentOS7 firewalld]# systemctl disable firewalld
3  rm '/etc/systemd/system/dbus-org.fedoraproject.FirewallD1.service'
4  rm '/etc/systemd/system/basic.target.wants/firewalld.service'
5  [root@CentOS7 firewalld]# systemctl start iptables
6  [root@CentOS7 firewalld]# systemctl enable iptables
```

Once we have saved or restored the configuration we can switch back to firewalld.

```
1  [root@CentOS7 firewalld]# systemctl disable iptables
2  rm '/etc/systemd/system/basic.target.wants/iptables.service'
3  [root@CentOS7 firewalld]# systemctl start firewalld
4  [root@CentOS7 firewalld]# systemctl enable firewalld
5  ln -s '/usr/lib/systemd/system/firewalld.service' '/etc/systemd/system/
   dbus-org.\
```

```
6   fedoraproject.FirewallD1.service'
7   ln -s '/usr/lib/systemd/system/firewalld.service' '/etc/systemd/system/
    basic.tar\
8   get.wants/firewalld.service'
```

10.2.2. Port Forwarding

In a similar way as we saw when talking about iptables, we can redirect ports too. If, for example, we want all connections to port 8000 in the local machine to be redirected to port 80, we can simply use the following command:

```
1   [root@CentOS7 firewalld]# firewall-cmd --add-forward-
    port=port=8000:proto=tcp:to\
2   port=80
3   success
```

Now, if we open a browser and try to open a connection to port 8000 in the server, we'll be redirected to port number 80.

10.2.3. Redirecting Traffic to a Different Host

It is also possible to redirect the traffic to a different host. To do this, the computer must be able to forward network traffic. To check this, we can see the value of the net.ipv4. ip_forward system parameter (see the preceding "Port Redirection" section).

Once the server is correctly configured, we can redirect the traffic with the following commands:

```
1   [root@CentOS7 firewalld]# firewall-cmd --add-masquerade
2   success
3   [root@CentOS7 firewalld]# firewall-cmd --add-forward-
    port=port=80:proto=tcp:toad\
4   dr=192.168.10.41
```

If we open a browser and type the address of our server, we'll be redirected to the server with IP address 192.168.10.41.

CHAPTER 11

OpenLDAP

By default, Linux systems keep a local registry of all their users. That registry is the /etc/passwd file. In this file, we can see a line for every registered user. So, in order to access a computer, we must have a user defined in that computer. This is OK when we have only a few computers, but if we have tens or hundreds of computers, it could be a nightmare to create new users or change a password in all of them.

The solution is to centralize user account management, that is, to have a common database in which to keep all information related to user accounts. There are many ways to accomplish this, but probably the most used today is the Lightweight Directory Access Protocol (LDAP) in one of its many variants.

LDAP keeps a central database in which users, computers, and, generally speaking, all network objects are registered. There are many implementations of the protocol, for example, Active Directory from Microsoft or eDirectory from Novell. Here we'll use OpenLDAP, a free implementation of the protocol.

11.1. Installing OpenLDAP

First, we have to install the openldap, openldap-servers, and openldap-clients packages.

```
1   [root@delphos ~]# yum install openldap openldap-servers openldap-clients
```

We make sure that the slapd service is configured to boot automatically, and we start the service.

In CentOS 6:

```
1   [root@delphos cn=config]# chkconfig slapd on
2   [root@delphos cn=config]# service slapd start
3   Starting slapd:                                    [  OK  ]
```

In CentOS 7:

```
1   [root@CentOS7 ~]# systemctl enable slapd
2   ln -s '/usr/lib/systemd/system/slapd.service' '/etc/systemd/system/
    multi-user.ta\
```

© Antonio Vazquez 2016
A. Vazquez, *Learn CentOS Linux Network Services*, DOI 10.1007/978-1-4842-2379-6_11

```
3   rget.wants/slapd.service'
4   [root@CentOS7 ~]# systemctl start slapd
```

11.2. Customizing the Installation

Once installed, we have to generate a password for the admin user. In this example, we use a simple password: "pass."

```
1   [root@delphos ~]# slappasswd
2   New password:
3   Re-enter new password:
4   {SSHA}Ftvq59j9XWVHRnfEplQvMiRBfthieUMU
```

Here, we're assuming that the root user and the OpenLDAP admin are the same person, but that's not always the case. If the latter were true, the OpenLDAP admin would have to change her password later.

Formerly, there was a file named /etc/openldap/slapd.d/slapd.conf in which the configuration of the OpenLDAP server was kept. But now the configuration is kept in the LDAP database itself. Nevertheless, the relevant files we need to modify are still in /etc/openldap/slapd.d.

```
1   [root@delphos ~]# ls /etc/openldap/slapd.d/
2   cn=config    cn=config.ldif
```

We can either modify these files directly or use the ldapmodify command. For a beginner, it is probably easier to edit the files, but as the recommended way to edit OpenLDAP is by using ldapmodify, this is what we'll do. We'll see in much more detail how to use ldapmodify in the upcoming sections. For now, just to initiate a working OpenLDAP installation, I'll describe the necessary steps briefly.

11.2.1. Modifying Objects

OpenLDAP actually stores its information in storage back ends. We could think of these back ends as the databases used by OpenLDAP. One of the most used back ends has always been the Berkeley DB back ends, such as bdb, or the more recent hdb. The information stored in the hdb back end can be found in the /etc/openldap/slapd.d/cn=config/olcDatabase={2}hdb.ldif file.

These are the contents of the /etc/openldap/slapd.d/cn=config/olcDatabase={2} hdb.ldif file after a fresh installation:

```
1   .
2   .
3   .
4   # AUTO-GENERATED FILE - DO NOT EDIT!! Use ldapmodify.
5   # CRC32 373d43d6
6   dn: olcDatabase={2}hdb
7   objectClass: olcDatabaseConfig
```

```
 8   objectClass: olcHdbConfig
 9   olcDatabase: {2}hdb
10   olcDbDirectory: /var/lib/ldap
11   olcSuffix: dc=my-domain,dc=com
12   olcRootDN: cn=Manager,dc=my-domain,dc=com
13   olcDbIndex: objectClass eq,pres
14   olcDbIndex: ou,cn,mail,surname,givenname eq,pres,sub
15   structuralObjectClass: olcHdbConfig
16   entryUUID: b8596292-eb3d-1034-860a-e7b4503cc451
17   creatorsName: cn=config
18   createTimestamp: 20150909125458Z
19   entryCSN: 20150909125458.235214Z#000000#000#000000
20   modifiersName: cn=config
21   modifyTimestamp: 20150909125458Z
22   .
23   .
24   .
```

LDIF (LDAP Data Interchange Format) is a text format designed to retrieve information from an LDAP server, as well as for updating it. In an LDIF file, we first identify the element we want to add, change, etc. To uniquely identify an element, we use the dn (distinguished name) attribute, which was created precisely for that reason. So, the first line of our LDIF file could be something like this:

```
1   dn: olcDatabase={2}hdb,cn=config
```

Next, we specify if we want to add an attribute, modify it, etc.

```
1   changeType: modify
```

If we want to modify an entry, we also must clarify whether we'll be replacing an attribute, deleting it, etc.

```
1   replace: olcSuffix
```

And, finally, we type the new value of the modified attribute.

```
1   olcSuffix: dc=olimpus,dc=local
```

You'll see many LDIF examples throughout the book, but for now, let's get back to the /etc/openldap/s- lapd.d/cn=config/olcDatabase={2}hdb.ldif file. We have to modify (at least) these two entries:

```
1   olcSuffix: dc=my-domain,dc=com
2   olcRootDN: cn=Manager,dc=my-domain,dc=com
```

And we have to add a new entry to store the admin's password (olcRootPW), where we'll store the password we just created with the slappasswd command.

To make all these changes with ldapmodify, we have to prepare an LDIF file such as this:

```
1   dn: olcDatabase={2}hdb,cn=config
2   changeType: modify
3   replace: olcSuffix
4   olcSuffix: dc=olimpus,dc=local
5   -
6   replace: olcRootDN
7   olcRootDN: cn=admin,dc=olimpus,dc=com
```

The first line identifies the main entry in the LDAP that we are going to change. Just a moment ago, we saw the parameter olcSuffix inside the /etc/openldap/ slapd.d/cn=config/olcDatabase={2}hdb.ldif file. In this file, the dn attribute is dn: olcDatabase={2}hdb, and as the file is inside the config folder, the full dn attribute is dn: olcDatabase={2}hdb,cn=config.

Another, and maybe better, way to identify the data we require to create the LDIF file could be to use the ldapsearch command.

```
1   [root@CentOS7-LPI300 ~]# ldapsearch -Y EXTERNAL -H ldapi:/// -b
    cn=config olcDat\
2   abase=\*
3   SASL/EXTERNAL authentication started
4   SASL username: gidNumber=0+uidNumber=0,cn=peercred,cn=external,cn=auth
5   SASL SSF: 0
6   # extended LDIF
7   #
8   # LDAPv3
9   # base <cn=config> with scope subtree
10  # filter: olcDatabase=*
11  # requesting: ALL
12  #
13
14  # {-1}frontend, config
15  dn: olcDatabase={-1}frontend,cn=config
16  objectClass: olcDatabaseConfig
17  objectClass: olcFrontendConfig
18  olcDatabase: frontend
19
20  # {0}config, config
21  dn: olcDatabase={0}config,cn=config
22  objectClass: olcDatabaseConfig
23  olcDatabase: {0}config
24  olcAccess: {0}to * by dn.base="gidNumber=0+uidNumber=0,cn=peercred,
    cn=external,c\
25  n=auth" manage by * none
26
27  # {1}monitor, config
```

```
28   dn: olcDatabase={1}monitor,cn=config
29   objectClass: olcDatabaseConfig
30   olcDatabase: {1}monitor
31   olcAccess: {0}to * by dn.base="gidNumber=0+uidNumber=0,cn=peercred,
     cn=external,c\
32   n=auth" read by dn.base="cn=Manager,dc=my-domain,dc=com" read by * none
33
34   # {2}hdb, config
35   dn: olcDatabase={2}hdb,cn=config
36   objectClass: olcDatabaseConfig
37   objectClass: olcHdbConfig
38   olcDatabase: {2}hdb
39   olcDbDirectory: /var/lib/ldap
40   olcSuffix: dc=my-domain,dc=com
41   olcRootDN: cn=Manager,dc=my-domain,dc=com
42   olcDbIndex: objectClass eq,pres
43   olcDbIndex: ou,cn,mail,surname,givenname eq,pres,sub
44
45   # search result
46   search: 2
47   result: 0 Success
48
49   # numResponses: 5
50   # numEntries: 4
```

We save the LDIF file with an appropriate name, for example, my_config.ldif, and we execute ldapmodify.

```
1   [root@CentOS7-LPI300 ~]# ldapmodify -Y EXTERNAL -H ldapi:/// -f
    my_config.ldif
2   SASL/EXTERNAL authentication started
3   SASL username: gidNumber=0+uidNumber=0,cn=peercred,cn=external,cn=auth
4   SASL SSF: 0
5   modifying entry "olcDatabase={2}hdb,cn=config"
```

Now we create another LDIF file (my_config2.ldif) to add the olcRootPW attribute.

```
1   [root@CentOS7-LPI300 ~]# cat my_config2.ldif
2   dn: olcDatabase={2}hdb,cn=config
3   changeType: modify
4   add: olcRootPW
5   olcRootPW: {SSHA}Ftvq59j9XWVHRnfEplQvMiRBfthieUMU
```

And we execute ldapmodify again.

```
1   [root@CentOS7-LPI300 ~]# ldapmodify -Y EXTERNAL -H ldapi:/// -f
    my_config2.ldif
2   SASL/EXTERNAL authentication started
```

```
3  SASL username: gidNumber=0+uidNumber=0,cn=peercred,cn=external,cn=auth
4  SASL SSF: 0
5  modifying entry "olcDatabase={2}hdb,cn=config"
```

To check the changes, we can use the ldapsearch command again.

```
1  [root@CentOS7-LPI300 ~]# ldapsearch -Y EXTERNAL -H ldapi:/// -b
   cn=config olcDat\
2  abase=\*
3  SASL/EXTERNAL authentication started
4  SASL username: gidNumber=0+uidNumber=0,cn=peercred,cn=external,cn=auth
5  SASL SSF: 0
6  # extended LDIF
7  #
8  # LDAPv3
9  # base <cn=config> with scope subtree
10 # filter: olcDatabase=*
11 # requesting: ALL
12 #
13
14 # {-1}frontend, config
15 dn: olcDatabase={-1}frontend,cn=config
16 objectClass: olcDatabaseConfig
17 objectClass: olcFrontendConfig
18 olcDatabase: frontend
19
20 # {0}config, config
21 dn: olcDatabase={0}config,cn=config
22 objectClass: olcDatabaseConfig
23 olcDatabase: {0}config
24 olcAccess: {0}to * by dn.base="gidNumber=0+uidNumber=0,cn=peercred,
   cn=external,c\
25 n=auth" manage by * none
26
27 # {1}monitor, config
28 dn: olcDatabase={1}monitor,cn=config
29 objectClass: olcDatabaseConfig
30 olcDatabase: {1}monitor
31 olcAccess: {0}to * by dn.base="gidNumber=0+uidNumber=0,cn=peercred,
   cn=external,c\
32 n=auth" read by dn.base="cn=admin,dc=olimpus,dc=local" read by * none
33
34 # {2}hdb, config
35 dn: olcDatabase={2}hdb,cn=config
36 objectClass: olcDatabaseConfig
37 objectClass: olcHdbConfig
38 olcDatabase: {2}hdb
39 olcDbDirectory: /var/lib/ldap
```

```
40   olcDbIndex: objectClass eq,pres
41   olcDbIndex: ou,cn,mail,surname,givenname eq,pres,sub
42   olcSuffix: dc=linuxaholics,dc=com
43   olcRootDN: cn=admin,dc=olimpus,dc=local
44   olcRootPW: {SSHA}Ftvq59j9XWVHRnfEplQvMiRBfthieUMU
45
46   # search result
47   search: 2
48   result: 0 Success
49
50   # numResponses: 5
51   # numEntries: 4OpenLDAPmodifying objectsldapsearch
```

We also have to allow access to the LDAP database to the admin user we just specified before (cn=admin,dc=olimpus,dc=local). If we take a look at the olcDatabase={1}monitor.ldif, file we'll see the following line:

```
1   olcAccess: {0}to *   by dn.base="gidNumber=0+uidNumber=0,cn=peercred,
    cn=external,\
2   cn=auth" read  by dn.base="cn=manager,dc=my-domain,dc=com" read    by *
    none
```

We'll have to edit the file or use ldapmodify to change the entry. If we use ldapmodify, the LDIF file should be something like this:

```
1   dn: olcDatabase={1}monitor,cn=config
2   changetype: modify
3   replace: olcAccess
4   olcAccess: {0}to * by dn.base="gidNumber=0+uidNumber=0,cn=peercred,cn=e
    xternal,c\
5   n=auth" read by dn.base="cn=admin,dc=olimpus,dc=local" read by * none
```

Once again, we execute ldapmodify by passing the new LDIF file as a parameter.

```
1   [root@CentOS7-LPI300 ~]# ldapmodify -Y EXTERNAL -H ldapi:/// -f
    my_config3.ldif
2   SASL/EXTERNAL authentication started
3   SASL username: gidNumber=0+uidNumber=0,cn=peercred,cn=external,cn=auth
4   SASL SSF: 0
5   modifying entry "olcDatabase={1}monitor,cn=config"
```

Now we can check with ldapsearch whether the value for the attribute was actually changed.

```
1   [root@CentOS7-LPI300 ~]# ldapsearch -Y EXTERNAL -H ldapi:/// -b
    cn=config olcAcc\
2   ess=\*
3   SASL/EXTERNAL authentication started
```

```
 4   SASL username: gidNumber=0+uidNumber=0,cn=peercred,cn=external,cn=auth
 5   SASL SSF: 0
 6   # extended LDIF
 7   #
 8   # LDAPv3
 9   # base <cn=config> with scope subtree
10   # filter: olcAccess=*
11   # requesting: ALL
12   #
13
14   # {0}config, config
15   dn: olcDatabase={0}config,cn=config
16   objectClass: olcDatabaseConfig
17   olcDatabase: {0}config
18   olcAccess: {0}to * by dn.base="gidNumber=0+uidNumber=0,cn=peercred,
     cn=external,c\
19   n=auth" manage by * none
20
21   # {1}monitor, config
22   dn: olcDatabase={1}monitor,cn=config
23   objectClass: olcDatabaseConfig
24   olcDatabase: {1}monitor
25   olcAccess: {0}to * by dn.base="gidNumber=0+uidNumber=0,cn=peercred,
     cn=external,c\
26   n=auth" read by dn.base="cn=admin,dc=olimpus,dc=local" read by * none
27
28   # search result
29   search: 2
30   result: 0 Success
31
32   # numResponses: 3
33   # numEntries: 2OpenLDAPmodifying objectsldapsearch
```

As we can see, the value was changed according to what we specified in the LDIF file. Another tool we can use to check the configuration is the slaptest command.

```
1   [root@CentOS7-LPI300 ~]# slaptest -u
2   config file testing succeeded
```

11.2.2. Adding Objects

Now we have to manually create an entry for dc=olimpus,dc=local in our LDAP server. The easiest way to do this is to create an LDIF file for this entry and pass it to the ldapadd command.

So, we create a file named olimpus.ldif, with the following content:

```
1   dn: dc=olimpus,dc=local
2   objectClass: dcObject
```

```
3   objectClass: organization
4   dc: olimpus
5   o: olimpus
```

We specify a series of attributes, such as distinguished name (dn), domain component (dc), and organization (o). We also define the new entry as an object of the type dcObject and organization.

Depending on the type of object we are creating, there are a series of attributes that can be optional or mandatory. We can check this by consulting the schema.

For example, if we want to know what attributes must be defined when adding an object of the organization type, we can check this on the schema. We should go to /etc/openldap/slapd.d/cn=config/cn=schema in CentOS 6 or /etc/openldap/schema in CentOS 7. In this location are all the files that define the OpenLDAP schema. If we are not sure where a certain object is defined, we can use the grep command (see Chapter 2). As far as our example is concerned, the object organization is defined in the cn={1}core.ldif file in CentOS 6, and in the core.schema file in CentOS 7, in which we will find an entry such as this:

```
1    objectclass ( 2.5.6.4 NAME 'organization'
2         DESC 'RFC2256: an organization'
3         SUP top STRUCTURAL
4         MUST o
5         MAY ( userPassword $ searchGuide $ seeAlso $ businessCategory $
6              x121Address $ registeredAddress $ destinationIndicator $
7              preferredDeliveryMethod $ telexNumber $
              teletexTerminalIdentifier $
8              telephoneNumber $ internationaliSDNNumber $
9              facsimileTelephoneNumber $ street $ postOfficeBox $
              postalCode $
10             postalAddress $ physicalDeliveryOfficeName $ st $ l $
              description ) )
```

As we can see, in this case, the only mandatory attribute is o.

Now we execute ldapadd and pass it the olimpus.ldif file as a parameter. We specify with (-f) the name of the file, the admin user (-D), and the password we defined for that admin user (-w).

```
1    [root@delphos ~]# ldapadd -f olimpus.ldif -D
     cn=admin,dc=olimpus,dc=local -w pass
2    adding new entry "dc=olimpus,dc=local"
```

We can check whether the entry was created successfully by using the ldapsearch command.

```
1    [root@delphos ~]# ldapsearch -x -b dc=olimpus,dc=local
2    # extended LDIF
3    #
4    # LDAPv3
```

```
 5   # base <dc=olimpus,dc=local> with scope subtree
 6   # filter: (objectclass=*)
 7   # requesting: ALL
 8   #
 9
10   # olimpus.local
11   dn: dc=olimpus,dc=local
12   objectClass: dcObject
13   objectClass: organization
14   dc: olimpus
15   o: olimpus
16
17   # search result
18   search: 2
19   result: 0 Success
20
21   # numResponses: 2
22   # numEntries: 1
```

You just saw how to add the object dc=olimpus,dc=local to our LDAP. Now you'll see how to add organizational units, groups, and users.

11.2.2.1. Adding an Organizational Unit

Maybe we'd like to have an organizational unit (OU) called users in which to store all LDAP users. To do so, we'll create a new LDIF file named users.ldif, with the following content:

```
1   dn: ou=users,dc=olimpus,dc=local
2   objectClass: organizationalUnit
3   ou: users
```

We execute ldapadd again to create the OU.

```
1   [root@delphos ~]# ldapadd -f users.ldif -D cn=admin,dc=olimpus,dc=local
    -w pass
2   adding new entry "ou=users,dc=olimpus,dc=local"
```

11.2.2.2. Adding a User

We can now include a user inside the organizational unit. The procedure is quite similar to what we have seen so far. First, we create a file named archimedes.ldif, with the following content:

```
1   dn: cn=Archimedes of Syracuse,ou=users,dc=olimpus,dc=local
2   cn: Archimedes
3   sn: Syracuse
```

```
4    objectClass: inetOrgPerson
5    userPassword: eureka
6    uid: archimedes
```

Then we execute ldapadd again.

```
1    [root@delphos ~]# ldapadd -f archimedes.ldif -x -D
     cn=admin,dc=olimpus,dc=local \
2    -w pass
3    adding new entry "cn=Archimedes of Syracuse,ou=users,dc=olimpus,dc=local"
```

In CentOS 7, we might receive this error:

```
1    [root@CentOS7 ~]# ldapadd -f archimedes.ldif -x -D
     cn=admin,dc=olimpus,dc=local \
2    -w admin
3    adding new entry "cn=Archimedes of Syracuse,ou=users,dc=olimpus,dc=local"
4    ldap_add: Invalid syntax (21)
5           additional info: objectClass: value #0 invalid per syntax
```

What this message means is that the object inetOrgPerson isn't loaded in the core schema, so we'll have to include it. In the /etc/openldap/schema folders, there are many LDIF files to extend the schema when we need it. We can see there is an inetorgperson.ldif file, which contains the schema definition for the inetOrgPerson object.

The schema itself is contained in the LDAP database, so we can add new definitions to it with the ldapadd command. As we're going to modify the configuration itself, instead of the data, we'll authenticate ourselves as the external root user (-Y EXTERNAL).

```
1    [root@CentOS7 ~]# ldapadd -Y EXTERNAL -H ldapi:// -f /etc/openldap/
     schema/inetor\
2    gperson.ldif
3    SASL/EXTERNAL authentication started
4    SASL username: gidNumber=0+uidNumber=0,cn=peercred,cn=external,cn=auth
5    SASL SSF: 0
6    adding new entry "cn=inetorgperson,cn=schema,cn=config"
7    ldap_add: Other (e.g., implementation specific) error (80)
8           additional info: olcObjectClasses: AttributeType not found:
           "audio"
```

As we can see, we get an error, because the attribute type audio isn't defined. So, we have to include this definition in the schema too.

If we perform a search of the string audio in the files located in the /etc/openldap/schema/ folder, we'll see that the attribute audio is defined in the cosine.ldif file. So, we extend the schema with this LDIF file first.

```
1    [root@CentOS7 ~]# ldapadd -Y EXTERNAL -H ldapi:// -f /etc/openldap/
     schema/cosine\
2    .ldif
```

```
3    SASL/EXTERNAL authentication started
4    SASL username: gidNumber=0+uidNumber=0,cn=peercred,cn=external,cn=auth
5    SASL SSF: 0
6    adding new entry "cn=cosine,cn=schema,cn=config"
```

Now we do the same thing with the inetorgperson.ldif file.

```
1    [root@CentOS7 ~]# ldapadd -Y EXTERNAL -H ldapi:// -f /etc/openldap/
     schema/inetor\
2    gperson.ldif
3    SASL/EXTERNAL authentication started
4    SASL username: gidNumber=0+uidNumber=0,cn=peercred,cn=external,cn=auth
5    SASL SSF: 0
6    adding new entry "cn=inetorgperson,cn=schema,cn=config"
```

Now we can add the user with the archimedes.ldif file we created before.

```
1    [root@CentOS7 ~]# ldapadd -f archimedes.ldif -x -D
     cn=admin,dc=olimpus,dc=local \
2    -w admin
3    adding new entry "cn=Archimedes of Syracuse,ou=users,dc=olimpus,dc=local"
```

If at some point we have to take a look at the currently used schema, we can use the slapcat command like this:

```
1    [root@CentOS7 ~]# slapcat -b "cn=schema,cn=config"
2    dn: cn=config
3    objectClass: olcGlobal
4    cn: config
5    olcArgsFile: /var/run/openldap/slapd.args
6    olcPidFile: /var/run/openldap/slapd.pid
7    olcTLSCACertificatePath: /etc/openldap/certs
8    olcTLSCertificateFile: "OpenLDAP Server"
9    olcTLSCertificateKeyFile: /etc/openldap/certs/password
10   structuralObjectClass: olcGlobal
11   entryUUID: bb38e2c0-4f85-1034-8587-e9dda2aed256
12   creatorsName: cn=config
13   createTimestamp: 20150223085725Z
14   entryCSN: 20150223085725.426340Z#000000#000#000000
15   modifiersName: cn=config
16   modifyTimestamp: 20150223085725Z
17   .
18   .
19   .
```

11.2.2.3. Adding a Group

To add a group, we repeat the same process. First we create the group.ldif file with the following content:

```
1   dn: cn=scientists,ou=users,dc=olimpus,dc=local
2   cn: scientists
3   objectClass: groupOfNames
4   member: cn=Archimedes of Syracuse,ou=users,dc=olimpus,dc=local
```

And we add the group with ldapadd.

```
1   [root@delphos ~]# ldapadd -f groups.ldif -x -D
    cn=admin,dc=olimpus,dc=local -w p\
2   ass
3   adding new entry "cn=scientists,ou=users,dc=olimpus,dc=local"
```

11.2.3. Deleting Objects

Apart from adding or editing, we can also delete objects from the LDAP server. The procedure is even easier, as we don't have to create any LDIF file. We just execute ldapdel with the cn we want to delete.

```
1   [root@CentOS7 ~]# ldapdelete "cn=Archimedes of Syracuse,ou=users,dc=oli
    mpus,dc=l\
2   ocal" -D cn=admin,dc=olimpus,dc=local -w admin
```

We can check that the entry was actually suppressed.

```
1   [root@CentOS7 ~]# ldapsearch -x -b "dc=olimpus,dc=local"
    "(cn=Archimedes)"    \
2   # extended LDIF
3   #
4   # LDAPv3
5   # base <dc=olimpus,dc=local> with scope subtree
6   # filter: (cn=Archimedes)
7   # requesting: ALL
8   #
9
10  # search result
11  search: 2
12  result: 0 Success
13
14  # numResponses: 1
```

11.3. Securing LDAP Connections with TLS

By default, when using LDAP connections, all information is sent in plain text. There's no need to insist again on the importance of ciphering all traffic transmitted between the client and the server.

We begin by creating a certificate. We have already seen this many times, but this time, we're going to take a different approach.

So far, we have created self-signed certificates in order to provide secure connections to known services. This is more than enough to secure the traffic in a local network.

A stricter use of certificates would require the use of a certificate signed by a certification authority, or CA. This is what Internet sites usually do. They request a signed certificate to a well-known CA.

In our case, however, we'll create our own CA and sign our certificate to use it with LDAP.

11.3.1. Creating a CA

After installing the openssl package, we should have a predefined tree structure under /etc/pki/CA.

```
1  [root@delphos ~]# cd /etc/pki/CA/
2  [root@delphos CA]# ls
3  certs  crl  newcerts  private
```

To keep track of the issued certificates, we create index.txt and serial files.

```
1  [root@delphos CA]# touch index.txt
2  [root@delphos CA]# echo 0001 > serial
```

Now we create the key for the CA.

```
1  [root@delphos CA]# openssl genrsa -aes256 -out /etc/pki/CA/private/
   ca.key.pem
2  Generating RSA private key, 512 bit long modulus
3  .................+++++++++++++
4  .....+++++++++++++
5  e is 65537 (0x10001)
6  Enter pass phrase for /etc/pki/CA/private/ca.key.pem:
7  Verifying - Enter pass phrase for /etc/pki/CA/private/ca.key.pem:
```

In this case, we haven't specified the number of bits used to generate the keys, so the default value of 512 bits is used. When working in a test environment, this is acceptable; however, for production environments, you should specify a higher value, such as 4096. This way, the keys will be much more secure.

Once we have the key file, we create the CA certificate itself.

```
1   [root@delphos CA]# openssl req -new -x509 -days 3650 -key /etc/pki/CA/
    private/ca\
2   .key.pem -    extensions v3_ca -out   /etc/pki/CA/certs/ca.cert.pem
3   Enter pass phrase for /etc/pki/CA/private/ca.key.pem:
4   You are about to be asked to enter information that will be
    incorporated
5   into your certificate request.
6   What you are about to enter is what is called a Distinguished Name or
    a DN.
7   There are quite a few fields but you can leave some blank
8   For some fields there will be a default value,
9   If you enter '.', the field will be left blank.
10  -----
11  Country Name (2 letter code) [XX]:ES
12  State or Province Name (full name) []:Madrid
13  Locality Name (eg, city) [Default City]:Madrid
14  Organization Name (eg, company) [Default Company Ltd]:olimpus
15  Organizational Unit Name (eg, section) []:
16  Common Name (eg, your name or your server's hostname) []:delphos.
    olimpus.local
17  Email Address []:
```

Now we are ready to generate the key and certificate files to use with openldap. It is very important that the common name matches the server's hostname.

```
1   [root@delphos CA]# openssl genrsa -out   private/ldap.olimpus.local.key
2   Generating RSA private key, 512 bit long modulus
3   ...+++++++++++++
4   ........+++++++++++++
5   e is 65537 (0x10001)
6
7   [root@delphos CA]# openssl req -new -key private/ldap.olimpus.local.
    key -out   \
8   certs/ldap.olimpus.local.csr
9   You are about to be asked to enter information that will be
    incorporated
10  into your certificate request.
11  What you are about to enter is what is called a Distinguished Name or
    a DN.
12  There are quite a few fields but you can leave some blank
13  For some fields there will be a default value,
14  If you enter '.', the field will be left blank.
15  -----
16  Country Name (2 letter code) [XX]:ES
17  State or Province Name (full name) []:Madrid
18  Locality Name (eg, city) [Default City]:Madrid
```

```
19   Organization Name (eg, company) [Default Company Ltd]:olimpus
20   Organizational Unit Name (eg, section) []:
21   Common Name (eg, your name or your server's hostname) []:delphos.
     olimpus.local
22   Email Address []:
23
24   Please enter the following 'extra' attributes
25   to be sent with your certificate request
26   A challenge password []:
27   An optional company name []:
```

We already have the certificate, but now we have to sign it with our CA.

```
1    [root@delphos CA]# openssl ca -keyfile private/ca.key.pem -cert certs/
     ca.cert.pe\
2    m -in certs/ldap.olimpus.local.csr -out certs/ldap.olimpus.local.crt
3    Using configuration from /etc/pki/tls/openssl.cnf
4    Enter pass phrase for private/ca.key.pem:
5    Check that the request matches the signature
6    Signature ok
7    Certificate Details:
8            Serial Number: 1 (0x1)
9            Validity
10                       Not Before: Oct    9 18:23:22 2014 GMT
11                       Not After : Oct    9 18:23:22 2015 GMT
12           Subject:
13               countryName                    = ES
14               stateOrProvinceName            = Madrid
15               organizationName               = olimpus
16               commonName                     = delphos.olimpus.
                 local
17           X509v3 extensions:
18           X509v3 Basic Constraints:
19               CA:FALSE
20           Netscape Comment:
21               OpenSSL Generated Certificate
22           X509v3 Subject Key Identifier:
23               9A:49:FC:6D:8C:E6:6D:03:4D:4F:D1:AF:0E:03:2F:49:
                 98:DF:F5:10
24           X509v3 Authority Key Identifier:
25               keyid:BF:40:C8:81:59:CC:B0:F0:89:41:E2:B9:01:
                 82:A8:A7:9A:F4:6B:ADOpenLDAPconnections with
                 TLScreation, CA
26
27   Certificate is to be certified until Oct    9 18:23:22 2015 GMT
     (365 days)
28   Sign the certificate? [y/n]:y
29
```

```
30
31   1 out of 1 certificate requests certified, commit? [y/n]y
32   Write out database with 1 new entries
33   Data Base Updated
```

When signing the certificate, we see this message: "Using configuration from /etc/pki/tls/openssl.cnf."

This only means that openssl will receive its default information from this file, asking for whatever data is not included in it. If we open the file, we'll see a lot of options whose values can be customized. We'll take a look at some of those most commonly used.

```
1    .
2    .
3    .
4    [ ca ]
5    default_ca    = CA_default                  # The default ca section
6
7    ####################################################################
8    [ CA_default ]
9
10   dir            = /etc/pki/CA             # Where everything is kept
11   certs          = $dir/certs             # Where the issued certs
     are kept
12   crl_dir        = $dir/crl               # Where the issued crl are
     kept
13   database       = $dir/index.txt         # database index file.
14   #unique_subject = no                    # Set to 'no' to allow
     creation of
15                                           # several ctificates with
                                             same subject.
16   new_certs_dir  = $dir/newcerts          # default place for new
     certs.
17
18   certificate    = $dir/cacert.pem        # The CA certificate
19   serial         = $dir/serial            # The current serial number
20   crlnumber      = $dir/crlnumber         # the current crl number
21                                           # must be commented out to
                                             leave a V1 CRL
22   crl            = $dir/crl.pem           # The current CRL
23   private_key    = $dir/private/cakey.pem # The private key
24   RANDFILE       = $dir/private/.rand     # private random number
     fileOpenLDAPconnections with TLScreation, CA
25   .
26   .
27   .
```

As we see, these are the default folders in which the keys and certificate files will be stored. We can also see the default database index file and serial number. Another use of this file could be to customize the default values for parameters such as country, city, organization, etc.

```
 1   .
 2   .
 3   .
 4   countryName_default            = XX
 5   .
 6   localityName_default           = Default City
 7   .
 8   0.organizationName_default     = Default Company Ltd
 9   .
10   .
11   .
```

Now that the certificate has been signed by the CA, we can see that the index.txt file has been updated.

```
1   [root@delphos CA]# cat index.txt
2   V        151009182322Z              01              unknown /C=ES/
    ST=Madrid/O=olimpus/CN=del\
3   phos.olimpus.local
```

We can also verify the issued certificate against our CA.

```
1   [root@delphos CA]# openssl verify -CAfile certs/ca.cert.pem certs/ldap.
    olimpus.l\
2   ocal.crt
3   certs/ldap.olimpus.local.crt: OK
```

After signing the certificate, we copy both the certificate and the key file to /etc/openldap/certs/. We also copy the CA certificate to /etc/openldap/cacerts/. Later, we'll have to modify the openldap configuration accordingly.

11.3.2. Securing the LDAP Protocol.

In CentOS 6, we have to create an LDIF file called tls.ldif, as follows:

```
1   dn: cn=config
2   changetype: modify
3   add: olcTLSCACertificateFile
4   olcTLSCACertificateFile:/etc/openldap/cacerts/ca.cert.pem
5   -
6   add: oclTLSCertificateFile
7   oclTLSCertificateFile:/etc/openldap/cacerts/ldap.olimpus.local.crt
```

```
 8    -
 9    add: oclTLSCertificateKeyFile
10    oclTLSCertificateKeyFile: /etc/openldap/certs/ldap.olimpus.local.key
```

Next, we modify the configuration with ldapmodify.

```
1    [root@delphos ~]# ldapmodify -Y EXTERNAL -H ldapi:/// -f tls.ldif
2    SASL/EXTERNAL authentication started
3    SASL username: gidNumber=0+uidNumber=0,cn=peercred,cn=external,cn=auth
4    SASL SSF: 0
5    modifying entry "cn=config"
```

Now we edit the /etc/sysconfig/ldap file and change the SLAPD_LDAPS parameter from no to yes.

SLAPD_LDAPS=yes

But in CentOS 7, the situation is different, as there are already default values for the TLS related attributes. We can see these values with slapcat.

```
 1    [root@CentOS7 ~]# slapcat -b "cn=config"
 2    dn: cn=config
 3    objectClass: olcGlobal
 4    cn: config
 5    olcArgsFile: /var/run/openldap/slapd.args
 6    olcPidFile: /var/run/openldap/slapd.pid
 7    olcTLSCACertificatePath: /etc/openldap/certs
 8    olcTLSCertificateFile: "OpenLDAP Server"
 9    olcTLSCertificateKeyFile: /etc/openldap/certs/password
10    structuralObjectClass: olcGlobal
11    .
12    .
13    .
```

We have to modify the values of the olcTLSCertificateFile and olcTLSCertificateKeyFile attributes. So, we create the following LDIF file:

```
 1    [root@localhost ~]# cat tls7.ldif
 2    dn: cn=config
 3    changetype:modify
 4    replace: olcTLSCertificateFile
 5    olcTLSCertificateFile:/etc/openldap/certs/ldap.olimpus.local.crt
 6    -
 7    replace: olcTLSCertificateKeyFile
 8    olcTLSCertificateKeyFile: /etc/openldap/certs/ldap.olimpus.local.key
 9    -
10    replace: olcTLSCACertificatePath
11    olcTLSCACertificateFile: /etc/openldap/cacerts/ca.cacert.pem
```

And we run the ldapmodify command with this LDIF file.

```
1   [root@CentOS7 ~]# ldapmodify -Y EXTERNAL -H ldapi:// -f tls7.ldif
2   SASL/EXTERNAL authentication started
3   SASL username: gidNumber=0+uidNumber=0,cn=peercred,cn=external,cn=auth
4   SASL SSF: 0
5   modifying entry "cn=config"
```

Now we edit the /etc/sysconfig/slapd file to add ldaps:/// to the SLAPD_URLS parameter.

```
1   SLAPD_URLS="ldapi:/// ldap:/// ldaps:///"
```

Then we restart the service.

```
1   [root@CentOS7 ~]# systemctl restart slapd
```

To make sure that TLS is working properly, we can check it by passing the -ZZ option to ldapsearch.

Thus, we're telling ldapsearch to establish a TLS connection.

```
1   [root@localhost ~]# ldapsearch -x -ZZ
2   # extended LDIF
3   #
4   # LDAPv3
5   # base <ou=users,dc=olimpus,dc=local> (default) with scope subtree
6   # filter: (objectclass=*)
7   # requesting: ALL
8   #
9
10  # users, olimpus.local
11  dn: ou=users,dc=olimpus,dc=local
12  objectClass: organizationalUnit
13  ou: users
14  .
15  .
16  .
```

When using ldapsearch, sometimes the system expects the certificate files to be in a special numeric format. This numeric format can be obtained with openssl, like this:

```
1   [root@Centos7 ~]# openssl x509 -in /etc/openldap/cacerts/ca.cert.pem
    -hash
2   48e13dbe
3   -----BEGIN CERTIFICATE-----
4   MIICkjCCAfugAwIBAgIJALzQ1SVNq43lMA0GCSqGSIb3DQEBCwUAMGIxCzAJBgNV
5   BAYTAkVTMQ8wDQYDVQQIDAZNYWRyaWQxDzANBgNVBAcMBk1hZHJpZDERMA8GA1UE
```

Alternatively, we can use the `cacertdir_rehash` script to do that automatically.

```
1   [root@Centos7 ~]# cacertdir_rehash /etc/openldap/cacerts/
2   [root@Centos7 ~]# ls /etc/openldap/cacerts/
3   48e13dbe.0  ca.cert.pem
```

11.4. Authenticating Users with LDAP

In previous sections of the book, the users always authenticated from local accounts locally stored on /etc/passwd. Now we'll see how to authenticate users with LDAP.

First, in the server, we'll have to allow incoming traffic to port ldap (389) and ldaps (636)

In CentOS 6:

```
1   [root@delphos ~]# iptables -I INPUT 2 -m state --state new -p tcp
    --dport 389 -j\
2   ACCEPT
3   [root@delphos ~]# iptables -I INPUT 2 -m state --state new -p tcp
    --dport 636 -j\
4   ACCEPT
```

In CentOS 7:

```
1   [root@CentOS7 ~]# firewall-cmd --add-service=ldap
2   success
3   [root@CentOS7 ~]# firewall-cmd --add-service=ldaps
4   success
```

In the client, we have to install a series of packages to allow LDAP authentication.

```
1   [root@prometheus ~]# yum install openldap-clients pam_ldap nss-pam-ldapd
```

Next, we can use the `system-config-authentication` command (Figure 11-1). If this command is not installed, we'll have to install the `authconfig-gtk` package with yum.

Figure 11-1. *system-config-authentication*

As we must to activate TLS to be able to authenticate with LDAP, we mark the corresponding check box and click the Download CA Certificate button (Figure 11-2). Now we type the URL from which the server certificate can be downloaded.

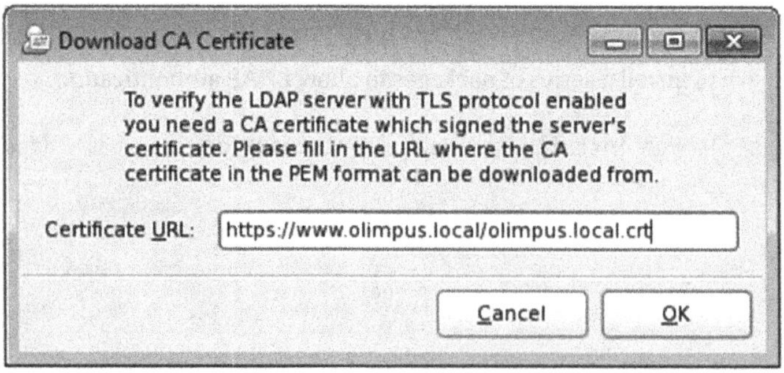

Figure 11-2. *Downloading the certificate*

When we created the certificate on the server, we placed it in /etc/openldap/
cacerts. In order to make it available to download, we can copy it to a web site, FTP site,
etc., as we have in previous sections of the book. In the figure, we have assumed that the
certificate was copied to the /www/docs/olimpus.local/ folder, where the web site is
hosted. For more details about configuring a web site, see Chapter 7.

When we click OK, this will automatically change a series of files that otherwise
would have to be changed by hand. For example, it will add the following lines to the /
etc/openldap/ldap.conf file:

```
1  URI ldap://192.168.1.20
2  BASE dc=olimpus,dc=local
3  TLS_CACERTDIR /etc/openldap/cacerts
```

If we haven't got a graphical environment available to execute system-config-
authconfig, we can get the same result with the authconfig command.

```
1  [root@delphos olimpus.local]# authconfig --enableldap --enableldapauth
   --ldapser\
2  ver=192.168.1.20 --ldapbasedn="dc=olimpus,dc=local" --enableldaptls
   --update
```

In order to authenticate as an LDAP user, when we create the user, we have to
include a series of fields, such as shell, uid, gid, etc. As an example, let's add the user
hypathia. We begin by creating the hypathia.ldif file, with the following content:

```
1   dn: uid=Hypathia,ou=users,dc=olimpus,dc=local
2   uid: Hypathia
3   cn: Hypathia
4   objectClass: account
5   objectClass: posixAccount
6   objectClass: top
7   objectClass: shadowAccount
8   userPassword:: Alexandria
9   shadowLastChange: 14846
10  shadowMax: 99999
11  shadowWarning: 7
12  loginShell: /bin/bash
13  uidNumber: 701
14  gidNumber: 500
15  homeDirectory: /home/hypathia
```

Nevertheless, if we're working with CentOS 7, there are a couple of things we have to
take into account before adding the new user.

First, we'll have to extend the schema again, this time with the ndis.ldif file.

```
1  [root@localhost ~]# ldapadd -Y EXTERNAL -H ldapi:/// -f /etc/openldap/
   schema/nis\
```

```
2   .ldif
3   SASL/EXTERNAL authentication started
4   SASL username: gidNumber=0+uidNumber=0,cn=peercred,cn=external,cn=auth
5   SASL SSF: 0
6   adding new entry "cn=nis,cn=schema,cn=config"
```

In addition, CentOS 7 seems not to recognize properly passwords written in clear text in the LDIF file. So, we'll get the encrypted equivalent with the slappasswd command.

```
1   [root@CentOS7 ~]# slappasswd
2   New password:
3   Re-enter new password:
4   {SSHA}9nI2t5F1oa8INTKb8a7SHQ3uAsGFUlM3
```

We type it in the LDIF file, like this:

```
1   dn: uid=Hypathia,ou=users,dc=olimpus,dc=local
2   uid: Hypathia
3   cn: Hypathia
4   objectClass: account
5   objectClass: posixAccount
6   objectClass: top
7   objectClass: shadowAccount
8   userPassword: {SSHA}9nI2t5F1oa8INTKb8a7SHQ3uAsGFUlM3
9   shadowLastChange: 14846
10  shadowMax: 99999
11  shadowWarning: 7
12  loginShell: /bin/bash
13  uidNumber: 1001
14  gidNumber: 500
15  homeDirectory: /home/hypathia
```

In addition, there is a new default rule that denies authentication to users with UIDs lower than 1000, except the root user, of course. So, we assign our user a uidNumber attribute greater than 1000.

Now we add this new user with ldappadd, as follows:

```
1   [root@delphos ~]# ldapadd -f hypathia.ldif -x -D
    cn=admin,dc=olimpus,dc=local -w\
2   pass
3   adding new entry "uid=Hypathia,ou=users,dc=olimpus,dc=local"
```

To ease the process of authentication, we should also install sssd.

```
1   [root@delphos olimpus.local]# yum install sssd
```

Now we'll be able to authenticate with an LDAP user.

```
1   login as: Hypathia
2   Hypathia@192.168.1.21's password:
3   [Hypathia@prometheus ~]$
```

11.5. PHPLDAPAdmin

So far, we have managed our LDAP server using mainly command-line utilities, but it is also possible to use a graphical tool. In this case, as we already have a working web server with PHP support, we'll install PHPLDAPAdmin.

PHPLDAPAdmin can be downloaded from its official site: http://phpldapadmin.sourceforge.net/wiki/index.php/D. Next, we uncompress the tar file in the folder we choose.

```
1   [root@delphos ~]# mkdir /phpldap
2   [root@delphos ~]# cp soft/phpldapadmin-1.2.3.tgz /phpldap/
3   [root@delphos ~]# cd /phpldap/
4   [root@delphos phpldap]# tar -xzvf phpldapadmin-1.2.3.tgz
```

We can rename the default name of the directory to something easier to remember.

```
1   [root@delphos phpldap]# ls
2   phpldapadmin-1.2.3   phpldapadmin-1.2.3.tgz
3   [root@delphos phpldap]# mv phpldapadmin-1.2.3 admin
```

Now we edit the apache config file to add a new virtual host.

```
1   .
2   .
3   .
4   <VirtualHost *:80>
5        DocumentRoot /phpldap/admin
6        ServerName ldap.olimpus.local
7        ErrorLog logs/ldap.olimpus.local-error_log
8        CustomLog logs/ldap.olimpus.local-access_log common
9            <Directory /phpldap/admin>
10                Order deny,allow
11           </Directory>
12   </VirtualHost>
13   .
14   .
15   .
```

We have to assign the right SELinux context to the folder.

```
1  [root@delphos config]# chcon -t httpd_sys_content_t -R /phpldap/admin/
```

And we have to install LDAP support for PHP.

```
1  [root@delphos ~]# yum install php-ldap
```

Now we restart the web service, for the changes to take effect.
In CentOS 6:

```
1  [root@delphos ~]# service httpd restart
2  Stopping httpd:                                              [ OK ]
3  Starting httpd:                                              [ OK ]
```

In CentOS 7:

```
1  [root@CentOS7 ~]# systemctl restart httpd
```

We also have to add a new register for ldap.centos.local. In this example, we'll edit the /var/named/- centos.local.zone file and add an alias (CNAME).

```
1  .
2  .
3  .
4  ldap      CNAME       delphos
5  .
6  .
7  .
```

We refresh the changes and ensure that our DNS can resolve this name.

```
1  [root@delphos phpldap]# dig  ldap.olimpus.local
2
3  ; <<>> DiG   9.7.3-P3-RedHat-9.7.3-8.P3.el6   <<>> ldap.olimpus.local
4  ;; global  options: +cmd
5  ;; Got answer:
6  ;; ->>HEADER<<- opcode: QUERY, status: NOERROR, id: 22037
7  ;; flags: qr aa rd; QUERY: 1, ANSWER: 2, AUTHORITY: 2, ADDITIONAL: 3
8  ;; WARNING: recursion requested but not available
9
10 ;; QUESTION  SECTION:
11 ;ldap.olimpus.local.             IN      A
12
13 ;; ANSWER SECTION:
14 ldap.olimpus.local.    172800   IN      CNAME     delphos.
   olimpus.local.
15 delphos.olimpus.local. 172800   IN      A         192.168.1.20
```

```
16   .
17   .
18   .
```

Next we access the `admin/config` directory and rename the `config.php.example`
file to `config.php`. We can edit the file if we want to customize the look and feel of the
application, but this is not necessary.

```
1   [root@delphos phpldap]# cd admin/config/
2   [root@delphos config]# ls
3   config.php.example
4   [root@delphos config]# mv config.php.example config.php
```

Now we can point our favorite browser to `http://ldap.olimpus.local`, and we'll
see the image shown in Figure 11-3.

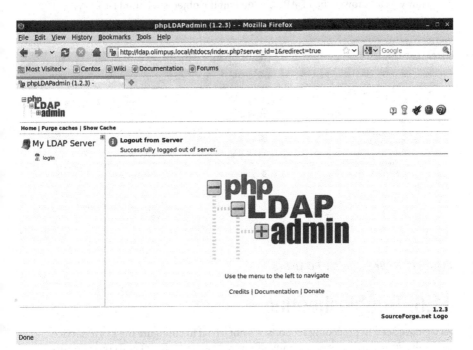

Figure 11-3. *PHPLDAPAdmin*

We click login and enter our login and password (Figure 11-4).

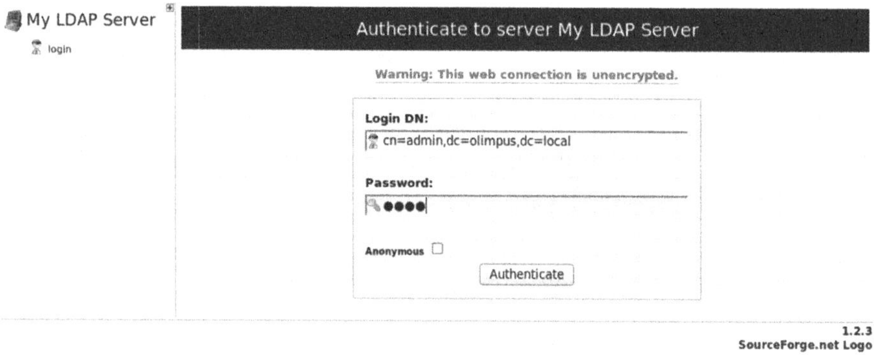

My LDAP Server
🔒 login

Authenticate to server My LDAP Server

Warning: This web connection is unencrypted.

Login DN:
🔒 cn=admin,dc=olimpus,dc=local

Password:
🔑 ●●●●|

Anonymous ☐

[Authenticate]

1.2.3
SourceForge.net Logo

Figure 11-4. *Login*

Now we can browse the LDAP tree and edit the objects (Figure 11-5).

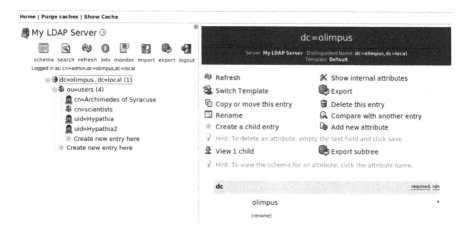

Figure 11-5. *Browsing the LDAP tree*

11.6. Troubleshooting

As we have seen in preceding sections, it's not trivial to configure the LDAP service correctly. Fortunately, there are some things we can do to detect and correct errors.

When querying the LDAP server with the ldapsearch command, the -d parameter shows debugging information, which can be very useful in order to diagnose problems.

```
1   [root@Centos7 ~]# ldapsearch -x -d1 -b dc=olimpus,dc=local -H ldap://
    ldap.olimpu\
2   s.local -ZZ
3   ldap_url_parse_ext(ldap://ldap.olimpus.local)
4   ldap_create
5   ldap_url_parse_ext(ldap://ldap.olimpus.local:389/??base)
6   ldap_extended_operation_s
7   ldap_extended_operation
8   ldap_send_initial_request
9   .
10  .
11  .
```

The sssd service is in charge of contact with the LDAP server to authenticate users. If we have any problem authenticating with a password, we can increase the log level by editing the /etc/sssd/sssd.conf file and including the following parameter:

```
1   debug_level=7
```

To solve problems with authentication, the /var/log/secure file is perhaps even more important. Following is an example of a failed authentication:

```
1   Feb  26  11:24:15 localhost su: pam_unix(su-l:auth): unrecognized
    ENCRYPT_METHOD  v\
2   alue [DES]
3   Feb  26  11:24:24 localhost  su: pam_unix(su-l:auth): authentication
    failure; logna\
4   me=root  uid=1001  euid=0  tty=pts/1  ruser=antonio  rhost=
    user=Hypathia2
5   Feb 26 11:24:24 localhost su: pam_succeed_if(su-l:auth): requirement
    "uid >= 100\
6   0" not met by user "Hypathia2"
```

Another interesting tool we can use to diagnose problems in OpenLDAP is slaptest. If we execute without options, it will check the syntax of the config file (Figure 11-6).

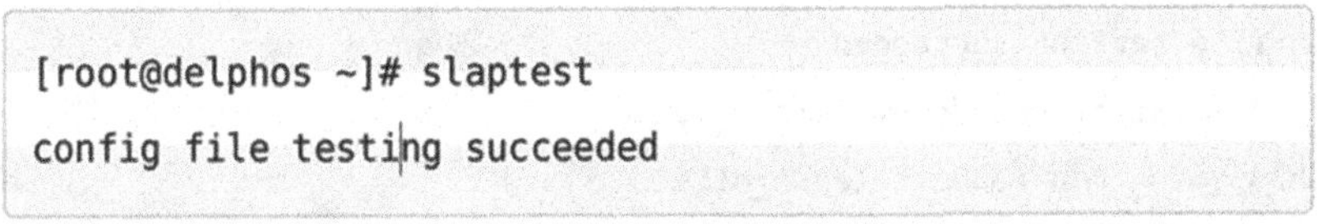

```
[root@delphos ~]# slaptest
config file testing succeeded
```

Figure 11-6. slaptest

We can also pass the -d (debug) parameter to get a bit more information (Figure 11-7).

```
[root@delphos ~]# slaptest -d 1
57ecfb34 <<< dnNormalize: <cn=backload>
57ecfb34 >>> dnNormalize: <cn=State>
57ecfb34 <<< dnNormalize: <cn=state>
57ecfb34 >>> dnNormalize: <cn=Runqueue>
57ecfb34 <<< dnNormalize: <cn=runqueue>
57ecfb34 >>> dnNormalize: <cn=Tasklist>
57ecfb34 <<< dnNormalize: <cn=tasklist>
57ecfb34 >>> dnNormalize: <cn=Start>
57ecfb34 <<< dnNormalize: <cn=start>
57ecfb34 >>> dnNormalize: <cn=Current>
57ecfb34 <<< dnNormalize: <cn=current>
57ecfb34 >>> dnNormalize: <cn=Uptime>
57ecfb34 <<< dnNormalize: <cn=uptime>
57ecfb34 >>> dnNormalize: <cn=Read>
57ecfb34 <<< dnNormalize: <cn=read>


57ecfb34 >>> dnNormalize: <cn=Write>
57ecfb34 <<< dnNormalize: <cn=write>
57ecfb34 backend_startup_one: starting "dc=olimpus,dc=loc
al"
57ecfb34 hdb_db_open: database "dc=olimpus,dc=local": dbe
nv_open(/var/lib/ldap).
config file testing succeeded
57ecfb34 slaptest shutdown: initiated
57ecfb34 ====> bdb_cache_release_all
57ecfb34 slaptest destroy: freeing system resources.
.
.
.
```

Figure 11-7. *Passing the* -d *(debug) parameter*

334

We have also at our disposal a valuable resource offered by OpenLDAP: the issue-tracking system at `http://www.openldap.org/its/` (Figure 11-8).

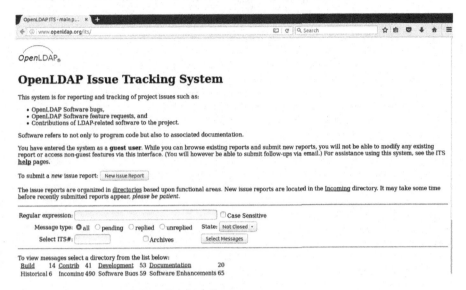

Figure 11-8. *OpenLDAP Issue Tracking System page*

With it, we can search for known issues or even submit a new issue report.

Index

© Antonio Vazquez 2016
A. Vazquez, *Learn CentOS Linux Network Services*, DOI 10.1007/978-1-4842-2379-6

Get the eBook for only $4.99!

Why limit yourself?

Now you can take the weightless companion with you wherever you go and access your content on your PC, phone, tablet, or reader.

Since you've purchased this print book, we are happy to offer you the eBook for just $4.99.

Convenient and fully searchable, the PDF version enables you to easily find and copy code—or perform examples by quickly toggling between instructions and applications.

To learn more, go to http://www.apress.com/us/shop/companion or contact support@apress.com.

Printed in the United States
By Bookmasters